JESUS 100 B.C.

MICHAEL THOMAS

authorHOUSE®

AuthorHouse™
1663 Liberty Drive
Bloomington, IN 47403
www.authorhouse.com
Phone: 1-800-839-8640

First published by AuthorHouse 1/28/2011

ISBN: 978-1-4567-1843-5 (e)
ISBN: 978-1-4567-1844-2 (sc)

Library of Congress Control Number: 2011900150

Printed in the United States of America

Any people depicted in stock imagery provided by Thinkstock are models, and such images are being used for illustrative purposes only. Certain stock imagery © Thinkstock.

This book is printed on acid-free paper.

CONTENTS

Thesis

In 1903, G.R.S. Mead wrote and published a book entitled Did Jesus Live 100 B.C.? Although Mead's book and his reasoning were deeply defective1 in many ways, nevertheless his thesis that Jesus may have lived approximately a century earlier than the commonly-accepted time has some substantial evidence to support it. In fact, Mead neglected some of the most important and powerful evidence in favor of the theory, apparently due to ignorance of his chosen subject-matter. We will seek to rectify this situation herein, presenting succinctly yet comprehensively all the relevant evidence in favor of the thesis that Jesus lived a century earlier than commonly supposed. We do not claim that this evidence constitutes conclusive proof, but nevertheless it is sufficiently significant to be made known. We will omit extraneous problems relating to the historical Jesus, and only touch on whatever directly or indirectly impinges upon our central thesis herein. Nevertheless there will be a wide variety of relevant subject-matter to consider, much of which is recondite, obscure, oblique, and even occult. Only after the complete evidence has been presented will a fair appraisal be possible. Even if a person decides that the evidence is insufficient to redate the historical Jesus it is wise to know just what that evidence is. Herein I will seek to briefly yet comprehensively present the full evidence that Jesus may have lived a century before the commonly-accepted time.

---

1   See chapter on Mead's errors, as well as discussion in the text.

People who are unfamiliar with this topic may be surprised that there is any evidence that Jesus lived a century before the commonly-accepted time. But in fact, there is a considerable body of evidence that such may have been the case. First, there is an obscure Jewish text known as the Toldoth Jeschu, which places Jesus (named Jeschu therein) in the days of Simeon ben Shetach, who lived in the early first century B.C. Then there is Daniel's prophecy of the seventy weeks. The weeks are symbolic of seven-year intervals, giving a total elapsed time of 490 years. According to the most natural reading of Daniel's text, the *terminus a quo* of the prophecy was the decree of King Cyrus the Persian. The prophecy states that the Messiah would come 483 years later. According to the standard chronology, the decree of King Cyrus was in 536 B.C. 483 years later gives us 53 B.C., which is clearly too early for Jesus Christ. Also, according to the prophecy, the Messiah would be a full-grown man at the *terminus ad quem* of the prophecy, not a baby. So even this date would make Jesus Christ late by about 85 years or so. But there is also a peculiar discrepancy between the standard chronology and the chronology of Josephus. The latter chronology places the decree of Cyrus approximately 45 years further in the past, thus making the time of fulfillment equivalently later. 53 B.C. + another 45 years further backwards in the past gives us 98 B.C., which might as well be 100 B.C. But once again, remember that the Messiah of the prophecy had to be a full-grown man, so the Jesus of the Gospels was late by about 130 years, according to the prophecy together with the chronology of Josephus.[2] This latter powerful and important evidence was completely overlooked by G.R.S. Mead, even though he made a fairly extensive use of Josephus. Aside from this powerful evidence, there is also evidence of chronological falsification in the Massoretic texts of Esther, Ezra, and Nehemiah that is directly pertinent to the matter under consideration. There is even some obscure evidence from the Dead Sea Scrolls that supports our thesis. There is also evidence from the Talmud that Jesus lived approximately a century before the commonly-accepted time. Finally, we offer some possible reasons why the Evangelists would have dislocated Jesus from

---

2   Josephus was a Jewish historian of the late first century A.D.

his true original time-period, as well as dealing with some possible objections or challenges to the thesis presented herein.[3]

Once again, we do not claim that the evidence presented herein is anything approaching conclusive proof, but rather that this evidence is sufficiently significant that it is of genuine interest to those interested in the question of the historical Jesus.

---

3   Mead's work was notoriously deficient in these respects.

Toldoth Jeschu

1. The beginning of the birth of Jeschu. His mother was Miriam [a daughter] of Israel. She had a betrothed of the royal race[1] of the House of David, whose name was Jochanan. He was learned in the law and feared heaven greatly. Near the door of her house, just opposite, dwelt a handsome [fellow]; Joseph[2] ben Pandera cast his eye[3] upon her.

It was at night, on the eve of the Sabbath, when drunken he crossed over to her door and entered in to her. But she thought in her heart that it was her betrothed Jochanan; she hid her face and was ashamed… He embraced her; but she said to him, Touch me not, for I am in my separation.[4] He took no heed thereat, nor regarded her words, but persisted. She conceived by him…

At midnight came her betrothed Rabbi Johanan. She said to him: What meaneth this? Never hath it been thy custom, since thou wast betrothed to me, twice in a night to come to me.

He answered her and said: It is but once I come to thee this night. She said to him: Thou camest to me, and I said to thee I was in my separation, yet heed'st thou not, but dids't thy will and wentest forth. When he heard

1 Mt 1:1-17; Lk 3:23-31.
2 Mt 1:1-25; 2:13-23; Lk 1:27; 2:1-16,43; Jn 1:45.
3 Mt 6:23; Lk 11:34.
4 Leviticus 15:19-27; cf Lev. 12:1-5 cp John 20:17 "Touch me not, for I am…"

this, forthwith he perceived that Joseph ben Pandera had cast an eye upon her and done the deed. He left her; in the morning he arose and went to Rabbi Simeon ben Shetach. He said to him: Know then what hath befallen me this night with my betrothed. I went in to her after the manner of men...; before I touched her she said: Thou hast already this night come once to me, and I said to thee I was in my separation, and thou gavest no ear to me, [didst] thy will and wentest forth. When I heard such words from her, I left her and [went forth]. Rabbi Simeon ben Shetach said to him: Who came into thy mind? He answered, Ben Pandera, for he dwelleth near her house and is a libertine.[5] He said to him: I understand that thou hast no witness for this thing, therefore keep silence; I counsel thee, if he have come once, then can he not fail to come a second time; act wisely; at that time set witnesses against him.

Some time after the rumour went abroad that Miriam was with child. Then said her betrothed Johanan: She is not with child by me; shall I abide here and hear my shame every day from the people? He arose and went to Babylon. After some [time she bore] a son, and they called his name Joshua after his mother's brother; but when his corrupt birth became known they called him Jeschu.

2. His mother gave him to a teacher, so that he might become wise in the *Halacha*, and learned in the *Torah* and the *Talmud*.[6] Now it was the custom of the teachers of the law that no disciple and no boy should pass on his way by them without his head being covered and his eyes cast to the ground, from reverence of the pupils towards their teachers.[7]

One day that rogue passed by, and all the wise were seated together at the door of the synagogue (that is, they called the school-house synagogue); that rogue then passed by the Rabbis, head on high and with uncovered pate, saluting no one, nay rather, in shameless fashion showing irreverence to his teacher.

---

5   cf Acts 6:9 "Then there arose certain of the synagogue, which is called *the synagogue* of the Libertines..."

6   An evident anachronism here and following, as in tractate *Nezekin*, etc.

7   This is evidently another grotesque anachronism; the custom of wearing a *yarmulkeh* was probably not adopted until well into the Common Era.

After he had passed by them, one of them began and said: He is a bastard (*mamzer*). The second began and said: He is a bastard and son of a woman in her separation (*mamzer ben ha-niddah*). Another day the Rabbis stopped in tractate *Nezekin*; then began that one to speak *Halachoth* before them. Thereupon one of them began and said to him: Hast thou then not learned: He who giveth forth a *Halacha* in the presence of his teacher, *without being asked*, is guilty of death? That one answered and said to the wise ones: Who is the teacher and who the disciple? Who of the twain was wiser, Moses or Jethro? Was it not Moses, father of the prophets and head of the wise? And the *Torah*, moreover, beareth witness of him: And from henceforth there ariseth no prophet in Israel like unto Moses.[8] Withal Jethro was an alien... yet taught he Moses worldly wisdom, as it is written: Set over them rulers of thousands, and of hundreds.[9] But if ye say that Jethro is greater than Moses, then would there be an end to the greatness of Moses.

When the wise heard this, they said: As he is so very shameless. Let us enquire after him. They sent unto his mother, [saying] thus: Tell us, pray, who is the father of this boy? She answered and said:...; but they say of him, that he is a bastard and son of a woman in her separation. Then began Rabbi Simeon ben Shetach: Today is it thirty years since Rabbi Jochanan her betrothed came to me; at that time he said to me: That and that hath befallen me. He related all that is told above,... how Rabbi Simeon answered Rabbi Jochanan, and how when she was with child, he [R.J.] for great shame went to Babylon and did not return; but this Miriam gave birth to this Jeschu, and no death penalty awaits her, for she hath not done this of her own will, for Joseph ben Pandera laid wait for her... the whole day.

When she heard from Rabbi Simeon that no death penalty awaited her, she also began and said: Thus was the story; and she confessed. But when it went abroad concerning Jeschu, that he was a bastard and son of a woman in her separation, he went away and fled to Jerusalem.

3. Now the rule of all Israel was in the hand of a woman who was called

---

8   Deuteronomy 34:10-12.
9   Exodus 18:17-22.

Helene.[10] And there was in the sanctuary a foundation-stone: and this is its interpretation: God founded it and this is the stone on which Jacob poured oil[11] and on it were written the letters of the *Shem*,[12] and whoever learned it, could do whatsoever he would. But as the wise feared that the disciples of Israel might learn them and therewith destroy the world, they took measures that no one should do so.[13] Brazen dogs were bound to two iron pillars at the entrance of the place of burnt offerings, and whosoever entered in and learned these letters- as soon as he went forth again, the dogs bayed {barked} at him; if he then looked at them, the letters vanished from his memory.[14]

This Jeschu came, learned them, wrote them on parchment, cut into his hip and laid the parchment with the letters therein- so that the cutting of his flesh did not hurt him- then he restored the skin to its place. When he went forth the brazen dogs bayed at him, and the letters vanished from his memory. He went home, cut open his flesh with his knife, took out the writing, learned the letters, went and gathered three hundred and ten of the young men of Israel.

4. He said to them: Behold then those who say of me I am a bastard[15] and son of a woman in her separation; they desire power for themselves and

---

10   This Helene was apparently one and the same as Queen Salome, otherwise also known as Alexandra, who was the widow of both Aristobulus and Alexander Jannaeus. She may also have been a composite of this Queen Salome-Alexandra and also Queen Helena of Adiabene. (cf Josephus, Antiquities of the Jews, 13.16.1-6; 20.2.1-5; War of the Jews, 1.5.1-4).

11   Genesis 28:18.

12   This *Shem* should not be confused with the famous four-letter *Tetragrammaton*, the Divine Name of God, which is inscribed thousands of times on the Hebrew Scrolls of *TaNaKh*. This must refer instead to the seventy-two-letter secret Name of God, otherwise spoken of as the *Shemhamphorasch*. This *Shemhamphorasch* or Secret Name of God is very important in mystical Judaism, and especially in Hasidic Judaism. See works on the Baal Shem Tov.

13   This is an absurd and ridiculous excuse for an absurd and ridiculous story. If the Jews had such a powerful secret weapon, they would never have been conquered by the Egyptians, Syrians, Assyrians, Babylonians, Greeks, Romans, or anyone else; neither would the holocaust have taken place.

14   Another absurd story.

15   cf John 8:41; cp Luke 19:14 cf *Talmud*.

seek to exercise lordship in Israel. But see ye, all the prophets prophesied concerning the Messiah of God, and I am the Messiah. Isaiah prophesied concerning me: Behold the virgin shall conceive, bear a son, and he shall be called Emmanuel.[16] Moreover, my forefather David prophesied concerning me and spake: The Eternal [Y.H.V.H.] said to me: Thou art my son; this day have I begotten thee.[17] He begat me without male congress with my mother; yet they call me a bastard![18] He further prophesied: Why do the heathen rage, and the kings in the country [nations] rise up against His Anointed?[19] I am the Messiah, and they, so to rise up against me, are children of whores, for so it is written in the Scripture: for they are children of whores.[20]

The young men answered him: If thou art the Messiah, show unto us a sign. He answered them: What sign do ye require that I should do for you? Forthwith they brought unto him a lame man, who had never yet stood upon his feet. He pronounced over him the letters, and he stood upon his feet. In the same hour they all made obeisance to him and said:

This is {Thou art} the Messiah.[21]

He gave them another sign: They brought to him a leper; he pronounced over him the letters, and he was healed. There joined themselves apostates from the children of his people.

When the wise saw that so many believed on him, they seized him and brought him before Queen Helene, in whose hand the land of Israel was. They said to her: This man uses sorcery and seduces the world.[22]

Jeschu answered to her as follows: Already of old the prophets prophesied concerning me: And there shall come forth a rod out of the stem of Isai

---

16   Isaiah 7:14 (LXX) cf Matthew 1:23.
17   Psalm 2:7.
18   John 8:41; cp Nicodemus 2:7; Luke 19:14.
19   Psalm 2:1-2.
20   Hosea 2:4, "And I will not have mercy on her children; for they be children of whoredoms".
21   Matthew 14:33.
22   Matthew 12:24; Mark 3:22; Luke 11:15.

(Jesse),[23] and I am he. Of him saith the Scripture: Blessed is the man that walketh not in the counsel of the ungodly.[24]

She said to them: Is this truly in your law, what he saith?

They answered: It is in our law; but it hath not been said concerning him, for it is said therein: And that prophet *that seeketh to lead thee astray to worship false gods, shall be put to death; so shalt thou* put the evil away from the midst of thee.[25] But the Messiah for whom we hope, with him are {greater} signs, and it is said of him: He shall smite the earth with the rod of his mouth.[26] *But* with this bastard these signs are absent.

Jeschu said: Lady, I am he, and I raise the dead. {*In some editions of the Toldoth, there follows a brief account of Jeschu raising a dead person to life*} In the same hour the queen was affrighted and said: That is a great sign. Apostates still joined themselves to him, were with him, and there arose a great schism in Israel.

5. Jeschu went to Upper Galilee. The wise assembled together, went before the queen and said to her: Lady, he practiceth sorcery and leadeth men astray therewith. Therefore sent she forth horsemen concerning him, and they came upon him as he was seducing the people of Upper Galilee and saying to them: I am the Son of God, who hath been promised in your law.[27] The horsemen rose up to take him away, but the people of Upper Galilee suffered it not and began to fight. *But* Jeschu said unto them: Fight not; have trust in the power of my Father in heaven.[28] The people of Galilee made birds out of clay; he uttered the letters of the *Shem* and the birds flew away.[29] At the same hour they[30] fell down before him. He said to them: Bring me a millstone. They rolled it to the sea-shore; he

---

23   Isaiah 11:1.

24   Psalm 1:1.

25   Deuteronomy 13:1-5.

26   Isaiah 11:4.

27   Isaiah 7:14; 9:6; Proverbs 30:4; Psalm 2.

28   Matthew 26:52-53.

29   cf Koran Sura 5:110; Infancy Gospel 15:1-6; Infancy Gospel of Thomas 1:1-10.

30   They. Presumably this refers to the people of Galilee, bowing down in homage to Jeschu.

spoke the letters, set it upon the surface of the sea, sat himself thereon, as one sits in a boat, went and floated on the water. They who had been sent, saw it and wondered; and Jeschu said to the horsemen: Go to your Lady[31] *and* tell her what ye have seen! Thereupon the wind raised him from the water and carried him onto dry land.

The horsemen came and told the queen all these things; the queen was affrighted, was greatly amazed, sent and gathered together the elders of Israel and spake unto them: Ye say he is a sorcerer, nevertheless every day he doeth great wonders.

They answered her: Surely his tricks should not trouble thee!

Send messengers, that they may bring him hither, and his shame shall be made plain. At the same hour she sent messengers, and his wicked company also joined itself unto him, and they came with him before the queen.

Then the wise men of Israel took a man by name Juda Ischariota, brought him into the Holy of Holies, where he learned the letters of the *Shem*, which were engraved on the foundation-stone, wrote them on a small [piece of] parchment, cut open his hip, spake the *Shem*, so that it did not hurt, as Jeschu had done before.

As soon as Jeschu and his company had returned to the queen, and she sent for the wise men, Jeschu began and spake: For dogs have compassed me.[32] And concerning me he [David] said: Tremble not before them.[33] As soon as the wise men entered and Juda Ischariota with them, they brought forward their pleas against him, until he said to the queen: Of me it hath been said: I will ascend to heaven.[34] Further it is written: If he take me, Selah! {Psalms} *Then* he raised his hands like unto the wings of an eagle and flew, and the people were amazed because of him: How is he able to fly twixt heaven and earth?!

Then spake the wise men of Israel to Juda Ischariota: Do thou also utter

31   Lady. A term of respect. Compare the term *Notre Dame*.
32   Psalm 22:16.
33   cf Psalms 23:4; 27:1-3; 56:4; 118:6.
34   Psalms 68:18-19; 139:8 cp Proverbs 30:4 cf Daniel 7:13-14.

the letters and ascend after him. Forthwith he did so; flew in the air, and the people marvelled: How can they fly like eagles?![35]

Ischariota acted cleverly, flew in the air, but neither could overpower the other, so as to make him fall by means of the *Shem*, because the *Shem* was equally with them both.[36] When Juda perceived this, he had recourse to a low trick; he befouled Jeschu, so that he was made unclean and fell to the earth, and with him also Juda.[37] It is because of this that they wail on their night, on account of what Juda did to him. At the same hour they seized him and said to Helene: Let him be put to death! If he be the Son of God, let him tell us who smote him.[38] So they covered his head with a garment and smote him with a pomegranate staff. As he did not know, it was clear that the *Shem* had abandoned[39] him, and he was now fast taken in their hands. He began and spake to his companions before the queen: Of me it was said: Who will rise up for me against the evil doers?[40] But of them he said: The proud waters.[41] And of them he said: Stronger than rocks make they their countenances.[42] When the queen heard this she reproved the apostates, and said to the wise men of Israel: He is in your hand.

6. They departed from the queen and brought him to the synagogue of Tiberias and bound him to the pillars of the ark.[43] Then there gathered

---

35   There is a curious legend about Simon Magus flying around in the city of Rome, trying to prove he was a God to the Romans. In one account, Simon Peter sees this and prays the "Our Father" and Simon comes crashing down to earth. The story is also found in the apocryphal Acts of Peter, 31-32. Apparently in one version of the story, Simon Magus, when he falls to earth, breaks his leg in three places and then is stoned by the Romans. This parallels the account of the stoning of Paul (Acts 14:19). In some of the Petrine (or pseudo-Petrine) literature, Simon Magus is a cypher for the apostle Paul, portrayed as a religious rival and enemy to Peter therein.

36   Zechariah 2:10-11; 11:10-14; 12:8; 13:7; 14:3-4; Isaiah 7:14; 9:6-7.

37   Talmud. Ritual impurity.

38   cf Luke 22:63-64 cp Mk 15:19; Mt 27:30; Peter 9 cf Micah 5:1.

39   Peter 19; Mt 27:46; Mk 15:34; Nicodemus 8:3 cf Judges 16.

40   Psalm 94:16.

41   Psalm 124:5.

42   Jeremiah 5:3.

43   It is customary in many synagogues to have a replica of the ark of the cov-

to him the band of simpletons[44] and dupes, who believed on his words, and desired to deliver him out of the hand of the elders; but they could not do so, and there arose great fighting between them.

When he saw that he had no power to escape, he said: Give me some water. They gave him vinegar in a copper vessel.[45] He began and spake with a loud voice: Of me David prophesied and said: When I was thirsty they gave me vinegar to drink.[46] On his head they set a crown of thorns.[47] The apostates lamented sore, and there was fighting between them, brother with brother, father with son; but the wise men brought the apostates low. He began and spake: Of me he prophesied and said: My back I gave to the smiters, *and my cheeks to them that plucked off the hair: I hid not my face from shame and spitting.*[48] Further of these the Scripture saith: Draw hither, sons of the sorceress.[49] And of me *it* hath been said: But we held him *smitten by God, and afflicted.*[50] And of me he said: The Messiah shall be cut off and he is not.[51] When the apostates heard this, they began to stone them with stones, and there was great hatred among them. Then were the elders afraid, and the apostates bore him off from them, and his three hundred and ten disciples brought him to the city of Antioch, where he sojourned until the rest-day of the Passover. Now in that year the Passover fell on the Sabbath,[52] and he and his sons came to Jerusalem, on the rest-day of Passover, that is on the Friday, he riding on an ass and saying to his disciples: Of me it was said: Rejoice greatly, Daughter of Zion, *shout, O Daughter of Jerusalem: Behold, thy King cometh unto thee: he is just, and having salvation; meek, and riding upon an ass,*

---

enant.

44   John 7:49 cf Isaiah 28:9 cf Mt 17:10 & Mk 9:11 cp Malachi 4:5-6 (3:23-24).

45   John 19:28-29 cp Mk 15:36 cf Mt 27:34,48; Peter 16.

46   Psalm 69:21.

47   Mt 27:29; Mk 15:17; Jn 19:2; Peter 8.

48   Isaiah 50:6 cp Mt 27:26,30; Mk 15:19; Lk 22:63-64; Jn 19:1.

49   Isaiah 57:3.

50   Isaiah 53:4.

51   Daniel 9:26. But see my interpretation of the verse below.

52   This is an important chronological marker; cf Jn 19:31 & Mt 28:1 (Greek); cp Mk 16:1 & Lk 23:56. Thus the Toldoth agrees with the Gospels that Jesus was crucified in a year in which the Passover fell on the Sabbath.

and upon a colt, the foal of an ass.[53] In the same hour they all cried aloud, bowed themselves before him, and he with his three hundred and ten disciples went into the sanctuary.

Then came one of them, who was called Gaisa [that is, Gardener], and said to the wise men: Do you want the rogue? They said: Where is he to be found? He answered: He is in the sanctuary; that is to say, in the school-house. They said to him: Show him unto us. He answered them: We, his three hundred and ten disciples, have already sworn by the commandments, that we will not say of him who he is; but if ye come in the morning, give me the greeting, and I will go and make obeisance before him, and before whom I make obeisance, he is the rogue.[54] And they did so.[55]

The disciples of Jeschu gathered together, went and gave their fellows the greeting, for they were come from all places to pray on the Mount of Olives on the Feast of Unleavened Bread. Then the wise men went into the sanctuary, where those were who had come from Antioch, and there was also the rogue among them. Thereupon Gaisa[56] entered with them, left the rest of the company, made an obeisance before the rogue Jeschu. Whereupon the wise men saw it, arose against him and seized him.[57]

---

53   Zechariah 9:9 cf Mt 21:1-11; Mk 11:1-10; Lk 19:29-38; Jn 12:12-15.

54   Mt 26:50; Mk 14:46; Lk 22:54; Jn 18:12. This is another absurd story, evidently intended to imitate what was written in the Gospels about the infamous kiss of Judas Iscariot. But the scene in the Garden of Gethsemane was at night, and hence there was some plausible reason for the need for such an identification. Here, it is merely another absurdity; the so-called "wise men" of Israel clearly knew what Jeschu looked like, and would recognize him in the morning-light.

55   Curiously, there is no mention of the thirty pieces of silver as the price for the betrayal in this account. But we ought not to be too surprised at the circumstance; the authors of the Toldoth would not want to allude to a fulfilled prophecy.

56   Gaisa is the traitor in the Toldoth. Juda Ischariota, clearly Judas Iscariot, has already been portrayed in the Toldoth not as a betrayer of Jesus (Jeschu) but instead as an agent of the Rabbis, and potentially a messianic rival. Gaisa, apparently meaning Gardener (according to the text), is the traitor, and the circumstance seems to be based upon the fact that a Gardener is mentioned in the Gospel of John (20:15).

57   cf Mt 26:50; Mk 14:46; Lk 22:54; Jn 18:12.

7. They said to him: What is thy name? He answered: Mathai. They said to him: Whence hast thou a proof from Scripture? He answered them: When *(mathai)* shall I come and see the face of God?[58] *But* they said to him: When *(mathai)* shall he die and his name perish?[59] Further they said to him: What is thy name? He answered: Naki. They said to him: Whence hast thou a proof from Scripture? He answered: With pure *(naki)* hands and a clean heart.[60] *But* they said to him: He remaineth not unpunished *(nakah)*.[61] Further they said to him: What is thy name? He answered: Boni. They said: Whence hast thou a proof from Scripture? He answered: My first-born son *(beni)* is Israel.[62] *But* they *answered him,* saying: Of thee it was said: Behold, I will slay thy first-born son.[63] Further they said to him: What is thy name? He answered: Netzer. They said: Whence hast thou a proof from Scripture? He answered them: A branch *(netzer)* shall spring up out of his roots.[64] *But* they said to him: Thou art cast forth from thy sepulchre, like an abominable branch *(netzer)*.[65] *Further they said to him: What is thy name? He answered: Todah. They said: Whence hast thou a proof from Scripture? He answered: A Psalm for Todah (Thanksgiving; Praise).*[66] But they answered him, saying, Whoso offereth Todah honoureth me.[67] And thus still more, as he gave himself many names. Forthwith they seized him, and his disciples could not deliver him, *as they had the first time.* When he saw himself brought to death he began and spake: Verily hath David prophesied of me and said: For thy sake are we smitten every day.[68] And of you said Isaiah: Your hands are full

---

58   Psalm 42:2.

59   Psalm 41:5.

60   Psalm 24:4.

61   Proverbs 16:5 cf Proverbs 19:5,9 cp Jeremiah 30:11; 46:28; 49:12.

62   Exodus 4:22 cp Hosea 11:1 cf Mt 2:15.

63   Exodus 4:23. This also confirms that Jeschu (Jesus) had sons, according to the Toldoth.

64   Isaiah 11:1 cp Zechariah 3:8; 6:12; Jeremiah 23:5; 33:15.

65   Isaiah 14:19.

66   Psalm 100:1 (Hebrew; heading).

67   Psalm 50:23.

68   Psalm 44:22 cf Romans 8:36.

of blood.[69] And of you said the prophet before God: They slew the prophets with the sword.[70]

The apostates began to lament and could not deliver him, *as they had before*. At the same hour was he put to death. And it was Friday the rest-day of the Passover and of the Sabbath.[71] When they would hang him on a tree (*Holz*), it brake, for there was with him the *Shem*.[72] For while he was yet alive he knew the custom of the Israelites, that they would hang him, he knew his death, and that they would hang him on a tree.[73] At that time he brought it to pass by means of the *Shem*, that no tree should bear him; but over the cabbage-stalk he did not utter the pronounced name, for it is not "tree" but green-stuff, and so *also plentiful, for {in the sixth year there are}* in Jerusalem cabbages with more than a hundred pounds [of seed] unto this day.

When they had let him hang until the time of afternoon prayer, they took him down from the tree, for so it is written: His body shall not remain all night upon the tree, *but thou shalt in any wise bury him that day, that thy land not be defiled, which the LORD thy God giveth thee for an inheritance.*[74] So they buried him on [Friday[75]] and the apostates of his people wept over the grave.

8. Some of the young men of Israel passed by them. They spoke to them in the Aramaic tongue: Why do the foolish ones sit by the grave? Let us look! The foolish ones said in their heart, that they [the young men] would see him in the grave, but they found him not. Thereupon the foolish ones sent to Queen Helene, saying: He whom they put to death was *the* Messiah, and very many wonders did he show while living, but

---

69   Isaiah 1:15.

70   I Kings 19:10 cf Romans 11:3.

71   cf Jn 19:31 cp Mt 28:1; Mk 16:1; Lk 23:56 cp Peter 34.

72   cp Judges 16:21-30. The power of the *Shemhamphorasch* returned to Jeschu after he was ritually cleansed from Juda's defilement.

73   Acts 5:30; 10:39; 13:29; I Peter 2:24 cf Galatians 3:13; Dt 21:22-23.

74   Deuteronomy 21:23.

75   Friday. This is an emendation of the text, which reads "Sunday"; but since this is clearly in conflict with the entire context, it must be a corruption in the text.

now after his death they buried him, but he is not in the grave, for he is already ascended to heaven, as it is written: For he taketh me, Selah![76] Thus did he prophesy concerning himself.

She went to the wise men and said: What have ye done with him? They answered her: We put him to death, for that was the judgment concerning him.

She said to them: If ye have put him to death, what have ye then done? They answered her: We have buried him.[77] Forthwith they sought him in the grave but found him not. Thereupon she said to them: In this grave ye buried him; where is he therefore? Then were the wise men affrighted and knew not what to answer her, for a certain one had taken him from the grave, borne him to the garden, and stopped the water which flowed into his garden; then digged he in the sand and buried him, and let the water flow again over his grave.

The queen said: If ye show me not *the body of* Jeschu, I will give you no peace and no escape. They answered her: Give us an appointed time and terms. When she had granted them an appointed time, all Israel remained in lamenting and fasting and prayer.[78] *Therefore* the apostates found occasion to say: Ye have slain God's Anointed *Prince!*[79]

And all Israel was in great anguish, and the wise men and all the land of Israel hurried from place to place because of great fear. Then went forth an elder of them, whose name was Rabbi Tanchuma; he went forth lamenting in a garden in the fields. When the owner of the garden saw him, he said to him: Wherefore lamentest thou? He answered: For this and this; because of that rogue who is not to be found; and lo, already is it the appointed time which the queen granted, and we are all in lamentation and fasting. As soon as he heard his words, that all Israel is as them who mourn, and that the rogues say: He is gone up to heaven,

---

76   Psalms.

77   cp Mk 15:42-46; Lk 23:50-55 cf Nicodemus 8:12-15; Jn 19:38-42; Mt 27:57-61.

78   This is blatant historical revisionism; by saying "all Israel..." the Jews have excluded the disciples of Jeschu from being Israelites, most unjustly.

79   Daniel 9:26.

the owner of the garden[80] said: Today shall joy and gladness reign in Israel, for I have stolen him away because of the apostates, so that they should not take him and have the opportunity for all time, *to claim that he has ascended to heaven,* and thereafter make trouble for the Israelites. Forthwith they went to Jerusalem, told them the good tidings, and all the Israelites followed the owner of the garden, bound cords to his [Jeschu's] feet, and dragged him {his body} to the queen and said: There {This} is he who is {has} ascended to heaven![81] *Then* they departed from her in joy, and she mocked the apostates and praised the wise men.

9. His disciples fled and scattered themselves in the kingdom; three of them went to Mount Ararat; three of them to Armenia; three to Rome; the others to other places, and misled the peoples, but everywhere that they took refuge, God sent his judgment upon them, and they were slain.[82] But many among the apostates of our people went astray after him; there was strife between them and the Israelites,...[83] confusion of prayers and much loss of revenue. Everywhere that the apostates caught sight of the Israelites they said to them: Ye have slain God's Anointed *Prince!* But the Israelites answered them: Ye are children of death, because ye have believed on {in} a false prophet![84]

---

80   cp John 19:41.

81   The evident absurdity and even impossibility of such a spectacle should be readily apparent to everyone who is not infatuated with Judaic fundamentalism and Talmudic revisionism; had such a scene ever occurred, there never would have been any such religion as Christianity in the world. But here the Toldoth testifies against the Jews that they would have been eager and willing to thus desecrate the body of Jesus; this provides the rationale and justification for the disciples to remove the body from the original tomb, and to rebury it secretly elsewhere, in a location unknown to the other Jews, lest they should thus defile and desecrate the body of Jesus. Thus the act of removal was neither a theft, nor sacrilege, nor was it a pretext to perpetrate a fraud, as the Jews allege. It was the final act of devotion by the loyal disciples of Jesus, to thus preserve the body of their Lord and Master from desecration. And if they later claimed that Jesus had ascended to heaven, the claim was made in good faith and a pure conscience, since they were speaking spiritually.

82   Thus the noble martyrdoms of the apostles and other early disciples are cleverly, conveniently, and disingenuously reinterpreted by the Rabbis as the vengeance of God.

83   It is noted that here occurs an uncertain word in the text.

84   Deuteronomy 13:1-5 cf Ezekiel 14:4-11.

Nevertheless they went not forth from the community[85] of Israel, and there was strife and contention among them, so that Israel had no peace.[86] When the wise men saw this they said: [It is now] thirty years[87] since that rogue was put to death, [but] till now we have had no peace with these misguided ones, and this hath befallen us because of the number of our sins, for it is written: They have moved me to wrath with *that which is not God; they have provoked me to anger with their vanities: and I will provoke them to anger with a foolish nation.*[88] That is, the Christians, who are not *a people;*[89] with a base people will I provoke them *to anger;* that is, the Ishmaelites.[90]

The wise said: How long shall the apostates profane the Sabbath… and the feasts, and slay one another? Let us rather seek for a wise man who may take these erring ones out of the community of Israel. It is now thirty years that we have admonished them, but they have not returned to God, because they have taken it into their heads that Jeschu[91] is the Messiah, and so may they go to destruction and peace be with us.

10. The wise men agreed on a man whose name was Elijahu, and he was learned in the Scripture, and they said to him: … We have agreed, that we will pray for thee, that thou shalt be counted as a good Israelite in the

---

85   Yahad.

86   cf Acts 18:2 cp Suetonius, Claudius, 25. "Because the Jews at Rome caused continuous disturbances at the instigation of Chrestus, he expelled them from the city". Of course the reign of Claudius was much later, and this edict expelling the Jews from Rome took place around 45 A.D., but this illustrates the fact that there were ongoing disputes among different groups of Jews respecting the alleged messianic status of Jesus.

87   Thirty years from the time of Jeschu's death (or supposed death). The reign of Queen Salome-Alexandra, who is otherwise identified as Queen Helene in the Toldoth, was from 78 to 69 B.C., according to the standard chronology; thirty years from 70 B.C. would be 40 B.C., or well within the Roman era of Judaean occupation.

88   Deuteronomy 32:21 cf Romans 10:19.

89   Hosea 1:6-10; 2:23 cf Romans 9:25-26 cp Deuteronomy 32:21.

90   Presumably the Muslims. However it is possible that this may allude to an earlier conflict between Messianic Jews and Arabs. There are some suggestive passages in Josephus.

91   Jeschu. That is, Jesus.

other world. Go, and do good for Israel, and remove the apostates from us, that they may go to destruction! Elijahu went to the Sanhedrin at Tiberias, *and* to Antioch, and made proclamation throughout the whole land of Israel: Whoso believeth on {in} Jeschu, let him join himself to me![92] Then he said to them: I am the messenger (apostle) of Jeschu, who sent me to you, and I will show you a marvel, as Jeschu did. They brought to him a leper, and he laid his hand upon him, so that he was healed. They brought unto him a lame man, he uttered the *Shem*, laid his hand on him, and he was healed and stood on his feet.[93] Forthwith they fell down before him and said: Truly thou art the messenger of Jeschu, for thou hast shown us marvels as he did. He said to them: Jeschu sendeth you his greeting and saith: I am with my Father in heaven at his right hand, until he shall take vengeance on the Jews, as David said: Sit thou on my right hand, *until I make thine enemies thy footsool.*[94] At the same hour they all lamented[95] and added foolishness to their foolishness.

Elijahu said to them: Jeschu saith to you: Whosoever will be with me in the other world, let him remove himself from the community of Israel and join himself not to them;[96] for my Father in heaven hath already rejected them and from henceforth requireth not their service, for so he said through Isaiah: Your new moons and feasts my soul hateth; *they are a trouble unto me; I am weary to bear them.*[97] But Jeschu saith to you: Whosoever will follow me, let him profane the Sabbath,[98] for God hateth it, but instead keepeth the Sunday; for on it God gave light to his world. And for Passover which the Israelites solemnize, keep ye it on the Feast of the Resurrection, for he is risen from his grave; for the Feast of Weeks, Ascension; for on it he ascended to heaven; for New

---

92   cf 2 Kings 10:18-19.
93   cp Acts 14:8-10.
94   Psalm 110:1 cf I Corinthians 15:25-27; Mt 22:44; Mk 12:36; Lk 20:42; Acts 2:34.
95   Lamented. Probably a corruption for "rejoiced".
96   Revelation 18:4.
97   Isaiah 1:14 cf Mt 21:43 cp Isaiah 54:9-10; 60:15; 65:17-19; 66:22-24; Jeremiah 31:35-37.
98   Colossians 2:16-17 cp Mt 24:20. The Sabbath was never changed from Saturday to Sunday in the New Testament.

Year, Finding of the Cross;[99] for the Great Fast Day [Day of Atonement], the Feast of the Circumcision;[100] for Chanuka [the Feast of Lights; the feast of the dedication[101]], Calendae [New Year]. The foreskin is naught; whosoever will circumcise himself, let him be circumcised; whosoever will not circumcise himself, let him not be circumcised.[102] Moreover, whatsoever God created in this world, from the smallest gnat to the mightiest elephant, pour forth its blood upon the ground[103] and eat it, for so it is written: As the green grass have I given you all *creatures for food.*[104] If one of them compel you to go a mile, go with him two;[105] if a Jew smite you on the left side, turn to him the right also;[106] if a Jew revile you, endure it and return it not again, as Jeschu endured it; in meekness he showed himself, therewith he showed you also meekness as he practiced it, that ye might endure all that any should do to you.[107] At the last judgment Jeschu will punish them, but do ye have hope according to your meekness, for so it is written: Seek ye the Lord, all ye meek of the earth, *which have wrought his judgment; seek righteousness, seek meekness: it may be ye shall be hid in the day of the LORD's anger.*[108]

Thus he spoke and taught, until he separated them from Israel. But Elijahu who gave them these laws, the not-good ones, did it for the welfare of Israel, and the Christians call him Paul.[109] After he had introduced these

---

99   Another grotesque anachronism.

100   Luke 2:21.

101   cf John 10:22-23 cf I Maccabees 4:56; 2 Maccabees 1:18.

102   Galatians 5:2-6; 6:12-15; Philippians 3:2; Romans 2:28-29 cf Barnabas 8:6.

103   Deuteronomy 12:16,23-24; 15:23; Leviticus 17:10-14; Genesis 9:3-4.

104   Genesis 9:3 cf I Timothy 4:4; Romans 14:2-3; I Corinthians 8:8; 10:27; Mk 7:15; Mt 15:10 cp Revelation 2:14-20 cf Acts 10:9-16; 15:29.

105   Mt 5:41.

106   Mt 5:39.

107   Mt 5:40-45; I Peter 2:19-24; 4:16; 2 Corinthians 11:24-26. Notice that this is a grotesque bastardization and corruption of the doctrine of meekness taught in the New Testament.

108   Zephaniah 2:3.

109   Paul. Thus the man otherwise named Elijahu in the Toldoth Jeschu is here identified as Paul. Hence the historical existence of Paul is not necessarily fatal to the thesis advocated herein. However see the chapter on the apostle Paul below. It is notable that the Jews portray Paul as one of their own agents in the Toldoth,

laws and commandments, the erring ones separated themselves from Israel, and the strife ceased.[110]

11. A long time after *these things* the Persian power arose; then a Christian departed from them, *and* made a mock of them, just as the heretics had laughed at the wise men [of Israel]. *This was Nestorius.*[111]

He said to them: Paul was in error in his scripture when he said to you: Circumcise yourselves not;[112] for Jeschu *himself* was circumcised.[113] Further hath Jeschu said: I am not come to destroy even one jot {yod} from the law of Moses, but to fulfill all his words.[114] And that is your shame, which Paul laid upon you, when he said: Circumcise yourselves not.[115] But Nestorius said to them: Circumcise yourselves, for Jeschu was circumcised.[116] Further said Nestorius: Ye heretics! Ye say that Jeschu is God, though he was born of a woman.[117] Only the Holy Spirit rested on him as on the prophets.[118]

Nestorius who began to argue with the Christians, persuaded their women; he said to them: I will enact that no Christian take two wives.[119] But as Nestorius became detestable in their eyes, there arose a strife between them, in so much that no Christian would pray to

---

just as Juda Ischariota (Judas Iscariot) also was so depicted therein.

110   As noted above, some of the commandments ascribed to Paul originate with Jesus himself, and are found in the Gospel of Matthew. However the passage denotes that Paul is associated with Christianity becoming primarily a Gentile movement. However Christianity probably did not become primarily Gentile until well into the second century. Indeed, there seems not to be very much of Gentile Christianity until the reign of the Emperor Hadrian, or later.

111   Nestorius. Nestorius taught that Jesus the man was overshadowed by the divine Christ, and that he became "the Son of God" by adoptionism, at his baptism by John the Baptist.

112   Galatians 5:2-6; 6:12; Philippians 3:2; Romans 2:28-29 cp Genesis 17:1-14.

113   Luke 2:21; Infancy 2:1 cf John 7:22-23 & 10:35.

114   Mt 5:17-18 cf John 10:35.

115   Galatians 5:2-6; 6:12; Philippians 3:2; Romans 2:28-29.

116   Luke 2:21 cf Galatians 4:4.

117   Galatians 4:4.

118   Thus Nestorius denied the alleged Deity of Christ.

119   Titus 1:6; I Timothy 3:2,12.

the abomination of Nestorius, nor the followers of Nestorius to the abomination of the Christians.

The Nestorians went to Babylon to another place, the name of which was Chazaza, and all fled before him, because Nestorius was a violent man. The women said to him: What requirest thou of us? He answered them: I require only that ye receive from me the bread-and-wine offering.

Now it was the custom of the women of Chazaza, that they carried large keys in their hands. He gave one of them the offering; *but* she cast it to the ground. Whereupon the women cast the keys in their hands upon him; smote him, so that he died, and there was for long strife between them.[120]

12. Now the chief of the Sanhedrin, his name was Shimeon Kepha[121] - and why was he called Kepha? Because he stood on the stone which Ezekiel had prophesied at the river Kebar, and on that stone it was that Shimeon Kepha heard a voice from heaven.[122] When the Christians heard that Shimeon Kepha was one of those who heard a voice from heaven, and that stores of wisdom were in him, they envied the Israelites, that so great a man was found in Israel;... God brought it into Shimeon's mind to go to Jerusalem... on the Feast of Tabernacles. And there gathered together all the bishops and the great ancient[123] of the Christians. They came to Shimeon Kepha to the Mount of Olives[124] on the day of the Feast of Willow-twigs. When the saw {heard} his wisdom, that [there was] not one in Israel like unto him, *they sought* to turn him to the religion of the Christians, and they constrained him, saying: If thou dost not profess our religion, we will put thee to death, and not leave one remaining in

---

120 Presumably this means between the Nestorians and the other Christians. I will not comment upon the absurdity of the story about the demise of Nestorius, other than merely observing how juvenile it is.

121 John 1:42; Galatians 2:9; Mt 16:15-19; Mk 3:16; Lk 6:14. It is interesting that here there appears to be an attempt to co-opt Jewish Christian traditions about the apostle Peter, as depicted in the *Acts of Peter* and the *Pseudo-Clementines*.

122 *Bath-kol, "Daughter of the Voice".*

123 Probably the Patriarch of Constantinople, or possibly the Pope of Rome.

124 Zechariah 14:4; Mt 21:1; 24:3; 26:30; Mk 11:1; 13:3; 14:26; Lk 19:29,37; 21:37; 22:39; Jn 8:1; Acts 1:10-12.

Israel to go into the sanctuary. When the Israelites perceived this, they besought him: Humour them, act according to thy wisdom, so shall neither sin nor guilt be on thee. Thereupon when he perceived the hard fate for Israel, he betook himself to the Christians, and said to them: On this condition do I become a convert to your religion, that ye put no Jew to death, that ye smite him not and suffer [allow] him to go in and out in the sanctuary. The ancient and the Christians accepted his words and all these conditions. He made a condition with them, that they would build him a tower; he would go into it, would eat no flesh, nor aught save bread and water and he would remain in the tower until his death. All this he did with respect to God, that he might not be stained and sullied by them, and that he might not mix with them; but to the Christians he spake in their sense as if he would mourn for Jeschu, and eat no flesh or aught else, but bread and water only. They built him a tower, and he dwelt therein; he sullied himself not with eating, and prayed not to the Cross.

Afterwards he composed in the tower *Keroboth, Jotzroth*, and *Zulthoth* in his name, like Eliezer ben Kalir. He sent and gathered together the elders of Israel, and handed over to their care all that he had found in his mind, and charged them that they should teach it to the leaders in prayer and use it for prayers, so that they might make mention of him for good.[125] They, moreover, sent it to Babylon to Rabbi Nathan, Prince of the Exile, and they showed it to the heads of the schools, to the Sanhedrin, and they said: It is good, and they taught it to the leaders in prayer of all Israel, and they used it for prayers. Whosoever would mention the name of Shimeon in his chanting did so. May his memory endure to the life of the other world. But God in his mercy *blessed* him as a good defender *of the true faith*. Amen. Selah!

Commentary on the Toldoth Jeschu

The Toldoth Jeschu is an ancient text that is common to both Orthodox and Karaite Jews. The written form of the Toldoth can easily be traced back to the third century, and possibly even as early as the late second century. The original language of the Toldoth was either Aramaic or

125   Nehemiah 13:31.

Hebrew, and the earliest extant manuscripts of the Toldoth are in Aramaic.[126] These earliest fragments were discovered by Solomon Schechter in the same Cairo Geniza in which he also discovered fragments of the famed Damascus Document.[127] The Damascus Document was also discovered among the Dead Sea Scrolls.[128] No doubt there was some oral form of the Toldoth Jeschu prior to the earliest writing thereof, but in any case both the oral and written forms of the Toldoth are reactive; the Toldoth presupposes the prior existence of a distinctly Christian movement, which arose from the matrix of Judaism. There are a number of recensions of the Toldoth, and Mead speaks of a "distinctly Karaite Toldoth."[129] The Toldoth appears to be a parody of the New Testament Gospels, and presents a Jewish interpretation of the life of Jesus. Therefore the virgin birth is replaced with a story of shameful bastardy, and the omnipotent power of the *Shem* is the "explanation" for how Jesus was able to perform miracles.[130] There is an unabashed attempt to claim Judas Iscariot, Paul the apostle, and Simon Peter as conscious agents of the Rabbis in the Toldoth. This may betray an intent to sabotage Christianity by casting doubt upon the legitimacy of some or all of the New Testament writings. For this very reason, the possibility exists that the chronological anachronism of Jesus living in the days of Queen Salome may also be an attempt to sabotage Christianity, by way of creating confusion respecting the time in which Jesus really lived. Indeed, we find the same kinds of anachronisms in the Talmud as well, but the very same argument still applies: we may have here nothing but an attempt at sabotage through disinformation. And if the thesis that Jesus lived (or may have lived) a century before the commonly-accepted time were based solely upon hostile sources, as appears to be the case in Mead's work, then we could dismiss the idea without further ado. But, as we will see, there are other sources which dovetail in such an unexpected and unsolicited way with

---

126   Mead., G.R.S., *DID JESUS LIVE 100 B.C.?*, (1903; 2005 by Cosimo Classics); pg. 255.

127   Ibid., pg. 253. Shanks, Hershel, (ed.), *UNDERSTANDING THE DEAD SEA SCROLLS.* (1992; Biblical Archaeology Society) (New York: Random House), pgs. 63-78.

128   Shanks., ibid.

129   Mead., op. cit., pg. 316.

130   See the chapter on the Shem below.

the thesis, that they deserve at least some consideration. We must at least consider the possibility that the Jews sought to sabotage Christianity chronologically, by deliberately dislocating Jesus from his true time. Mead pretends that such an idea is an impossibility, and doesn't even consider it or mention it. Mead is guilty, either consciously or unconsciously, of disregarding Christian evidence, in the sense that he grants more favour to Jewish and occult sources of information, rather than to the New Testament or other Christian sources. But there may also have been other motives on the part of the Jews to dislocate Jesus from the canonical timeframe. One is as a form of camouflage. In other words, by placing Jesus in a much earlier time, they provided themselves with some degree of "plausible deniability" if ever the text of the Toldoth were to fall into Christian hands. Indeed, the fact that Queen Salome-Alexandra is not distinctly mentioned by name in the Toldoth, but she is called therein "Queen Helene", which seems to make her a composite of Queen Salome and Queen Helena of Adiabene, may have been intended as a form of camouflage, by placing the events narrated therein in some "never-never land" of pure fantasy. I suppose that some would argue that the Rabbis were responding to a story they believed was a fantasy in the same coin. This is possible, but it does not lead to any definitive conclusions respecting the historical Jesus. It is also just barely possible that the anachronism was due merely to carelessness. In the Talmud there are frequent anachronisms, particularly in respect to Jesus and Mary. We would certainly expect the Christians to have much more reliable information about their own Lord and Savior, including the time in which he lived and was crucified, all other things being equal. And the New Testament is consistent in respect to the time in which Jesus was crucified. By contrast, the anachronisms of the Talmud are notoriously inconsistent; sometimes placing Jesus or Mary either before or after the canonical timeframe. Although it was also pointed out by Mead that, the "anachronisms" placing Jesus in the days of Alexander Jannaeus are statistically significant, in the sense of occurring much more frequently, than other such anachronisms. The version of the Toldoth above is a comparatively late one; the reference to Nestorius places it no earlier than the fifth century. And if indeed the reference to the Ishmaelites refers to Muslims then this would make the recension at least as late as the seventh century, or later. However, these portions of the Toldoth clearly seem to be later additions to an older text and tradition. The reference to the "Finding of the Cross" once again places the recension as late as the fourth century, but once again, there no doubt were earlier forms of the Toldoth, both written and oral. The wildly satirical nature of much of the story may evince that it had never been intended as a serious rebuttal to the claims of Christianity. Returning briefly to Queen Helene, the fact that she may be a composite of Queen Salome-Alexandra and Queen Helena of Adiabene may suggest that the Rabbis understood the Jesus of the Gospels to be a composite figure. Helena, a convert to Judaism, helped the Jews in Jerusalem in a time of famine.[131] For this reason she was likely well-esteemed by the Jews. Queen Salome, the widow of Alexander Jannaeus, ruled over the Jews for nine years, and allowed the Pharisees to rule the country in all but name.[132] Therefore she also would have been greatly beloved by the Rabbis who were descendants of those Pharisees, both ideologically and biologically. Therefore it is quite possible that the Queen Helene of the Toldoth is a composite of these two women, who lived at different times. But Simeon ben Shetach, who is also mentioned in the Toldoth, was also a contemporary of Alexander Jannaeus. So the preponderance of evidence from the text of the Toldoth points to the time of Queen Alexandra (Salome) as being the time in which Jesus lived. True this could be merely camouflage and/or disinformational sabotage, but by placing Jesus in the days of Alexandra, the Jews would be forfeiting a classic "disclaimer" in respect to the crucifixion: "The Romans did it." Over and over we constantly hear this refrain today, like a broken record. If Jesus really lived in the days of the Roman occupation of Judaea, and was crucified by the Romans (as the New Testament maintains), then the Jews would have had a perfect alibi vis-à-vis the crucifixion; they could just blame it on the Romans. So any value that such chronological camouflage would have, or value as a form of sabotage by casting doubt upon the veracity of the New Testament documents, would seem to be outweighed by the political advantage of having such a convenient alibi. Furthermore doubt is cast upon the camouflage/disinformation scenario, due to the fact that the Toldoth was

---

131   Jos. Ant. 20.2.1-5.
132   Jos. Ant. 13.16.1-6; War. 1.5.1-4.

written by Jews for Jews, and generally circulated exclusively among Jews. Jews had been prohibited by the Rabbis from reading any works of the Christians,[133] and Christian clergy probably inculcated the same attitude among their flock towards Jewish writings.[134] So the Toldoth does present some evidence that Jesus may have lived back in the Hasmonean era. This evidence is supplemented in part by the Talmud, and also by the book of Daniel. In the Toldoth, Jesus is twice captured by the Rabbis. The first time he is delivered by his disciples. But the second time he does not escape. The hanging from a cabbage-stalk is curious. As we will see, there are some curious verses in the New Testament that speak of Jesus having been slain and hanged from a tree. This is distinctly different from the traditional form of crucifixion. This is evidence from the very pages of the New Testament itself, that Jesus may in fact not have been crucified by the Romans, but instead he was executed in the Hasmonean era. The problem is that the Toldoth was apparently completely unknown to Christians in the early centuries of the Common Era, so there are no discussions of it or answers to the anomalous chronology found therein. Some critics may cite this as evidence that the Toldoth really is a late document, however Tertullian does respond to a tradition that is found within it. However he does not comment on the chronology of the text, so he may have only heard a story that circulated among Jews in his time. The incident with Juda Ischariota flying in the air with Jeschu is curious and worth briefly commenting on. The text says that Juda Ischariota "befouled" Jeschu, but it is unclear from the text whether this denotes urination or defecation. However there is an argument from the Talmud that suggests the former, rather than the latter. There is a Talmudic argument that ritual uncleanness can indeed travel back upstream, from an unclean vessel, back into the (formerly) clean vessel from which the water (or other liquid) was poured. Orthodox Rabbis took this position. Therefore apparently the text means that Juda Ischariota urinated upon Jeschu while they were both in flight, and, since Jeschu was now defiled, he fell to the earth. But since Juda's own ritual impurity also travelled back upstream through the stream of urine, he also became defiled, and thus fell to earth. We hear no more of Juda Ischariota after this (even

---

133   Mead., op. cit., pgs. 237-240.
134   Save the Scriptures.

though he now had the omnipotent power of the *Shem* to do whatever he wanted), so it would seem that the story was a gratuitous mockery of Jesus which was introduced to uphold the Rabbinical determination in respect to ritual impurity. Of course after Jeschu became ritually purified once again he once again wielded the power of the *Shem*. But curiously, we never again hear of Juda Ischariota; presumably he had served his purpose within the context of the Toldoth. Thirty years after the death (or apparent death) of Jeschu, Paul is introduced as Elijahu, an agent of the Rabbis. Presumably very early forms of the Toldoth would have ended with the story of Paul, or perhaps with an account of Shimeon Kepha, who seems to be an appropriation of the Jewish-Christian version of Simon Peter in some early traditions. The account of Nestorius was apparently added to later editions of the Toldoth to make it more complete. The Toldoth Jeschu was apparently intended as an explanation to Jews for the rise and existence and continuity of Christianity. There would have been no social need for this, except for the fact that Christianity claimed to be based upon the prophecies of the Jewish prophets. The Messianic status of Jesus was the all-or-nothing question that could not be set aside in any controversy between the opposing parties. Curiously, the Toldoth is somewhat less scathing in its indictment of Jesus than certain passages of the Talmud are. The expediency of the Shem leaves Jesus free to have performed his marvels by truly divine, rather than diabolical, power.[135] Nor is there any mention of Jesus being punished in the midst of boiling filth and excrement, as found in some Talmud passages.[136] Mary also does fairly well. She is not accused of being a deliberate adulteress, as she is shamefully charged in some Talmud passages.[137] In fact, nowhere is Mary ever in jeopardy of being stoned for adultery, either in the New Testament, the New Testament Apocrypha, nor in any Jewish writings. This proves that Jesus had not been accused of illegitimacy in his own days. By the same token, Jesus himself probably never laid claim to having been born of a virgin, despite what is written in the Toldoth. Nowhere in the New Testament does Jesus ever claim any such thing. Of course it could be argued by Christians

---

135   cp Mt 12:24-32; Mk 3:22-29; Lk 11:14-26.
136   Mead., op. cit., pgs. 204-207.
137   Ibid., pgs. 152-166.

that Jesus indirectly laid claim to this, by claiming to have been the Son of God. An appeal could certainly be made to Bible prophecy, which does foretell a virgin birth.[138] The Greek text of Isaiah leaves no doubt, however much contemporary Jews may protest to the contrary. And the Greek text would have been that used by those who composed the Gospels in Greek. Actually this casts a new light on Mark 3:21, where the family of Jesus accuses him of being "beside himself"; it may have been a sort of disclaimer in respect to his messianic claims, lest they be in danger of a death penalty by the Sanhedrin. This would have been especially the case with Mary, who would not want to unjustly suffer the death penalty for adultery. But it is quite possible that the earliest disciples of Jesus interpreted his ontological status as "the Son of God" in a spiritual sense, which would not require a literal virgin birth. In other words, it was in reference to his spiritual nature, rather than to his flesh-and-blood body, that such Sonship would apply. In fact, there is some evidence of an earlier adoptionist view of the divine Sonship of Jesus in the New Testament.[139] Miriam (Mary) at least seems to be relatively unscathed in the Toldoth, compared with some portions of the Talmud. She is betrothed to a man of the house and lineage of David, just as in the New Testament Gospels. By implication this means that she herself was also of the tribe of Judah, since according to Numbers 36, the Israelites had been commanded by God to only marry within their ancestral tribe. By contrast, there is some evidence from the Gospel of Luke that Mary (and therefore Joseph) were of the tribe of Levi, rather than Judah. She is the kinswoman of Elizabeth, who is said to be of the daughters of Aaron.[140] Therefore presumably Mary and Joseph were also Levites, and therefore so also would be Jesus. Despite this, Luke still supplies Jesus with a Davidic genealogy,[141] but this almost appears to be an afterthought, and an attempt to provide Jesus with a gratuitous messianic credential.

The attitude of Jochanan, the betrothed of Miriam, is in stark contrast

---

138   Isaiah 7:14 (LXX).
139   Nestle-Aland., NOVUM TESTAMENTUM GRAECE. (26th critical edition of the Greek New Testament; Deutsche Bibelgesellschaft Stuttgart © 1979); pgs. 158, 159, 162.
140   Luke 1:5.
141   Luke 3:23-31.

with that of Joseph of the Gospels. We read of Joseph: "When his mother Mary, being espoused to Joseph, was found to be with child by holy spirit, before they were married. Then Joseph her husband, being a just man, and not willing to make her a public spectacle, mused on sending her away secretly."[142] This is in stark contrast with the attitude of Jochanan of the Toldoth, who openly repudiated Miriam, and abandoned her, departing to Babylon. Interestingly, the passage in Matthew commends Joseph for not exposing Mary to the shame of bearing an illegitimate child, and possibly from the fate of a public stoning. But the mind-set of the Toldoth is mired in the legalism of Rabbinical Judaism, in all its tortured logic. Despite itself, the Toldoth fails miserably. It cannot account for how and why generation after generation of Jews continued to claim that Jeschu (Jesus) was the Messiah. Jeschu still comes out smelling like a rose, compared to the so-called "wise men of Israel". The absurd stories that abound throughout the Toldoth are an insult to the intelligence. Perhaps this is because the Rabbis felt that Christianity was an absurd religion and unworthy of a serious refutation.[143] Returning the question of the lineage of Jesus, it is quite possible that Jesus was not even ethnically Jewish at all. According to the Gospel texts, he was native to Galilee, which is called in Scripture "Galilee of the Gentiles."[144] Galilee was one of several regions in the neighborhood of Syria that had been conquered generations before by John Hyrcanus, who imposed the religion of Judaism upon the native inhabitants of that land.[145] Therefore these people, who formerly had been Canaanites and Syrians, now became known as Jews, albeit it was true only in the religious sense. In fact, since these were forced conversions, the sincerity of such Judaism is open to question. In any case, a critical appraisal of the question of the descent of the historical Jesus suggests that quite possibly Jesus was neither a Jew[146] nor a Levite, but rather a

---

142   Matthew 1:18-19.

143   Proverbs 26:5.

144   Isaiah 9:1; Matthew 4:15 cf I Maccabees 5:15.

145   Jos. Ant. 13.9.1. War 1.2.6.

146   Jew. In the strictly ethnic sense, a lineal descendant of the tribe of Judah. This is the original meaning of the term "Jew". Indeed, throughout the Hebrew *TaNaKh*, this is the distinctive meaning of the word *Yehudiy*; in Esther 8:17, where it says in the King James Version "And in every province, and in every city, withersoever the king's commandment and his decree came, the Jews (*Yehudim*)

Canaanite. Therefore the monotonous, "politically correct" carping that Jesus was a Jew is probably not even true. It is also interesting that the text of the Toldoth accords with the Septuagint reading of Isaiah 7:14, which clearly says "the virgin" shall conceive, and bear a son, and call his name Immanuel., etc.[147] Since Jesus (Jeschu) clearly lived long after the time of the first fulfillment[148] of the prophecy, thereafter the prophecy had definitely taken on Messianic proportions, and had thus been so interpreted by the Septuagint translators. In fact, the text of the Toldoth argues against the constant carping of Jews that the original Hebrew of Isaiah 7:14 reads "*almah*" which does not require the interpretation of *virgo intacta*. The Toldoth Jeschu, a Jewish text, written by Jews and for Jews, thus supports the reading of the Septuagint text, a text which had been interpreted and translated by Jews from the original Hebrew. Furthermore the Latin Vulgate text also confirms the Septuagint reading, as does also the Greek New Testament.[149] Possibly the concept of a virgin

had joy and gladness, a feast and a good day. And many people of the land became Jews (*Yahadim*); for the fear of the Jews (*Yehudim*) fell upon them.", as one can see, in the underlying Hebrew, two distinctly different Hebrew words are used; therefore one cannot become a Jew (*Yehudiy*) in the primary sense; one can instead join the community (*Yahad*); this latter term being found in the famous Damascus Document. The term "Jew" as originally used, and as confirmed by the etymological derivation, denotes a person descended from the tribe of Judah; but the term has come to be used as an umbrella term to include Levites, Benjaminites, the remnants of the other tribes of Israel who remained faithful to the Jerusalem cultus after the division of the kingdom in the days of Rehoboam, and ultimately to all converts to Judaism, and their descendants. But here I am using the term in its original, biblical, sense. Josephus confirms my interpretation of the word "Jew" in his Magnum Opus, the *Antiquities of the Jews:* "So the Jews prepared for the work: that is the name they are called by from the day that they came up from Babylon, which is taken from the tribe of Judah which came first to these places, and thence both they and the country gained that appellation." (Jos. Ant. 11.5.7; 173).

147   SEPTUAGINTA., Deutsche Bibelgesellschaft Stuttgart (Alfred Rahlfs, editor; 1935, 1979; Deutsche Bibelgesellschaft Stuttgart), pg. 575. (vol. 2; Duo volumina in uno).

148   Within 65 years of the prophecy; cf Isaiah 7:8.

149   BIBLIA SACRA VULGATA., (IUXTA VULGATUM VERSION-EM); Deutsche Bibelgesellschaft Stuttgart (1969)., pg. 1103. Nestle-Aland., op. cit., pg. 3.

birth may have been derived from Zoroastrianism, which had some influence upon pre-Christian Judaism. In any case by the third century B.C., when the Hebrew *Torah* Scrolls were first translated into Greek, the idea that the Messiah would indeed be born of a virgin had taken firm hold upon the Jewish imagination, and was largely accepted. This remains true, despite any protests by contemporary Jews to the contrary, or the carpings of those seduced by Talmudic revisionism. Thus to claim to be the Messiah was equivalent to claiming to be the Son of God. However this was not *necessarily* the same as claiming an equality with God, as post-Nicene Christians might think. The stark monotheism of postexilic Judaism would not permit any rival to the Godhead. However it is likely that there was also a spectrum of opinions regarding the alleged ontological status of the Messiah among different groups of Jews. The Messianic passages of the book of Enoch are proof against any nay-saying pseudoscholars who would pretend that the Jews never looked forward to a superhuman Messiah. And *Enoch* was apparently a normative Scripture to the Qumran community, who would have shunned any hint of idolatry or polytheism. Such pseudoscholars have never grasped the subtleties of Arianism.[150] One can detect a childishly mocking tone in the answers that the "wise men" give to Jeschu; even within the Toldoth, their answers seem far more out-of-context than the ones Jeschu provides. It is quite possible that the Toldoth only played a relatively marginal role in Judaism. Nevertheless it does provide some degree of circumstantial evidence in favor of the postulate that Jesus lived approximately a century before the canonical timeframe. As such, it is a crucial part of the complete evidence that Jesus may have lived 100 B.C. However the Toldoth also provides a clear chronological marker for us, inasmuch as it testifies, perhaps inadvertently, that the year in which Jesus was crucified was one in which the Passover fell on the Sabbath. This is also in accordance with the Gospel testimony. But this also places constraints, and possibly some degree of testability, to the theory proposed herein. If none of the nine years in which Queen Alexandra reigned was one in which the Passover fell on the Sabbath, then the theory advocated herein can be safely ruled out. And we know

---

150   Arianism. Named after Arius, a bishop of the third and fourth centuries, who maintained that Jesus was the Son of God, but not God the Son.

from records that the Passover fell on a Sabbath in the year 27 A.D., which is in accord with the standard chronology in respect to Christ. Furthermore 27 A.D. also is congenial to an interpretation that the seventh year of Artaxerxes[151] was the *terminus a quo* of Daniel's prophecy of the seventy weeks. We would also have to determine whether any years from 53 B.C. to 46 B.C. inclusive were years in which Passover fell on the Sabbath. This is the final test for the theory advocated herein.

---

151   457 B.C., according to the standard chronology.

SEVENTY WEEKS

Daniel's prophecy of the seventy weeks is a crucial part of the evidence that Jesus may have lived in the first century B.C., and this key evidence was completely overlooked by G.R.S. Mead. Apparently Mead was not sufficiently acquainted either with the book of Daniel or the chronology of Josephus to realise how these two sources dovetail together to confirm the 100 B.C. date for Jesus. Mead certainly makes some use of Josephus, as well as the Jewish Scriptures, but this relevant evidence escaped his scrutiny. And there can be no doubt that, had Mead known of this admittedly somewhat obscure evidence, he would have mentioned it in his book.

We will examine the prophecy in some detail, but first I would like to say a few words about the book of Daniel. There is not unanimous agreement among Bible scholars respecting the origin of the book of Daniel. Critical Bible scholars believe it is a late *pseudepigraphon* of the second century B.C., while conservative Bible scholars believe the book is genuine, and thus dates from the sixth century B.C. Strong and valid arguments are to be found on both sides of this controversy, which is far from settled. Indeed, this controversy has raged since the days of Porphyry.[1] Sincere Christians and Jews devoutly believe the work to be genuine, and a key component of their faith.[2] Nevertheless in a historical inquiry of this

---

1   Porphyry was a polemicist against Christianity in the third century.
2   This is especially so in the case of Christians.

nature we cannot be shackled by theological preconceptions. Without pretending to resolve the dispute between critical and conservative biblical scholars respecting the book of Daniel, I will simply state that, considering the question *holistically*, I am more inclined to believe that the book is a *pseudepigraphon*. One thing that both conservative and critical Bible scholars are agreed on is that *Daniel* was written before the first century B.C., which is the time period in question. Therefore we will proceed with an examination of the prophecy without further ado.

The prophecy was supposedly revealed to Daniel in the first year of Darius the Mede, who was the son of Ahasuerus.[3] Daniel understood that, according to the prophecies of Jeremiah, the time of the seventy year captivity of the Jews was coming to an end.[4] But rather than expecting an automatic fulfillment of the prophecies, Daniel prays to God for forgiveness for his people.[5] Then Daniel has a vision of an angel, who proceeds to reveal a prophecy.[6] I would like to offer my translation of the prophecy, since I believe portions of it have been mistranslated in most Bibles.

24 Seventy weeks[7] are determined upon thy people and upon thy holy city, to finish the transgression, to make an end of sins, to make reconciliation for iniquity, to bring in everlasting righteousness, to seal up vision and prophecy, and to anoint the Most Holy.

25 Know therefore and understand, From the going forth of the commandment to restore and to build Jerusalem, unto the Messiah the Prince, Seven weeks, and sixty-two weeks: the street shall be built again, and the wall, even in troublous times.

26 And after sixty-two weeks shall Messiah make a covenant,[8] but not

---

3   Daniel 9:1. This was approximately 537 B.C., according to the standard chronology.
4   Jeremiah 25:8-13; 29:10.
5   Daniel 9:3-19. We will sometimes write "as if" Daniel were a genuine prophet of the sixth century, for the sake of economy.
6   Daniel 9:20-27.
7   Seventy weeks., I.e., seventy weeks of years, or 490 years. Cp Numbers 14:34.
8   Heb., *karath*. Cf BIBLIA HEBRAICA STUTTGARTENSIA. Deutsche

in his own *name,* and the people of the Prince that shall come shall spoil the city and the sanctuary; and the end thereof *shall be* with a flood, and unto the end of the war desolations are determined.

27 And he shall confirm the covenant with many for one week,[9] and in the midst of the week he shall cause the sacrifice and the oblation to cease, and for the overspreading of abominations shall he make it desolate, even unto the consummation, and that decreed shall be poured upon the desolate.

First and foremost I will seek to justify my reading of *karath* as meaning "make a covenant" rather than the more familiar "shall be cut off". While it is true that the Hebrew word *karath* very often has the meaning of "cut off" as in being killed, the central idea has to do with cutting, and is also associated with the idea of making a covenant, as in circumcision, etc. In fact, the above reading is permitted by the Hebrew Dictionary found in ABINGDON'S STRONG'S EXHAUSTIVE CONCORDANCE OF THE BIBLE WITH HEBREW, CHALDEE & GREEK DICTIONARIES. One has but to look at the prophecy in context to see that the reading "cut off" is inappropriate when applied to the Messiah, for whom the Jews were all eagerly awaiting. It would be absurd for the Messiah to appear, only to be killed immediately. There is no evidence that the Jews were awaiting a dying Messiah, much less a crucified Messiah.[10] Furthermore how could the Messiah "confirm the covenant with many for a week" following this, if he had already been killed? Furthermore the reference to "the covenant" in verse 27 confirms the reading of "make a covenant" in verse 26. The proof that my translation of *karath* is the correct one in this verse is based upon simple common sense. The Messiah, whom the Jews identified with the coming Son of man,[11] was supposed to be granted "an everlasting dominion, which shall not pass away, and his kingdom which shall not

---

Bibelgesellschaft Stuttgart. (EDITIO FUNDITUS RENOVATA; K. Elliger & W. Rudolph; Textum Masoreticum curavit H.P. Ruger MASORAM ELABORAVIT G. E. Weil.); pg. 1404.

9   The final seven-year period of the prophecy.

10   There are even passages in the New Testament that confirm this: John 12:34 & Acts 8:27-34 cf Isaiah 53:7-8.

11   John 12:34.

be destroyed."[12] How could the Messiah be granted "an everlasting dominion" if he were to be "cut off"? No Jew who lived at that time could have thus interpreted the prophecy in such a way as to anticipate an early martyrdom for the Messiah. Not only would this idea have been foreign to the expectations of the Jews, but such an interpretation of the prophecy would have made the position of Messiah an unenviable one indeed, in terms of any men who otherwise would have sought to lay claim to the title at that time.[13] My argument is that the reading "shall be cut off" must have only post-dated the time when Jesus actually was martyred, or presumably martyred. Some critical Bible scholars have sought to identify the "anointed one" who is "cut off" with the high priest Onias, but this explanation is unsatisfactory, since Onias lived far too early to have been the intended "Messiah" of the prophecy. Regardless of one's reading of *karath* in this verse, if the decree of Cyrus[14] is taken as the *terminus a quo* of the prophecy, then the *terminus ad quem* would be 46 B.C., which was long after the time in which Onias lived. Even subtracting the final seven years of the prophecy, that would still give us 53 B.C., which is still far later than the time of Onias. Therefore regardless of when *Daniel* was written, Onias could not have been the intended "Messiah" or "anointed one" of the prophecy; therefore my reading of *karath* seems to be the more probable reading, as it was originally understood. Only after the time that Jesus was martyred did the reading of *karath* in Daniel 9:26 become changed from "shall make a covenant" to "shall be cut off". At least that seems most probable to me. Another point of contention is whether there is any distinction between "the Messiah the Prince" of verse 25 and "the Prince that shall come" of the following verse. Common sense would tell us that there is no such distinction, although translators have sought to perpetuate this impression, by using a lower-case "p" for the latter instance, while using a capital "P" for the former. But in Hebrew there is no distinction between upper and lower-case letters; all the letters are the same. There is nothing in the passage itself that clearly distinguishes between the two instances of the same Hebrew word, used in such close

---

12   Daniel 7:14.
13   I.e., at the time when the Messiah was supposed to come, according to the prophecy.
14   536 B.C., according to the standard chronology.

proximity, in the very same prophecy; and it seems only the theological prejudices of the translators that have so dictated their reading of the passage. They apparently stumble on the notion that the Messiah could be the one to "cause the sacrifice and the oblation to cease", as we read in verse 27. And admittedly this does require some explanation. Some Christians have interpreted this verse as meaning that the sacrifices and oblations of the temple would cease "to be effective as offerings to God" after the "perfect and final sacrifice of Christ upon the cross", and one can readily understand their rationale. However in critical terms, there was no cessation of sacrificial offerings in the temple immediately after the supposed time of Christ's crucifixion; those sacrifices continued on till the temple was destroyed by the Romans in 70 A.D. That was a good thirty to forty years after the time Jesus was crucified, according to the standard chronology. Therefore such an interpretation of supposedly "fulfilled" prophecy is an absurd begging of the question and an example of special pleading. Furthermore we are inquiring into the original interpretation of the prophecy, rather than later reinterpretations thereof. It would certainly have been a paradox to a Jew to suppose that the Messiah would "cause the sacrifice and the oblation to cease", and that may be one reason why Jews as well as Christians have thus made a distinction between the two occurrences of "prince" in the prophecy. But there were some Jews who were opposed to blood sacrifices, known as *Ebionim*. In the eyes of the *Ebionim* the Messiah would bring an end to sacrifice and oblation, since they were grievous to God.[15] Therefore quite possibly this prophecy in Daniel is a passage that either originated with or was influenced by the *Ebionim*, as certain other Scripture passages seem to have been. This explanation may not be satisfying to everyone, however. Most contemporary Christians identify this latter "prince" with the antichrist. Critical Bible scholars who may wish to identify him with Antiochus Epiphanes are refuted by the fact that Antiochus lived far too early to be the "prince" of the prophecy. Even adding the 45 years of the discrepancy between the chronology of Josephus and the standard chronology would still give us from 98 B.C. to 91 B.C. as the final "week"

---

15   Cf Isaiah 1:10-15; I Samuel 15:22; Micah 6:6-8; Hosea 6:6; Psalms 40:6-8; 50:7-15; 51:16-17; 107:22; 116:17; Proverbs 15:8; 21:3,27; Ecclesiastes 5:1; Jeremiah 7:22.

of the prophecy, which is clearly much later than 168 B.C. And it does seem to be a bit too much to suppose that the author of Daniel would have reckoned an additional seventy years backwards to the decree of Cyrus.[16] So there seems to be no basis to distinguish between "the Messiah the Prince" of verse 25 and "the Prince that shall come" of verse 26. They are one and the same. Thus, the final verse of the prophecy seems to predict a messianic abrogation of the Levitical law of blood sacrifices. This actually seems to be in accord with the earlier part of the prophecy, which speaks of "making an end of sins[17] making reconciliation for iniquity, bringing in everlasting righteousness, sealing up vision and prophecy, and anointing the most holy". The finality of the prophecy overshadows anything found in the *Torah* proper.[18] There may seem to be a conflict with the latter half of Ezekiel, which does depict perpetual sacrifices.[19] But if in fact Daniel is a late *pseudepigraphon*, then it ought not to be too surprising to find a more spiritual vision of the *eschaton*.[20]

Another potential objection against identifying the "Prince that shall come" of verse 26 with "the Messiah the Prince" of verse 25 is the fact that it is said that "the people of the Prince that shall come shall spoil the city and the sanctuary", which makes it hard to imagine that any group of Jews would thus spoil the city and the sanctuary. Unless there was some sort of civil war among the Jews. And this is precisely the kind of situation that is depicted in the reign of Alexander Jannaeus.[21] Furthermore we must remember that some of the *Ebionim* may have felt so passionate about their convictions that all animal sacrifices should be abolished that they would spoil the city and the sanctuary, if it served their purpose. Therefore the objections against the identification of the "Prince" mentioned in the two successive verses in the very same prophecy are insufficient to warrant. The more natural reading of the

---

16   This would create a discrepancy of 115 years between such a chronology and the standard chronology. This is an absurdity.

17   This could actually even denote sin-offerings.

18   I.e., the books attributed to Moses, as distinguished from the other Jewish Scriptures, known collectively as *TaNaKh*.

19   Ezekiel 40-48.

20   I.e., one without such blood sacrifices.

21   Jos. Ant. 13.13.1-5; 13.14.1-3.

prophecy implies that they are one and the same man. Only theological preconceptions cloud the judgment of those who otherwise would clearly see the meaning of the text. A person from a Buddhist or Hindu background would not so stumble over the text, as do Christians and Jews.

Significantly, Jeschu (Jesus) refers to the prophecy of Daniel 9:26 in the Toldoth, and refers the fulfillment of the prophecy to himself. This is certainly highly significant, in my view. Of course in the Toldoth itself it has been translated according to the currently-accepted reading of "shall be cut off and he is not" rather than "shall make a covenant, but not *in* his own *name*", as I have interpreted it. But this in no way disproves my reading of *karath*. The Toldoth is a reactive document, and presumably was written no earlier than the very late second century at the earliest; more likely the third century. By then, Christians had already appropriated the text of Daniel and reinterpreted the prophecy and the reading of *karath* therein to mean "shall be cut off", in accordance with the "suffering servant" view of the Messiah, as portrayed in the passion of Jesus Christ. And the other Jews would have effectively relinquished any real claim upon the literal fulfillment of the prophecy, since the time of predicted fulfillment had already come and gone. Indeed, after the abortive Bar Kochbah uprising the Rabbis incorporated the concept of *gilgulim*[22] into calculations of when the promised Messiah would appear. The ambiguity of the term *karath* would remain in any Hebrew or Chaldee text, and the earliest extant versions of the Toldoth are in Chaldee (Syriac; Aramaic). I suppose that some could appeal to the Greek Septuagint to discredit my reading of *karath*, but I think it would be difficult to find a Greek text of Daniel dated to before the Common

---

22   Gilgulim. Heb., rollings. The term denotes transmigration. See Eisenmenger, Johann Andreas., THE TRADITIONS OF THE JEWS. (ENTDECKTES JUDENTHUM; 1700; (Johann Andreas Eisenmenger 1654-1704); translated from German to English by John Peter Stehelin 1732-1734; published in two volumes as Rabbinical Literature; or, The Traditions of the Jews; reprinted in 1742 and 1748. One volume edition reproduction of the 1748 edition, by Michael A. Hoffman II, 2006; published by Independent History and Research P.O. Box 849 Coeur d'Alene, Idaho 83816. Available @ http://www.RevisionistHistory.org; pgs. 441-503.

Era.[23] Of course I cannot rule out the possibility that there may be some future discovery of some scroll or fragment of a Greek text of Daniel with the relevant portion, which may prove me wrong. But if my reading of *karath* is wrong, then we would have to postulate two Messiahs, one of whom was to die a martyr's death.[24] There actually is evidence that the Jews are expecting two Messiahs. I remember when I was a college student some of the Jewish students on campus confided to me privately that they were waiting for two Messiahs. And in fact there are Rabbinical traditions of two Messiahs.[25] Ironically one of these Messiahs is called the Son of Joseph.[26] There is also evidence from the Dead Sea Scrolls that at least some Jews were expecting two Messiahs as far back as two thousand years ago. In one of the scrolls, known as the Manual of Discipline, it says: "They shall govern themselves using the original precepts by which the men of the *Yahad* began to be instructed, doing so until there come the Prophet and the Messiahs of Aaron and Israel."[27] So inasmuch as the Jews (or at least some Jews) have been expecting two Messiahs for two millennia I am not making my entire thesis hinge upon my reading of *karath*. Nevertheless I still feel that my reading is preferable and more highly probable as the original reading. Furthermore if the Jews expected this Messiah to die almost as soon as he appeared, his role would be most unenviable. Neither Jesus nor any other man would be eager to lay claim to such a title, if it involved an early death. I suppose in all fairness it is possible that the reading of *karath* may have denoted "shall be cut off" but a supernatural resurrection would thus revive the Messiah, to fulfill the remainder of the prophecy. However it is impossible to determine whether or not any Jews living at that time so understood the prophecy. I doubt that any young Jewish male would want to make an experiment of it, regardless how devout.

---

23   As far as I know the earliest text of the Septuagint dates to the third century.

24   Or even a sacrificial death.

25   Eisenmenger., op. cit., pgs. 701-702.

26   Ibid.

27   Wise, Michael, with Martin Abegg, Jr., and Edward Cook., *THE DEAD SEA SCROLLS: A NEW TRANSLATION*. (San Francisco: Harper Collins; 1996); pg. 139. [1QS, 4Q255-264a, 5Q11; (Manual of Discipline; Col. 9:10-11)].

But if we assume the *terminus a quo* of the prophecy to be the decree of Cyrus, then this gives us a *terminus ad quem*[28] of 483 years later, or 53 B.C., according to the standard chronology. And, since the Messiah is definitely a full-grown man in the prophecy, rather than a baby, the temporal discrepancy is even greater. We are told that Jesus began his ministry when he was thirty.[29] Therefore if the decree of Cyrus is the true *terminus a quo* of the prophecy, then Jesus was too late by 83 years to be the Prince Messiah of the prophecy. Of course this embarrassing result calls for some clever chronological juggling on the part of Christian scholars. As such, we are told that it was *not* the decree of Cyrus that was the starting-point of the prophecy, but rather the decree of Artaxerxes, some 92 years later. Of course this still does not yield an absolutely pristine result, since then Jesus would have been slightly too early; but nevertheless it is still tolerably close, and with even more clever chronological juggling, the expositors can assure Christian "sheep" that Jesus appeared at just the right time to fulfill the prophecy. We will inquire into this question more deeply in the next chapter. But here I would simply point out that, there is nothing in the text of the prophecy as it stands in Daniel that would even remotely hint that any other decree had been intended than the famous decree of Cyrus. Ironically, the position of the conservative Bible scholars respecting the date of Daniel only serves to strengthen the contention that the decree of Cyrus was the *terminus a quo* of the prophecy, rather than any later decree. For if Daniel himself was truly a man who lived in the sixth century, he would have lived in the very time of that decree, and long before any latter decree, whether by Darius[30] or Xerxes or Artaxerxes. On the other hand, if Daniel is really a late *pseudepigraphon*, then the author *could* have had one of these other decrees in mind. The problem in either case is that, there is absolutely nothing within the text of the prophecy itself that even slightly or remotely hints that it was any other such decree, and it is very difficult to imagine that the author would have left such

---

28   Terminus ad quem. I.e., a modified terminus ad quem, in which the final seven years of the prophecy have been subtracted; the Messiah the Prince being expected at the very beginning of the final week of the prophecy.

29   Luke 3:23.

30   Darius the Persian, not to be confused with Darius the Mede, who preceded him.

an item unaddressed. Of course in the latter case it is possible that the author was deliberately obscure. But a natural, straightforward reading of the text implies that the famous decree of Cyrus must have been the intended starting-point of the prophecy. Certain Christian polemicists may carp that the text speaks of "the commandment to restore and to build Jerusalem" rather than merely the temple; whereas the decree as it is recorded in Ezra 1:1-4 only mentions the rebuilding of the temple. But this argument is weak and lacks all true conviction, since the decree, as it is recorded in Josephus, is more complete, and does indeed contain the permission to rebuild the city, as well as the temple.[31] Not only that, but even Scripture itself associates King Cyrus with the rebuilding of both the city and the temple: "That sayeth of Cyrus, My shepherd, who shall perform all my pleasure: even saying to Jerusalem, Thou shalt be built; and to the temple, Thy foundation shall be laid."[32] Therefore it is disingenuous to say the least for any Christian expositor to protest that it was not the decree of Cyrus that had been intended as the starting-point of the prophecy. Dispensational premillennialists are notorious for this. But in fact the prophecy itself even distinguishes between the time of the "going forth of the commandment to restore and to build Jerusalem" and the time when the street and wall of the city would be rebuilt, which would be forty-nine years later, according to the prophecy. In Nehemiah we read of the rebuilding of the wall of Jerusalem. But as we will see in the next chapter, there is evidence that there has been some chronological falsification in the texts of Ezra, Nehemiah, and Esther. In the case of Ezra and Nehemiah I suspect that the falsification was done deliberately in order to secretly extend the expected time of fulfillment of the prophecy of the seventy weeks past the original time, based upon the decree of Cyrus as the *terminus a quo* of the prophecy. This was apparently done with a view to validating the claims of some latter-day would-be messiahs, most prominently Bar Kochbah.

One little-known fact also strengthens our thesis. The Dead Sea Scrolls were written for the most part in the first century B.C. Yet there is a scroll that, by implication, admits that the time for the fulfillment of

---

31   Jos. Ant. 11.1.1-2.
32   Isaiah 44:28.

prophecy had come and gone, without any fulfillment. Daniel's prophecy of the seventy weeks is not explicitly mentioned, and in fact the relevant text is a commentary on Habakkuk, but one can only suspect that the prophecy of the seventy weeks must have been in mind, since it is the only prophecy in the Jewish Scriptures that provides a prophetic timetable for when the Messiah was supposed to appear. There is no dispute that the Habakkuk *pesher* was written in the Roman era of Judaean occupation; the only debate is whether the writer is speaking of the invasion of 63 B.C., or 69 A.D. Most scroll scholars incline towards the former view.[33] The point is that, if the writer of the Habakkuk *pesher* wrote of the first Roman invasion of Judaea, then the expected time of fulfillment of the prophecy had already come and gone, with a miserable failure; this in turn points to an earlier *terminus ad quem* for the prophecy, rather than a later one, which argues in favor of the decree of Cyrus being the true *terminus a quo* of the prophecy.

"God told Habakkuk to write down what is going to happen to the generation to come; but when that period would be complete He did not make known to him. When it says. "so that with ease someone can read it," this refers to the Teacher of Righteousness, to whom God made known all the mysterious revelations of his servants the prophets. "For *the* prophecy testifies of a specific period; it speaks of that time and does not deceive." This means that the Last Days will be long, much longer than the prophets had said; for God's revelations are truly mysterious."[34]

When it says that the Last Days will be "much longer than the prophets had said" this is an unmistakable reference to Daniel's prophecy of the seventy weeks, for the simple reason that there literally is no other prophecy in the Jewish Scriptures that gives a specific timetable for the coming of the Messiah. As such, the *pesher* indicates that the expected time of fulfillment had already come and gone. If the majority view on

---

33   However it should be readily apparent that the scroll was not composed during or even immediately after the events it interprets. Presumably, the scroll was written some time after 46 B.C., which would have been the *terminus ad quem* of Daniel's prophecy of the seventy weeks, according to the standard chronology.

34   Wise, Abegg & Cook., op. cit., pg. 119. [1QpHab; Col. 7.1-7].

the dating of the Habakkuk *pesher* is correct,[35] then the *pesher* actually helps to confirm the decree of Cyrus as the original *terminus a quo* of Daniel's prophecy of the seventy weeks. And this evidence is so obscure, so unexpected, and so unsolicited that it has a unique evidential value.

Finally, as I stated above, I feel that the fact that Jeschu (Jesus) applies the prophecy of Daniel to himself in the Toldoth is highly significant. However, taking a critical view of the matter, the significance does not *necessarily* denote that Jesus himself explicitly applied the prophecy to himself, either openly or secretly to his disciples. But what it no doubt does signify is that by the second century the Christians had applied the prophecy to Jesus, retroactively. In other words, now that Jesus had been murdered by the Rabbis, the prophecy was retroactively applied to Jesus, and the reading of *karath* was henceforth interpreted as meaning "shall be cut off" to denote the sacrificial martyrdom of Jesus. Unfortunately there are no surviving original Hebrew documents written by the earliest disciples of Jesus, who presumably would have spoken Hebrew, rather than Greek.[36] The Greek Septuagint has two alternate readings of *karath*, found in two different texts.[37] The two Greek words found are *apostathesetai* and *exolethreuthesetai*,[38] which denote *uprooted* and *completely destroyed*, respectively. Needless to say, these readings of *karath* are at variance with the one I have proposed herein, but once again, as far as I know, there is no proof that these readings originate from earlier than the first century B.C., the time when, according to my thesis, Jesus lived

35   And there is strong reason to suppose so; the *pesher* speaks of the invasion as a horrible novelty; this would not have been the case in the latter half of the first century A.D., when the Romans had already been occupying Judaea as over-lords for well over a century. It is more likely speaking of the first Roman invasion of Judaea, which took place in 63 B.C.

36   Contrary to popular belief, Hebrew never became a "lost tongue"; postexilic Jews spoke Hebrew much more commonly than Aramaic. The word *Syristi* does not so much as appear anywhere in the Greek New Testament, although it does occur in the Greek Septuagint. Instead, the New Testament uses the word *Hebraisti*, which denotes Hebrew rather than Syriac (Aramaic, Chaldee). Furthermore only about one-sixth of the Dead Sea Scrolls were written in Aramaic, while the vast majority were written in Hebrew; cf Wise, Abegg & Cook., op. cit., pg. 9. However some of the Scrolls were composed in Greek; ibid., pg. 10.

37   Or more likely, text-types; i.e., families of Greek texts.

38   SEPTUAGINTA., op. cit., pg. 924. (volume two; Duo volumina in uno).

and died. If in fact Jesus really did live during that time, then no doubt he would have laid claim to being the one spoken of in the prophecy. In fact, this is in a sense the very crux of the argument; while critics might argue that the fact that the Jesus of the Gospels lived at the wrong time makes it seem more realistic and hence more likely that he actually did live at the commonly-accepted time, and this would be a good argument, all other things being equal, except that, in such a view, no man would have stepped forward at (or shortly after) the supposed time when the prophecy was to be fulfilled, claiming to be the Anointed Prince of the prophecy. Actually what we read of Aristobulus in Josephus makes it seem as if he was implicitly laying claim to being the Anointed Prince of the prophecy.[39] Furthermore it is crystal clear from what Josephus wrote in that passage that Aristobulus lived almost exactly at the right time for the fulfillment of the prophecy.[40] Unfortunately for him, Aristobulus only reigned for about a year, so he just missed reigning at precisely the right time to be the Prince Messiah of the prophecy. In other words, unless we are going to insist that the Jews were always passive with respect to the fulfillment of prophecy, then it would be strange to suppose that no man or men laid claim to being the Messiah the Prince of the prophecy right at the very time that Daniel had predicted. Certainly there was a plenitude of would-be messiahs after this time, so we would expect that there would have been at least one man who openly laid claim to being the Messiah spoken of in the prophecy at that time. And, since there are Jewish traditions that Jesus (Jeschu) lived around that time, then the two streams of evidence dovetail together in an unsolicited way to confirm the postulate that Jesus lived a century earlier than the canonical date. And we also have supplementary evidence that the Jews were not always passive with respect to the fulfillment of prophecy. In Josephus we read of a Jew named Onias, the son of Onias the high priest, who built a temple to God in Egypt, to fulfill a prophecy of Isaiah.[41] We shall have more to say of this temple hereafter. But the point is that the Jews did not always take a passive stance towards the fulfillment of prophecy. Therefore it is

---

39   Jos. Ant. 13.11.1.

40   481 years & 3 months after the people had been delivered from the Babylonish slavery; ibid.

41   Jos. Ant. 13.3.1-3. Cf Isaiah 19:18-19.

reasonable to suppose that at least one man would have stepped forward and laid claim to being the Messiah the Prince of the prophecy at the fulfillment of the time, according to the chronology of the prophecy. Whatever man did step forward at that time, whatever other qualities he would have to recommend him, the fact that he was "on time" in respect to the fulfillment of the prophecy would have been a great advantage, especially in the eyes of his disciples. Why not Jesus?

Xerxes & Artaxerxes

The information to be presented in this chapter is crucial to our thesis. However it is a bit complex, so the reader must be patient and diligent in studying the material presented. But once the significance of the material is grasped, then it can be clearly discerned how it is relevant to our theme. I do not mean to put to reader off by this *caveat;* neither is it intended as some sort of disclaimer respecting the relevance of the information. But I will be building on information that has already been presented, and one must appreciate the cumulative nature of the evidence. In one sense, it is like putting the pieces of a huge jig-saw puzzle together. Once the pieces are in place one can see the complete picture.

The evidence presented in this chapter is directly related to Daniel's prophecy of the seventy weeks, discussed in the preceding chapter; as such, this evidence was completely overlooked by G.R.S. Mead in his study. However when this evidence is added together with evidence that Mead offered, the thesis that Jesus lived a century earlier than the commonly-accepted time is greatly strengthened. The evidence I shall discuss is somewhat recondite, but not so obscure as to be beyond the comprehension of the average person, once it has been clearly pointed out.

Josephus, the famous first-century Jewish historian, mentioned not only the famous Persian King Cyrus, but also a latter king also named

Cyrus, who was called by the Greeks Artaxerxes.[1] Quite possibly the circumstance of two different Persian kings, each named Cyrus, may have become a source of confusion to Jews living at a later time, in respect to chronology. However, what the evidence seems to bear out is rather that at some point subsequent to 46 B.C., certain Jews deliberately sought to falsify chronology through forged documents, in order to cleverly but artfully extend the supposed time of the fulfillment of Daniel's prophecy of the seventy weeks beyond the original *terminus ad quem*. Ironically, these forged documents later came to be accepted as canonical Scripture by the Jews, and in turn, by the Christians. The documents in question are the biblical books of Ezra and Nehemiah. There is also a third book somewhat implicated, but not as an original document; I am speaking of the Hebrew Massoretic text of Esther, which not only is less complete than the Greek Septuagint version of that book, but which also follows a different (and impossible) chronology. The motive for such chronological falsifications was simply to "prove" that the time for the Messiah's advent was not overdue. Needless to say, if the thesis herein is correct, and Jesus truly lived during the time in question, namely the first century B.C., then the men who conspired to produce such forged documents were not followers of him. Because the followers of Jesus would have had no need or desire to "prove" that the time of fulfillment of the prophecy was still pending; in their case the effort would have been instead to reinterpret the meaning of the prophecy in such a way as to "prove" that Jesus (Jeschu) had fulfilled it.

The Jewish Scriptures[2] are often called by the Jews *TaNaKh*, a term which is an acronym denoting the threefold division of the Scriptures of the law, the prophets, and the writings.[3] The books of Ezra, Nehemiah, and Esther are classed within *Kethuvim*. The book of Daniel is also now so classed, but there is overwhelmingly strong evidence that it was originally classed within *Nehevim*. In the New Testament, Jesus himself

---

1   Jos. Ant. 11.6.1; 184.
2   I prefer the term Jewish Scriptures to Hebrew Scriptures, since the latter term may imply those books only in the original Hebrew, or in accordance with the Hebrew Massoretic text.
3   In Hebrew, *ha-Torah, ha-Nehevim,* and *ha-Kethuvim,* respectively.

speaks of Daniel as "the prophet"[4] and Josephus consistently speaks of Daniel as a prophet, and even "one of the greatest prophets" in his writings.[5] Josephus depicts Daniel as a genuine prophet who lived back in the days of the first King Cyrus. Therefore Josephus, a Jewish source, provides unimpeachable evidence that Daniel had been classed within *Nebevim*, rather than *Kethuvim*, in the first century. In fact, I suspect that Daniel was not demoted from *Nebevim* to *Kethuvim* until at least the third century. The available evidence strongly suggests that this was done in defiance of Christians, who claimed that the prophecies of Daniel proved that Jesus was really the Messiah. The evidence to be presented in this chapter will clarify the point in terms of motive.

Within *TaNaKh* itself, the name Cyrus always refers to the first King Cyrus, and never to Artaxerxes.[6] According to Josephus, it was the Greeks who called the latter Cyrus Artaxerxes. Ezra and Nehemiah likewise refer to the same king as Artaxerxes, rather than Cyrus. This might possibly serve as evidence that Ezra and Nehemiah were not written until the late fourth century B.C. or later.[7] If so, these books must be classed as *pseudepigrapha*. But there is actually much more and stronger evidence that these two books are forgeries.

According to Josephus, the first King Cyrus was the one who issued the famous decree allowing the Jews to return to Palestine, and to rebuild their temple and city.[8] This is in accord with what we find written in Isaiah 44:28: "That saith of Cyrus, My Shepherd, who shall perform all my pleasure; even saying to Jerusalem, Thou shalt be built; and to the temple, Thy foundation shall be laid." Josephus also draws attention to the fact that Isaiah prophesied the events in question 140 years before the temple had been destroyed by the armies of King Nebuchadnezzar.[9] According to the standard chronology, the Jerusalem temple was

---

4   Mt 24:15; Mk 13:14.

5   Jos. Ant. 10.11.4 & 10.11.7.

6   Isaiah 44:28; 45:1-4; Daniel 1:21; 6:28; 10:1; 2 Chronicles 36:22-23; Ezra 1:1-8; 3:7; 4:3-5; 5:13-17; 6:3,14.

7   I.e., after the time of Alexander the Great, when Greek became a fairly common language in parts of the Middle East.

8   Jos. Ant. 11.1.2.

9   Jos. Ant. 11.1.2; 6.

destroyed by the Babylonians in 587 B.C.; that gives us 727 B.C. for the date of Isaiah's prophecy. Of course critical Bible scholars are skeptical of the authenticity of Isaiah, or portions of it. But Josephus does provide us with somewhat of a chronological framework. However, as we will see in the following chapter, his chronology was somewhat different from the currently-accepted, standard chronology.

Josephus tells us that Cyrus authorized the rebuilding of Jerusalem and the temple thereof with revenue from the royal treasury.[10] But then we are told that the Jews were hindered in their rebuilding of the temple by the Cutheans (Samaritans), and that, after the death of King Cyrus, King Cambyses forbade the Jews from building their city or temple.[11] Then, after the death of King Cambyses, King Darius (the Persian; not to be confused with Darius the Mede, of the book of Daniel[12]) allowed Zerubabel/Zorobabel to return to Jerusalem and rebuild the temple.[13]

Curiously, Josephus includes an account that is also contained in the *apocryphal* book known as I Esdras, in which King Darius proposes that his three bodyguards each answer a riddle as to which is strongest: wine, women, or the truth?, and promises to grant royal favours and privileges to whomever he finds the wisest in his answers.[14] Then Josephus narrates how the temple in Jerusalem was finally rebuilt, even though the Cutheans sought to obstruct the rebuilding of the temple.[15] Significantly, these Cutheans first offered to help the Jews rebuild their temple, but were rather rudely rebuffed by the Jews.[16] Curiously, this account is also paralleled in the biblical book of Ezra, but in Ezra, the episode is depicted

---

10   Jos. Ant. 11.1.3.
11   Jos. Ant. 11.2.1-2.
12   Daniel 5:31; 6:1,6,9,25,28; 9:1; 11:1. Every other mention of Darius within *TaNaKh* is of Darius the Persian.
13   Jos. Ant. 11.3.1-10.
14   Jos. Ant. 11.3.2 cf I Esdras 3:1-24; 4:1-63. The text of Josephus is evidently superior to that of I Esdras; in the latter, it is the three bodyguards who themselves spontaneously think of the contest, but in Josephus, it is proposed by the king, which is more believable. In any case, Zerubabel prevails, and is granted his wish to return to Jerusalem with a grant from the king to rebuild the temple.
15   Jos. Ant. 11.4.1-9.
16   Jos. Ant. 11.4.3.

as occurring in the reign of Cyrus, rather than Darius.[17] Comparatively speaking, the chronology of events as found in Ezra seems confused[18] compared to that of Josephus. The reason will soon be evident.

There is clearly a chronological discrepancy between the account of Josephus and the *apocryphal* book of I Esdras on the one hand, and that of Ezra and Nehemiah, on the other. And, despite the fact that the latter two books are considered canonical Scripture by both Jews and Christians, the evidence suggests that in fact they postdate both *I Esdras* and Josephus. This is highly significant, especially in relation to our central thesis. First there is the formidable fact that we have two independent sources that mutually confirm each other's chronology.[19] Therefore the weight of evidence automatically suggests that the chronology common to both sources is correct, and that what we find in Ezra and Nehemiah is more likely to be a chronological revision.

According to Josephus, after the death of King Darius the Persian, his son Xerxes reigned.[20] Significantly, Josephus places Ezra (therein called Esdras, according to the Greek transliteration) and Nehemiah in the reign of Xerxes.[21] But the biblical books of Ezra and Nehemiah both place the events narrated therein within the reign of Artaxerxes, the son of Xerxes.[22] This discrepancy is highly significant, as we will see. Josephus also places the events narrated in the book of Esther in the reign of Artaxerxes, the son of King Xerxes.[23] Very significantly, the Greek version of Esther, as found in the Septuagint, also places the episode of Esther and Mordecai in the reign of Artaxerxes.[24] So once again we have

---

17   Ezra 4:1-6.

18   Ezra 4:4-7.

19   I.e., Josephus and I Esdras, respectively. By contrast, the two books of Ezra and Nehemiah can hardly be construed as two independently written works; early on, they were inscribed on the very same scroll and considered as one book. In any case it was clearly recognised by all concerned parties that the books emanated from the same or very similar source.

20   Jos. Ant. 11.5.1; 120.

21   Jos. Ant. 11.5.1-8.

22   Ezra 7:12-26; Nehemiah 2:1 cp Jos. Ant. 11.5.1.

23   Jos. Ant. 11.6.1-13.

24   SEPTUAGINTA., op. cit., pgs. 951-973. (volume one; Duo volumina in uno).

an instance of chronological agreement from two independent sources, which are contradicted by what is found in the Hebrew Massoretic text. Protestant Christians often make a false pretence that those portions of the book of Esther which are found neither in the ancient Hebrew or Chaldee of *TaNaKh*, but are found only in the Greek, are merely additions or embellishments to the original book of Esther, which is supposedly identical with the Hebrew Massoretic text found within *TaNaKh*. However this can definitely be disproven; the very fact that Artaxerxes rather than Ahasuerus is identified as the reigning king is really enough proof that there has been some chronological doctoring in the case of Esther. But even stronger proof, in my view, is the fact that, at the very end of the Greek edition of Esther there is a colophon clearly stating that the Greek translation of the work was made in the fourth year of the reign of Ptolemy and Cleopatra, by Lysimachus, the son of another Ptolemy of Jerusalem, who sent the epistle regarding *Purim* by Dositheus and his son Ptolemy, who were both Levitical priests, to Egypt.[25] One tends to get a false impression by reading the merely chopped up pieces of Esther in the Apocrypha, since the passages are isolated from their proper context, and the very last fourteen verses are unaccountably placed first. But one will not be able to make sense of it by some patchwork-quilt method of reconstruction, and trying to place the portions found in the Apocrypha together with the Massoretic text of Esther. The chronology would still be skewed, which is a clue that something is wrong.

Not only are the text of Josephus and the more complete text of Esther in agreement in placing the events of Esther in the reign of Artaxerxes, rather than Ahasuerus, who was the father of Darius the Mede,[26] but the text of Josephus also more closely corresponds to the more complete account, including the various letters of King Artaxerxes, and the accusation against Haman as being a conspirator against the king, and (in Josephus) of being an Amalekite.[27] In fact, in almost all details, the

---

25   Ibid., pg. 973.

26   Daniel 9:1.

27   Jos. Ant. 11.6.1-13. In the Greek Septuagint text, Haman is accused of being a conspirator of the seed of the Macedonians, who sought to overthrow the Persians.

account of Josephus corresponds to the Greek edition of Esther; Josephus merely omits any mention of the prophetic dream of Mordecai, and its interpretation. And the colophon at the end of the Greek edition of Esther precludes any supposition that those portions not found within the Massoretic text of *TaNaKh* were merely gratuitous embellishments upon an earlier Hebrew text lacking them; the evidence suggests, to the contrary, that the entirety of the Greek version of Esther is a translation of an earlier Hebrew original. The mere fact that a shorter version of Esther is found within the Massoretic text of *TaNaKh* does not in the least lend the slightest hint of any credibility to the supposition that only those portions found therein are genuine. If so, we would have to ask why the entire Greek text was altered chronologically, to make it say that the events occurred in the reign of Artaxerxes, rather than Ahasuerus, if that had been the case, rather than the reverse. And as we will soon see, any such supposition is close to impossible.

There is a rather curious parallel to the circumstances noted immediately above in that, in codex editions of *TaNaKh*, the book of Esther is placed immediately before the book of Daniel; this is a logical sequence if we are to suppose that the events narrated in Esther occurred before those narrated in Daniel, which would have to be the case if those events (of Esther) took place in the reign of Ahasuerus, the father of Darius the Mede, rather than in the reign of Artaxerxes, the son of Xerxes (the Persian), as narrated in both Josephus and the Greek edition of Esther. Furthermore, in Christian codices of the Bible, Esther is placed after Nehemiah, which is a logical sequence if we were to suppose that the events of Esther took place in the reign of Artaxerxes, the son of Xerxes, rather than in the days of Ahasuerus, the father of Darius the Mede. In other words, the very placement of the book of Esther in Christian Bibles implies the chronology found in both Josephus and the Greek Esther; in Josephus, Ezra and Nehemiah lived in the days of Xerxes, the father of Artaxerxes; while Esther and Mordecai lived in the days of Artaxerxes the son of Xerxes. So what we find in Josephus corresponds more closely to what is found in Christian Bibles, rather than what is found in contemporary codices of *TaNaKh*. This is definitely evidence of chronological tampering on the part of the Jews.[28]

---

28 Of course one may suspect on this account that the Jews' placement of

The reason why the Massoretic chronology of Esther is not very believable compared to the chronology found in the Greek edition of Esther, and also in Josephus,[29] is because King Ahasuerus, the father of Darius the Mede, never had any such universal dominion over the great Median-Persian empire, according to the account of Daniel. And in this case <u>all</u> the texts and accounts of Daniel are in agreement, including the Massoretic text. According to Daniel, Belshazzar the Babylonian king was succeeded by Darius the Median.[30] Therefore it is absurd to propose that the father of Darius (Ahasuerus) could possibly have reigned over the great empire of 127 provinces, "from India to Ethiopia", as the Massoretic edition of Esther claims.[31] The chronological sleight-of-hand practiced by the Jews would have been another motive for them to demote Daniel from *Nehevim* to *Kethuvim*. But Artaxerxes the son of Xerxes did inherit such an extensive empire. Therefore it is more believable that the events narrated in the book of Esther, if they ever happened at all, occurred in the reign of Artaxerxes, rather than in the much earlier reign of Ahasuerus. But I strongly suspect that the chronological tampering to the text of Esther was necessitated by the forged documents of Ezra and Nehemiah, which presented a completely false chronology of events, apparently with the intent to "prove" that Daniel's prophecy of the seventy weeks was still awaiting fulfillment, by some latter-day Messiah. This should become clearer as more evidence is presented.

The first King Artaxerxes mentioned by Josephus is further identified by William Whiston in the notes as Artaxerxes Longimanus.[32] He is thus further distinguished from another, later Artaxerxes, known as Artaxerxes Mnemon.[33] A person reading the texts of Ezra or Nehemiah

---

Jesus (Jeschu Ben Pandera) in the days of Simeon Ben Shetach is yet another instance of such chronological tampering. Although this is possible, we have already briefly touched upon this, and found the counter-arguments to be equally valid.

29   I.e., aside from this agreement of two independent sources, which in itself is a formidable form of evidence that the Massoretic-text chronology of Esther is false.

30   Daniel 5:30-31.

31   Esther 1:1.

32   JOSEPHUS: THE COMPLETE WORKS., Thomas Nelson Publishers., pg. 357.

33   Ibid., pg. 365. Cf Jos. Ant. 11.7.1.

would not immediately be able to discern exactly which Artaxerxes was the king mentioned, and thereby the *terminus ad quem* of Daniel's prophecy could thereby be further removed from the originally intended time, by pretending that it was the decree of one of these later kings named Artaxerxes, that was the intended *terminus a quo* of that prophecy. This appears to have been the intent behind the chronological tampering. Indeed, this is the only explanation for the otherwise unaccountable chronological discrepancy. Clearly the intent behind such chronological tampering was to allow for a later appearance of the Messiah, to justify the supposed legitimacy of several latter-day would-be messiahs; the most notable and last of whom being Simeon Bar Kochbah. This explanation is more credible than mere carelessness; it is unlikely in the extreme that the Jews would have been lax in their reckoning of chronology precisely at a time when they ought to be eagerly awaiting their promised Messiah, according to Daniel's prophecy.

So far we have seen at least some evidence of chronological tampering by the Jews; there is also much more to consider. But if we give due consideration to the motivation for such chronological doctoring, we find that the only reason sufficiently strong would be to somehow artificially extend Daniel's prophecy of the seventy weeks further into the future, to allow for the Messiah to come. If the thesis herein is true, and Jesus was the original Messiah, or a man who claimed to be such, living at the expected time, and yet in the eyes of the majority of the Jews failed in his messianic claims, then it is understandable that from that time, the Jews would question why the prophecy failed. One possible reason that may have been offered was that the time had been miscalculated; another may have been that the time had been delayed due to the people's unworthiness; these and similar reasons would probably have been offered by the religious experts to keep the hope of the people alive. But to bolster the first explanation, efforts may have been undertaken to recalculate the time, and no doubt a supposedly "pious" motive would thereafter exist to falsify the respective chronology, to make it appear as if the time of the decree was more recent than it really was. Efforts would also have been made to dislocate the decree of Daniel's prophecy from that most famous decree of King Cyrus, to that of the later Cyrus, otherwise known as Artaxerxes. And even Artaxerxes Mnemon might thereby become confused with Artaxerxes Longimanus. The Hebrew Massoretic-text books of Ezra and Nehemiah clearly seem to fit into this pattern. In fact, the evidence makes it rather glaringly obvious that there has been some chronological doctoring, and the messianic motivation vis-à-vis the prophecy of Daniel seems to be the best explanation to account for such doctoring.[34]

When one compares the text of Josephus with the Massoretic texts of Ezra and Nehemiah, the chronological discrepancy becomes quite glaring; a decree issued by Xerxes in Josephus is quoted almost verbatim in Ezra, but is ascribed to Artaxerxes.[35] Furthermore Josephus himself would have had no reason to alter the chronology from the time of Artaxerxes to that of his predecessor Xerxes. But certain Jews no doubt did have a motivation to alter the chronology in the opposite direction, to seek to artificially extend Daniel's prophecy of the seventy weeks further into the future, to allow for the legitimacy of some later messianic pretender.

There is an absence of clear evidence that the books of Ezra and Nehemiah existed any time earlier than 135 A.D.[36] Neither book is quoted from

34   In fact, there does not appear to be any alternative explanation. Carelessness has been ruled out, and in fact is no explanation.

35   Jos. Ant. 11.5.1. Cf Ezra 7:11-26.

36   No doubt I will be admonished by certain Scroll scholars that fragments of these two books were found among the Dead Sea Scrolls. But therein lies a problem; much of the contents of those two books can also be found in the apocryphal book of I Esdras. It is certainly quite possible, even probable, that the Greek version of I Esdras may be merely a translation from a Hebrew (or possibly Aramaic) original. Therefore whatever tiny fragments of these two books were supposedly discovered in the caves of Qumran, they may be merely fragments of this other book, which is not in accord with the chronology found in those other two books. No English translation of the entire Qumran corpus has so far been published; only the sectarian texts have been translated and published, in various editions. Furthermore even if it can be proven that those portions which are unique to Ezra and Nehemiah (and which are therefore absent from I Esdras) are found among the fragments of texts of the Dead Sea Scrolls, it does not thereby prove the genuine antiquity of those texts; none of those texts can be dated to earlier than the late first century B.C., at the very earliest. This is notably after the time of Jeschu, according to the Toldoth, and after the time when the Messiah

in the New Testament. And most of what Josephus wrote respecting Ezra and Nehemiah can also be found in in the apocryphal books of I Esdras and Ecclesiasticus (Sirach). Not only this, but there is also an outrageously glaring circumstance that virtually proves that those two books postdate the apocryphal book of I Esdras. In the Greek Septuagint, the *apocryphal* book of I Esdras is placed first in the Codex, and called "Esdras Alpha", while the *canonical* books of Ezra and Nehemiah are placed immediately after it, and labelled (as one book) "Esdras Beta".[37] How can this be anything but the most glaring anachronism, if we are to suppose, as apparently most Bible scholars would have us suppose, that the biblical books of Ezra and Nehemiah actually predate the book of Esdras, rather than the reverse? How can this be interpreted as anything but overwhelmingly strong evidence that the Massoretic-text books of Ezra and Nehemiah postdate the document otherwise known as I Esdras? As strong as this evidence is, there is yet more. For one thing, we can be sure that the text of Nehemiah is at least partly pseudepigraphal, since Nehemiah mentions the high priest Jaddua, who lived long after the time of Nehemiah.[38] Not only that, but nowhere is any distinctive book ascribed to Nehemiah in either Sirach 49:13 or in 2 Maccabees 1:20-36 or 2:13, where we would definitely have expected to find mention of such a book, had Nehemiah himself written any such definitive book as ascribed to him in *TaNaKh*.

It will be illuminating to read the accounts written in second Maccabees.

13 The same things also were reported in the writings and commentaries of Nehemiah; and how he founding a library gathered together the acts of the kings, and of the prophets, and of David, and *also* the epistles of the *Persian* kings concerning the holy gifts. (2 Maccabees 2:13)

Although there is mention made of writings (in the plural) and commentaries (once again in the plural) of Nehemiah, and that he even

---

was supposed to come, according to the prophecy of Daniel (i.e., after 53 B.C., according to the standard chronology).

37   SEPTUAGINTA., op. cit., pgs. 873-950. (volume one; Duo volumina in uno).

38   Nehemiah 10:21; 12:11,22 cf Jos. Ant. 11.5.1-8 & 11.8.1-7.

founded a library, and gathered together the acts of the kings (presumably of Israel and Judah) and of the prophets, and of David, and also the epistles of the kings of Persia respecting the holy offerings, nowhere does the verse mention any such distinctive book of Nehemiah as is found within *TaNaKh*. Neither do we read in the canonical book of Nehemiah that he founded a library. Furthermore there is the very suspicious circumstance that, the two books of Ezra and Nehemiah contain the epistles of the Persian kings in question, which epistles are very important, since they provide a legal justification for the rebuilding of both the temple and the city of Jerusalem, but the verse omits any mention of a distinctive book written by Nehemiah, or even any book written by Ezra. So this evidence suggests that the books of Ezra and Nehemiah are both pseudepigraphal, and are based upon epistles ascribed to Artaxerxes, rather than Xerxes, who, according to the history narrated by Josephus, was the reigning Persian monarch at the time when Ezra and Nehemiah actually lived. So even the original factual basis of those two books has been falsified, in a calculated act of chronological sleight-of-hand. In fact, the very epistles are almost otherwise identical to what is found written in Josephus, except the name "Artaxerxes" has been substituted for "Xerxes". This virtually proves that a chronological manipulation has taken place. It may also be instructive to look at the other relevant passage from 2 Maccabees concerning Nehemiah.

19 For when our fathers were led into Persia [Babylon], the priests that were then devout took the fire from the altar secretly, and hid it in a hollow place of a pit without water, where they kept it secure, so that the place was unknown to all men.

20 Now after many years, when it pleased God, Nehemiah, having been sent by the king of Persia, sent to the posterity of those priests who had hidden the fire; but when they told us {him} that they found no fire, but *instead some* thick "water",

21 then he commanded them to draw it up *from the pit*, and to bring it *to him*; and when the sacrifices were laid on *the altar*, Nehemiah commanded the priests to sprinkle the wood and the things laid thereon with that "water".

22 When this was done, and the time came that the sun shone, which before had been hidden by clouds, there was *immediately* a great fire kindled *on the altar,* so that everyone marvelled.

31 Now when the sacrifice was consumed, Nehemiah commanded the "water" that was left to be poured on the great stones.

32 When this was done, there was *again* kindled a flame; but it was consumed by the fire that shined from the altar.

33 So when this matter became known, it was told to the king of Persia, that in the place where the priests that had been led away had hidden the fire, there appeared *this strange* "water", and that Nehemiah purified the sacrifices with it.

34 Then the king, enclosing the place, sanctified it, after he had proven the truth of the report.

35 And the king bestowed many gifts on those whom he would gratify.

36 But Nehemiah called this thing *Nephthar,* which means "a cleansing"; but many men call it *Nephthai.* (2 Maccabees 1:19-22,31-36)

This very curious episode is not related anywhere in the biblical book of Nehemiah, which would be an incredibly suspicious omission, assuming that the incident related is true, and that Nehemiah really wrote the book ascribed to him. Unfortunately in the passage above, the king of Persia is not named, so we are left without an important piece of evidence that is directly relevant to our inquiry. But it seems fairly evident that this strange incident, which is faintly reminiscent of the legend of *Hanukkah,* concerns the curious discovery of *naphtha,* which is a clear, colourless flammable mixture of light hydrocarbons. Apparently naphtha is derived from petroleum, and is a raw material for many petrochemicals. Men who did not understand the scientific basis for this substance and its chemical properties, might think that a miracle occurred when they saw something ignite from the action of this substance. Possibly Nehemiah did know the actual use of *naphtha,* but decided that it was wiser to keep it secret. That might possibly account for why the incident is not recorded in the book of Nehemiah. However, from what we have already seen above, it is fairly evident that the book of Nehemiah is pseudepigraphal, or at least partially pseudepigraphal. Otherwise why would no such distinctive book of Nehemiah be mentioned in either the passage above, or in 2 Maccabees 2:13, or in Sirach 49:13? Furthermore, even if Nehemiah wanted to keep the true knowledge of the properties of *naphtha* a secret, he still could have, should have, and presumably would have recorded some account of the incident in the book of Nehemiah, had he actually written the book ascribed to him. He could have recorded it as a genuine miracle. If the incident really took place, then it is unlikely that it would have been kept secret from the people. But any priests who did know the true secret properties of *naphtha* would have kept that knowledge secret. Indeed, in that pre-scientific age, most likely any men acquainted with the substance would have thought of it as a magical substance with miraculous properties. And I dare say that the incident is far more interesting than anything narrated in the rather tedious biblical text of Nehemiah.

But not only is there all this overwhelmingly strong evidence that Ezra and Nehemiah are pseudepigraphal; there is still more. The apocryphal book of II Esdras[39] is introduced as "the second book of the prophet Esdras [Ezra]" (1:1). In the Apocrypha, the book is placed immediately after I Esdras. And, as we have seen above, the Greek Septuagint Bible places I Esdras as Esdras Alpha, and the canonical Ezra-Nehemiah (as one book) as Esdras Beta. The clear implication of this is that even the book of II Esdras (IV Ezra) actually predates the canonical books of Ezra and Nehemiah. Ezra and Nehemiah, although presumably originally written on two separate scrolls, were later inscribed together on a single scroll; this accounts for them being counted as only one book in the codex of the Greek Septuagint. But the fact that they are rendered as Esdras Beta, while the apocryphal I Esdras is rendered as Esdras Alpha, is fatal to any supposition that those books predated the apocryphon.[40] And II Esdras claims to be "the <u>second</u> book of the prophet Ezra", which seems to clearly imply, not the biblical book of Ezra as being the first such book, but rather the apocryphal book of I Esdras. Most Bible scholars date the

---

39   Otherwise also known as IV Ezra, IV Ezrae, or the Apocalypse of Ezra.

40   Apocryphon. A secret book. In this case, IV Ezra (II Esdras).

writing of II Esdras to 100 A.D.[41] This would thereby place *Ezra* and *Nehemiah* in the second century. In fact, many Bible scholars consider the first two chapters of II Esdras to be a later Christian addition to a Jewish work. And, since it is the very first verse of the very first chapter that introduces the book as "the second book of the prophet Esdras"[42] this implies an even later origin for *canonical* Ezra and Nehemiah. William Whiston, in his notes and commentaries on the works of Josephus, expresses the opinion that neither Ezra, Nehemiah, nor the Massoretic text of Esther were even written until the second century A.D.[43] The evidence supports this opinion. In the case of Esther, no fragments of it were found in the caves of Qumran. And in the case of fragments of Ezra and Nehemiah supposedly discovered at Qumran, what we have written above respecting such things in an earlier note seems adequate to dispel any carping upon the alleged antiquity of those texts. In other words, even if fragments from Qumran could "prove" that Ezra and Nehemiah predated 135 A.D., they could not prove that those texts predated 46 B.C.

So to briefly summarize the evidence we uncovered in this chapter, we found indisputable evidence of chronological tampering in the texts of Ezra, Nehemiah, and the Massoretic text of Esther. The only discernible motive for such chronological tampering is the desire to artificially extend the *terminus ad quem* of Daniel's prophecy of the seventy weeks, by implicitly postulating an alternative and later *terminus a quo* for the prophecy, such as a decree by Artaxerxes, rather than the decree of Cyrus. The motivation behind all this was to justify potential messianic claims made by latter-day messianic pretenders, most notably Simeon Bar Kochbah. As obscure as this evidence is, it is fairly easily understandable, once it is presented in detail. In fact, the messianic explanation is the only

---

41   Based upon the reference to thirty years after the ruin of Jerusalem; 3:1. There are both merits and limitations to such a dating of the book, but it is the general consensus among Bible scholars. While not necessarily "set in stone" this estimate will do, for the purposes of our discussion.

42   Although admittedly some manuscripts of IV Ezrae omit the word "second"; cf BIBLIA SACRA VULGATA., op. cit., pg. 1931.

43   JOSEPHUS: THE COMPLETE WORKS., op. cit., pgs. 1012-1031; pg. 365, *n*.

explanation that accounts for otherwise unaccountable chronological discrepancies between these texts and what we find written in Josephus, and in various apocryphal texts, which otherwise agree with one another. In fact, even if our central thesis is not true, the evidence presented herein remains evidential and the messianic explanation still applies as the only valid explanation. But the fact that this evidence and this explanation dovetail together so well with the supposition that Jesus lived back in Hasmonean times, together with evidence from the Toldoth Jeschu, that we consider the thesis to be greatly strengthened thereby. And this convergence of evidence from diverse sources is so unexpected and so unsolicited that the evidential value seems even more pungent. Of course we do not want to be guilty of overstating our case; but as we proceed, we must keep in mind the cumulative nature of the evidence.

CHRONOLOGY

A s noted above, there is an approximately 45-year discrepancy
between the standard chronology and the chronology of Josephus.
It is uncertain how and why such a large discrepancy arose, but it is
something that must be taken into account in our study. One possible
reason for such a discrepancy may have been that Josephus, in writing
of Moses, the great law-giver of the Hebrews, sought to place him back
in the remotest possible antiquity, to elevate his status in the eyes of the
Greeks and Romans. This may partially account for the discrepancy, but
there has also been controversy surrounding the subject of chronology
for quite some time. Unfortunately chronology has become a subject
of controversy in some instances due to the theological prejudices of
certain persons who tenaciously cling to a long-discredited religious
fundamentalism. Other aspects of the problem lie in the unpliable nature
of dogmatic academic orthodoxy. Egyptian chronology in particular
has become a subject of great controversy, but once again this has to due
with the inevitable interconnection with the religious chronology of the
Jews. As such, the standard chronology is merely a more-or-less general
consensus vis-à-vis biblical chronology.

When we scrutinize the writings of Josephus, however, it soon becomes
evident that there is a major discrepancy between his chronology and the
standard chronology. In fact, one can find somewhat[1] of a discrepancy

---

1   I.e., a ten-year discrepancy; cf Jos. War. 1.3.1 cp Jos. Ant. 13.11.1.

between the earlier chronology of Josephus, which he used in his *War*, and the later chronology used in his *Antiquities*. Presumably the latter work corrected the chronological inaccuracies of the former, but this is not necessarily the chief point. The chief point is the question of what sort of chronology was in use by the common people during the first century B.C. If, according to the commonly-accepted chronology then in use, the time for the coming of the Messiah was at hand just when Jesus himself came on the scene and claimed messianic status, then no doubt the chronological element of the supposed fulfillment of prophecy was a key point exploited by Jesus in his bid for messianic status.

Josephus wrote in his *War* that Aristobulus assumed the kingship 471 years and three months after the people returned from the Babylonian Captivity; in the *Antiquities* he "corrected" this to 481 years and three months. But since here we note a ten-year discrepancy between the two different chronologies, it is also a distinct possibility that the people who lived back in Hasmonean times used a still different system of chronology. What Josephus wrote of Aristobulus makes it appear that Aristobulus himself was a sort of messianic pretender. However Aristobulus only reigned for about a year, and came to a tragic end. His widow, Salome, who was also known as Alexandra, married his brother, Alexander Jannaeus. After Alexander Jannaeus died, Alexandra reigned over the Jews for nine years. During her reign the Pharisees held sway. The Toldoth seems to depict the events narrated therein as occurring during the reign of Alexandra.

According to the chronology Josephus used for his *Antiquities of the Jews*, the decree of Cyrus was 582 years before the assession of Cyrenius to the procuratorship of Syria. The latter date was the time of the birth of Jesus, according to the Gospel of Luke.[2] 582 minus 483 equals 99; in other words, Jesus was too late by 99 years to be the Messiah of Daniel's prophecy, according to the chronology of Josephus. In fact, it is much worse than that, since the Messiah had to be a full-grown man at the time of the seventieth week of the prophecy; therefore Jesus was actually late by almost 130 years or so, according to the chronology of Josephus.[3] Of

---

2   Luke 2:1-7.
3   Together with Daniel's prophecy of the seventy weeks.

course this is assuming the decree of Cyrus as the *terminus a quo* of the prophecy, rather than some later decree. But we have already discussed this question, and have seen that the most natural, straightforward reading of Daniel's prophecy implies the decree of Cyrus and no other as the starting-point of the seventy weeks. Unfortunately these chronological issues are further complicated by the fact that, according to the standard chronology, the assession of Cyrenius (Quirinius) did not take place until about 6 or 7 A.D. And yet, according to the Gospel of Matthew, Jesus was born in the days of King Herod I, who died in 4 B.C., according to the standard chronology. Also the account in Matthew implies that Jesus had been born two years previously, giving us a date of at least 6 B.C., if not a year or so earlier. For one reason or another, most scholars have favoured, or tended to favour, the Matthew date over the Luke date. One possible reason may have been that there was hope from an inscription that Cyrenius may have been twice made governor of Syria, thus allowing a possible reconciliation between Luke and Matthew on this point. But apparently all such hope of any such reconciliation has been given up by all except terminal fundamentalists.

Strangely, according to the chronologies[4] used by Josephus, the time of the fulfillment of Daniel's prophecy of the seventy weeks falls in the reign of Alexander Jannaeus. Alexander Jannaeus had a long reign of 27 years, and there is no record recounted by Josephus of any events similar to what we find written in the Toldoth Jeschu. Neither do we find any such account narrated in the reign of Alexandra-Salome. This silence of Josephus is one possible argument against the thesis advocated herein. If indeed there was a crisis in Judaism, indeed the very central crisis of Judaism, of a man claiming to be the Messiah the Prince of Daniel's prophecy, who lived at just the right time, who performed miracles,[5] but who was ultimately rejected by the religious leaders, and who maintained a loyal following of disciples to his legacy even after his death, then we cannot account for the silence of Josephus respecting such monumental events in the history of his people. Of course there is debate as to whether Josephus was truly silent in respect to Jesus living in the days of Pontius

4   In both the *War* and the *Antiquities*.
5   According to both the Toldoth and the Gospels Jesus performed many miracles.

Pilate.[6] The silence of Josephus in respect to Jesus is an enigma, but it is not necessarily any more of a problem for our thesis than it is for the supposition that Jesus lived in the days of Pilate. There are certainly limits to any argument from silence. But admittedly in this case the silence is rather glaring, if not deafening. Josephus himself was no doubt well acquainted with the prophecies of Daniel, and especially the prophecy of the seventy weeks, and therefore the great chronological significance of that prophecy could not have escaped his notice. And yet in both of his major works covering the period in question, the chronologies used by Josephus point to the reign of Alexander Jannaeus as the time of alleged fulfillment of the prophecy. Did Josephus mean to silently imply that Alexander Jannaeus himself was the Anointed Prince of the prophecy?

One important point relevant to our immediate discussion is that, of the two chronologies used by Josephus in his two major works,[7] the chronology used in his earlier work[8] is actually closer to the standard chronology than that in his latter work. Once again this may be due to an attempt on the part of Josephus to place Moses at the remotest possible antiquity, so that he would thereby gain the venerability of a hoary antiquity in the eyes of the Greeks and Romans. And this circumstance is borne out by the fact that the *War* begins with the invasion of Jerusalem by Antiochus Epiphanes, while the *Antiquities* begins with Adam and Eve. So not every "correction" of Josephus in his latter work is necessarily a valid correction; the earlier work may be more accurate in some chronological respects.

Although the Toldoth does not speak specifically of Daniel's prophecy in a highly detailed way,[9] it does at least mention it and Jeschu himself quotes from it, in relation to himself. Even taking a critical view of this,

---

6   Although the infamous *Testimony Flavium*, which is placed in the 18th book of the *Antiquities*, in the procuratorship of Pontius Pilate, is generally disregarded as a Christian interpolation by the general consensus of historians, scholars, and literary critics. It is never quoted from in any document earlier than the fourth century.

7   I.e., the *War of the Jews* and the *Antiquities of the Jews*, respectively.

8   *War*.

9   Nor would we expect it to, since it would only lend credence to the claims of the disciples of Jesus, that he was really the Messiah of the prophecy.

it is evident at least that the disciples of Jesus must have laid claim to the pivotal prophecy as being fulfilled in their Lord and Master. And no doubt the common perception among the Jews, or at least among the disciples of Jeschu, was that the proper *terminus ad quem* of the prophecy occurred at exactly the right time. And it is doubtful that there could have been too much of a chronological discrepancy between their system of reckoning and that of the other Jews. If this key point is not strongly evident in the text of the *Toldoth Jeschu* we ought not to be greatly surprised by the fact, since it would only serve to justify and legitimize the claims made for Jesus by his disciples. And if the thesis advocated herein is correct, then of course we cannot expect to find confirmation from within the texts of the New Testament itself, since those texts were composed after a unanimous agreement to portray Jesus as having lived in the days of Herod and Pilate.[10]

According to the chronology of Josephus used in his *magnum opus, the*

Antiquities of the Jews, the decree of Cyrus was issued 581 years and five months before Cyrenius became governor of Syria. The latter date is biblically significant because it was, according to the testimony of Luke, when Jesus was born.[11] But this is definitely bad news for Christians, unless they can justify using a later decree as the *terminus a quo* of Daniel's prophecy of the seventy weeks. In fact this is exactly what Christian apologists and chronologists have sought to do, but with little in the way of real conviction. According to the *Antiquities*, Aristobulus assumed kingship 481 years and three months after the return from the Babylonian Captivity. According to the *War*, this assession took place 471 years and three months after the Babylonian Captivity. The chronology of the *War* is at least closer to the standard chronology. So comparing the two accounts, we find that, according to Josephus' earlier work, Aristobulus began to reign as king of the Jews 110 years and two months before Jesus was born, according to Luke's Gospel. Therefore either Jesus lived far too late to fulfill the key prophecy of Daniel, or the *terminus a quo* of that prophecy must be recalculated from another time,

---

10   We will discuss possible motives for such a chronological dislocation in the next chapter.

11   Luke 2:1-7.

much later than the decree of Cyrus. Or, the thesis proposed herein is correct, and Jesus actually did live approximately a century earlier than the commonly-supposed time. It should be fairly evident that I am not writing this with a motivation to uphold some preconceived theological superstructure, but instead proceed with an historical inquiry free from the restraints of theological shackles.

Let us suppose, for the sake of discussion, that initially the *terminus ad quem* of the prophecy had passed without any detectable fulfillment. Would not this failure of prophecy in itself have created a major crisis of faith for the Jews? And in the aftermath would it not have been likely that the fertile imaginations of the religious leaders would have come up with one excuse after another for why the time must have been miscalculated? And in such an environment, would it not have been likely that charismatic figures were likely to spring up, claiming messianic status for themselves? At the very least we would expect one such man would so come forward, claiming to be the Messiah. And why not Jesus? Why could not the original, historical Jesus have been such a man? Of course if he could perform miracles, or convince people that he performed miracles, then so much the better for his claims.[12] Of course, it is doubtful that Jesus ever performed any miracles, regardless of when he lived. There are a few considerations that bolster this sound judgment. First, there is evidence from the New Testament itself that the performance of miracles was not a messianic requirement. We are told that the people were wondering whether John the Baptist may have been the Messiah,[13] despite the fact that he performed no miracles.[14] Furthermore we have what appears to be a disclaimer of sorts in some of the Gospels; oftentimes, after Jesus performed a miraculous healing, he admonished the beneficiary of the cure to "tell no man".[15] Would Jesus have issued such a strange and inexplicable commandment, if he had truly performed such miracles? Of course not. Finally, Jesus himself is recorded to have said that "no

---

12   Either through some hypnotic power or the strength of his personal charm.

13   Luke 3:15.

14   John 10:41.

15   Mark 7:36; 8:26; Luke 5:14; 8:56 cf Mark 9:9; Matthew 17:9; Luke 9:21.

sign shall be granted" to his generation.[16] Clearly he could not have made any such statement if he had been performing routine miracles left and right, as he supposedly did, according to the Gospel texts. Therefore the question of the miraculous can be safely ruled out, without any *a priori* philosophical objection against the possibility of miracles, in the case of Jesus. The miracles recounted in the *Toldoth* were merely gratuitous pandering to the ubiquitous superstition of the common people living in those times. To paraphrase an earlier writer, "It would have been a miracle if they hadn't believed in miracles". We must remember the essentially reactive nature of the Toldoth. In that text, the miracles serve a completely different theological function- to justify the belief in the supernatural power of the *Shemhamphorasch*, the secret Divine Name of God. This concept became very important in *Hasidic* Judaism.

According to the standard chronology, the twentieth year of Artaxerxes, when Nehemiah[17] asked permission of the king to rebuild the city of Jerusalem, was approximately 444 B.C. If this were used as the *terminus a quo* of Daniel's prophecy, 483 years later would bring us to approximately 39 A.D. Of course this is too late for Jesus, even for the crucifixion,[18] and furthermore we have the additional constraint of the Passover falling on the Sabbath in the year in question.[19] Some have placed the *terminus a quo* of the prophecy, not in the twentieth year of Artaxerxes, but rather the seventh year.[20] But this assumption is chiefly the weak point in terms of evidence. It does not seem to be much of an official decree at all, in contrast to the famous and unprecedented decree of

---

16   Mark 8:12.

17   Nehemiah 2. But see discussion above on Xerxes & Artaxerxes.

18   Which, according to some historicist interpreters of biblical prophecy, should correspond to the "midst of the week", i.e., the final, seventieth week of the prophecy, when "he shall cause sacrifice and oblation to cease" cf Daniel 9:27.

19   According to both the Toldoth and also the Gospels.

20   457 B.C., according to the standard chronology; cf Ezra 7:1-26 cp Jos. Ant. 11.5.1. This would seem to provide a pristine *terminus a quo*, with a pristine *terminus ad quem*, granting 27 A.D. as a year falling "in the midst" of the seventieth "week" of years, in which Christ abolished the efficacy of oblation and sacrifice, by his perfect and final sacrifice on the cross. This is exactly why this interpretation is favoured by Seventh-Day Adventists. Also, in 27 A.D. Passover fell on the Sabbath. Perfect.

King Cyrus. Not only that, but there is the rather inconvenient evidence we find from Josephus, that Ezra and Nehemiah lived, not in the days of Artaxerxes, but in the days of Xerxes, the father of Artaxerxes. This would necessarily have placed any such decree by Xerxes correspondingly earlier in time, thus also giving an earlier *terminus a quo* and *terminus ad quem* to the prophecy. In fact, in Josephus, we read that the wall of the city was completed in the 28th year of the reign of Xerxes.[21] We have no reason to suspect that Josephus lied in his reckoning of chronology, or that he was careless in his calculations. In fact, the discrepancy between the chronology of Josephus and what we find written in Ezra, Nehemiah, and the Massoretic text of Esther is further evidence that those latter texts are forgeries. Because Josephus would have had no reason to contradict what had been written in an earlier, venerable account. Furthermore the prophecy of Daniel speaks of a *Jubilee* period of 49 years between the time of the decree and the building of the street and the wall of the city.[22] Therefore if we were to use 444 B.C.[23] as the *terminus a quo* of the prophecy, this would mean that the walls of Jerusalem were not completed until 395 B.C., which was long after the reign of Artaxerxes I. There is no hint in the book of Nehemiah that there had been any change of kingship among the Persians; furthermore we would have to imagine that Nehemiah, who was the cup-bearer to Artaxerxes, and obtained permission from him for the rebuilding of Jerusalem, labored for almost fifty years before completing his task. In that case, Nehemiah must have been quite elderly by the time his work was done. But of course there is not the slightest hint of this in the text of *Nehemiah*, which once again confirms that it was merely a forgery, rather than an original document written by Nehemiah. Christians are unlikely to delve too deeply into these chronological issues, so the bogus chronology is upheld by general ignorance of the subject. And those few Christians who might be determined to examine the chronology in question, would typically be so fanatical in their religious beliefs that it is a mere matter of confirming what they have already decided is true.

21   Jos. Ant. 11.5.8; 179.
22   Daniel 9:25-26.
23   This may be 445 B.C., according to some sources. But the difference is negligible, in terms of centuries and millennia, which we are considering in our chronology.

Therefore any subterfuge or rationalization will be employed in their dubious arguments to uphold the superstructure of their beliefs. Anyone who has attempted to have a rational conversation with such persons knows exactly what I am talking about. I should know, because I used to be a born-again Christian myself.

The Queen Helene of the Toldoth Jeschu is evidently intended to represent Queen Salome-Alexandra, the widow of Alexander Jannaeus. But some may object that, if so, she ought to have been more clearly identified by name, rather than have the mysterious name "Helene" ascribed to her, for some unknown reason. And this is a fair objection, that must be addressed. First of all, the name Helene may be a combination of Salome and Helena, the latter person having been a queen of Adiabene, who converted to Judaism with her son Izates.[24] Queen Helena helped the Jews of Jerusalem in a time of famine by providing corn[25] for them. Thus she no doubt became greatly beloved in the memory of the Jews. No doubt Queen Salome-Alexandra also was greatly beloved, since she allowed the Pharisees to hold sway over the people. This was in stark contrast to the policy of her late husband, who bitterly persecuted the Pharisees, based upon a feud with them going back to the days of his father, John Hyrcanus. But the Queen Helene of the *Toldoth* would thus seem to be a composite of Salome and Helena. Helena lived after the alleged time of Jesus.[26] But Salome lived long before the canonical time of Jesus. Why would the Jews have confounded these two queens in the Toldoth Jeschu? And furthermore, does not such confusion weaken the thesis advocated herein? The only explanation that springs readily to mind is the attempt at camouflage; in other words, that if a text of the *Toldoth* had fallen into the hands of Christians, the uncertainty respecting the identity of the queen, and also of Jeschu himself, might have supplied some degree of *plausible deniability* that the text was speaking of the Jesus Christ of the Christians. This explanation may not be fully satisfying to everyone.[27] But there is also one important detail that ought not to be

---

24 Jos. Ant. 20.2.1-5.

25 Corn. Thus reads the translation of Josephus by Whiston; presumably it means wheat. Cf the King James Bible.

26 According to the standard chronology.

27 One alternate explanation is that the Rabbis regarded the tale of Jesus as a

overlooked in connection to this question. That is the fact that the famed Rabbi Simeon Ben Shetach also is a character in the story. And in this instance, the Rabbi in question is a definitely-recognizable historical person, who lived in the early first century B.C., and was a contemporary of both Alexander Jannaeus and Alexandra. In fact, we will have more to say of Rabbi Simeon Ben Shetach when we examine evidence from the Talmud. But the point here is that even from the Toldoth, the mention of Simeon Ben Shetach in relation to Jeschu and Queen Helene places Jeschu (Jesus) in the Hasmonean era.[28] Therefore the evidence from the Toldoth dovetails together with the evidence we have seen from Daniel's prophecy of the seventy weeks, and also with evidence yet to be considered from the Talmud, in favour of the thesis advanced herein.

I suppose if there is one criticism I have of both the *Toldoth* and the *Talmud* vis-à-vis Jesus it is that, there seems to have been some degree of cultural revisionism at work. In other words, Jesus is given the Hebrew name Jeschu, and the context of the stories are very much presented within the context of a Pharisaic-Rabbinical *milieu,* to such an extent that one seems to acquire a caricatured image of Jesus as being Jewish in a cultural sense that was unlikely to have been historically true, regardless of when he lived.[29] One has but to read Josephus to see that, after the time of Alexander the Great, many Jewish men had Greek names. Not only that, but Greek culture, language, philosophy, and aesthetics became very commonplace throughout the Levant during that time. Jesus was probably known more commonly by the Greek form of his name[30] than

---

fantasy, and Jesus himself as merely fabulous; therefore they only offered a mocking satire in response to the Gospels.

28   Hasmonean era. The Hasmonean era can be dated from the uprising of the Maccabees to overthrow the tyrant Antiochus Epiphanes, all through their high-priestly dynasty, up until the time that Judaea was invaded by Pompey in 63 B.C. Although technically, it was Herod I who murdered the last of the Hasmonean line, even though they were his own sons by Mariamne.

29   I.e., either in the first century B.C. or the first century A.D.

30   Iesous. Pronounced "YAY-soos". Josephus mentions over a dozen men with the name Jesus. Jesus is the Latin form of the name, but in English translations, when we read "Jesus" in such Greek texts, it is evident that the Greek form is in the underlying Greek; therefore the historical Jesus was probably more commonly known as Jesus, rather than Jeschu or Joshua (Yeshu or Yeshua).

by any Hebrew or Syriac form of the name, despite what some Hebrew Christian groups like "Jews for Jesus" might claim to the contrary. And, as we have seen above, Jesus was probably not even ethnically Jewish either; the supposed descent from King David is virtually an afterthought in the Gospels,[31] and appears to be merely a gratuitous pandering to the necessity for proper Messianic credentials. So it seems at least plausible if not probable, that Jesus was somewhat influenced by Hellenistic thought in his teachings. There are certainly significant parallels with the school of the Cynics.[32]

Returning to the question of chronology, if we take the decree of Cyrus[33] as the *terminus a quo* of Daniel's prophecy of the seventy weeks, and we then subtract the first *Jubilee* period of seven weeks,[34] this brings us to 488 B.C., which is well within the reign of Xerxes.[35] And, according to Josephus, it was in the reign of Xerxes that Nehemiah completed the walls of Jerusalem, within a period of three years.[36] So once again, we can see that the decree of Cyrus is the more natural *terminus a quo* for Daniel's prophecy of the seventy weeks. One may argue with the exact precision of the standard chronology, however. Yet in general terms, it

---

31   Found in only two of the four Gospels, namely Matthew and Luke, which royal genealogies nevertheless contradict each other. Furthermore these two Gospels, at least in their current form, each claim a virgin birth for Jesus, thus obviating any such supposed royal pedigree.

32   And also more than a hint of Platonism in John. Epicureans and Stoics are also explicitly mentioned in the New Testament; cf Acts 17:18.

33   537 B.C., according to the standard chronology.

34   I.e., 49 years, or seven weeks of years.

35   The Wikipedia article is wrong in respect to the chronology of his reign; it has his reign from 485 B.C. to 465 B.C., when (supposedly) his son Artaxerxes succeeded him. But this is definitely in error, since we have the explicit statement by Josephus that Xerxes reigned (At least) 28 years; (Jos. Ant. 11.5.8; 179) and I would rather give credit to Josephus than to the "geniuses" who set up Wikipedia. The Wikipedia articles, while apparently following the standard chronology, may be in error. The standard chronology is in itself somewhat suspect, if it has been established by Christians who had a vested interest in falsifying the chronology in the service of evangelicalism. Either that, or we would have to charge Josephus either with carelessness, or with deliberate falsification of the chronology, to sabotage Christianity. This could also account for the silence of Josephus about Christ.

36   Jos. Ant. 11.5.6-8.

seems to be correct. But of course our thesis involves not the accuracy of the standard chronology in a general sense, but rather the question of whether Jesus himself may have lived at a time earlier than what is commonly supposed. And so far we have seen that there is at least some significant evidence that this may have been the case.

We will not get a complete picture from any one source, but by combining accounts from several diverse sources, and considering some obscure but relevant evidence, a more complete portrait of Jesus will emerge. I will ask the reader to be patient and give due consideration of all the evidence to be presented herein. Only after all the evidence has been presented will it be possible to reevaluate the case for Jesus having lived in the first century B.C.

According to the implicit chronology of the *Antiquities,* the decree of Cyrus was issued in 574 B.C.; according to that of the *War,* the same decree was issued in 564 B.C. According to the standard chronology, the decree of Cyrus was issued in 537 B.C. or 536 B.C.[37] So we can see that there is a 37 or 38 year discrepancy between the standard chronology and the one used by Josephus in his *Antiquities,* while there is a 27 or 28 year discrepancy in the case of his earlier work, the *War.* So of the two, his earlier work was closer to the standard chronology. So there is a ten-year discrepancy between the implicit chronologies employed by Josephus in two of his major works of history. Since the earlier chronology allowed for the *terminus ad quem* of Daniel's prophecy to be closer to the reign of Alexandra, it is quite possible that an earlier chronology still, used by the Jews during the time in question, may have allowed for that same expected time of fulfillment to fall in her reign. So it is not so far-fetched to imagine that the original, historical Jesus may have lived during that time, and thus laid claim to Messianic status on the basis of the prophecy.[38]

We have already seen evidence from one Jewish source that Jesus lived in the first century B.C., and we will also later examine some evidence

---

37   In terms of chronology, one or two years' difference is negligible, on such large time-scales. Nevertheless chronologists still strive for absolute accuracy.
38   And other unknown credentials.

from the Talmud in favour of this theory. However against this some will protest that, on the Christian side, _all_ the sources agree in placing Jesus in Roman times, rather than Hasmonean. And while it is certainly true that all Christian sources place the crucifixion of Christ in the procuratorship of Pilate, and all the primary Christian sources[39] also place the nativity of Christ in the Roman era, there is one glaring exception among early Christian writings, that places the birth of Christ back in the days of Alexandra-Salome and Alexander Jannaeus. This highly significant exception was pointed out by Mead in his book. The exception is found in the works of Epiphanius. It will be worthwhile to examine exactly what Epiphanius wrote along these lines.

"Now the throne and kingly seat of David is the priestly office in Holy Church; for the Lord combined the kingly and high-priestly dignities into one and the same office, and bestowed them upon His Holy Church, transferring to her the throne of David, which ceases not as long as the world endures. The throne of David continued by succession up to that time- namely, till Christ Himself- without any failure from the princes of Judah, until it came to Him for whom were "the things that are stored up" who is Himself "the expectation of the nations". For with the advent of the Christ, the succession of the princes from Judah, who reigned until the Christ Himself, ceased. The order [or succession] failed and stopped at the time when He was born in Bethlehem of Judaea, in the days of Alexander, who was of the high-priestly and royal race; and after this Alexander this lot failed, from the time of himself and Salina, who is also called Alexandra, for the time of Herod the King and Augustus Emperor of the Romans; and this Alexander, one of the anointed (or Christs) and ruling princes placed the crown on his own head ... After this a foreign king, Herod, and those who were no longer of the family of David, assumed the crown."[40]

Mead then comments on this curious passage from Epiphanius:

"This passage is perhaps the most remarkable in the whole range of Patristic [sic] literature; it might very well be called the "Riddle of

39   I.e., the New Testament documents.
40   Mead., op. cit., pgs. 392-393.

Epiphanius" *par excellence*, for it is the most enigmatic of all his puzzles. It is remarkable for many reasons, but most of all because no Father [sic] has given more minute indications of the date of Jesus, according to canonical data helped out by his own most positive assertions, than Epiphanius. Nevertheless here we have the Bishop of Salamis categorically asserting, with detailed reiteration, so that there is no possibility of escape, that Jesus was born in the days of Alexander and Salina, that is of Jannai and Salome; not only so, but he would have it that it must needs have been so, in order that prophecy, and prophecy of the most solemn nature, should be fulfilled that there should be no break in the succession from the tribe of Judah, as it had been written. There is no way of extricating ourselves from the crushing weight of the incongruity of this statement of Epiphanius by trying to emend the reading of the text; for not only does the whole subject of his argument demand such a statement, but he supports it by a number of subsidiary assertions."[41]

If we can overlook Mead's melodramatic flourish, we can see that he at least has somewhat of a point here. A few pages later, he also supplements this first passage by another similar one from Epiphanius:

"From the time that Augustus became Emperor, for four years, more or less, from [the beginning of] his reign, there had been friendship between the Romans and Jews, and contribution of troops had been sent, and a governor appointed, and some portion of tribute paid to the Romans, until Judaea was made [entirely] subject and became tributary to them, its rulers having ceased from Judah, and Herod being appointed [as ruler] from the Gentiles, being a proselyte, however, and Christ being born in Bethlehem of Judaea, and coming for the preaching [of the Gospel], the anointed rulers from Judah and Aaron having ceased, after continuing until the anointed ruler Alexander and Salina who was also Alexandra; in which days the prophecy of Jacob was fulfilled: "A ruler shall not cease from Judah and a leader from his thighs, until he come for whom it is laid up, and he is the expectation of the nations"- that is, the Lord who was born."[42]

---

41   Ibid., pgs. 393-394.
42   Ibid., pgs. 396-397.

Both of the passages from Epiphanius are highly significant in terms of placing the nativity of Jesus back in the days of Alexander Jannaeus and Alexandra-Salome, but there also seems to be some degree of confusion in respect to the chronology, since it also seems to at least partially accord with the canonical chronology in respect to Jesus being born in Bethlehem in the days of King Herod I, etc. Furthermore the evidential value of these passages are greatly weakened, in my estimation, by the fact that Epiphanius is not basing his pronouncements upon any verifiable historical sources or circumstances, but his argument is completely based upon perceived theological necessity. Mead should have picked up on this, and not ostentatiously trumpeted these passages as if they were proof of his theory.[43] Once again, however, these very passages illustrate the fact that, from Christian sources, the question of history and chronology is made subservient to theological considerations. This very fact may have facilitated the chronological dislocation of Christ from his original time period.[44] In the case of Epiphanius, he was trying to rationalize and justify how Christ supposedly fulfilled messianic prophecy, by having been born at just the right time. Unfortunately for his credibility, his chronology is skewed and he seems oblivious to the fact that Jesus would have been well over a hundred years old by the time of Pontius Pilate, assuming he had been born back in the days of Alexander Jannaeus. So the evidence from Epiphanius, while worth noting, is not nearly as highly significant, in my estimation, as Mead seems to suppose.

Mead also is clueless as to why the Rabbis did not level criticism against the Christians for having falsified the chronology in respect to Jesus.[45] But aside from begging the question, here Mead really exposes the inadequacy of his study. It may be illustrative to see exactly what Mead wrote:

"It all seems so senseless, so useless; if it was untrue, what purpose could

---

43   Indeed I consider this a very serious mistake by Mead. It is far too easy to find strange passages within such literature, and seek to create a controversy with it. Such documents are vastly less important than the New Testament texts in any genuine historical inquiry into the origin of Christianity.

44   I.e., assuming that such had been the case. I do not want to be accused of begging the question in respect to my thesis.

45   Ibid., pg. 419.

it possibly serve? If it was the truth, why did not the Rabbis invariably put it in the forefront of all their polemics, and bend all their energies on making their tradition consistent, even as the Christians devoted all theirs to making their story uniform? [sic] But this is just what we do not find; there is not a single word on the Christian side to show that the Rabbis ever argued that the Christian tradition was one hundred years out; no early writer, no Church Father [sic] (if we except Epiphanius, who does so indirectly), breathes a word of such a terrific indictment of the fundamental historicity of the Christian tradition. Whatever we learn of the controversy from the Christian side, it all seems to show that the Rabbis spent all their energies on combatting dogmas- such as the virgin-birth, the divinity of Jesus, the Messiah claim, etc. It is true that Celsus categorically accuses the Christians of continually altering the Gospel history to suit dogmatic considerations; but is it credible that the Rabbis could have had so potent a weapon in their hands as an ancient and authentic tradition that Jesus lived 100 B.C., and yet have refrained from using it on every occasion?"[46]

Here Mead really shows his ineptitude in gaudy colours. If he had dug a little bit deeper, as I have done, he would have known exactly why the Rabbis were in no position to use "so potent a weapon" in their hands as the knowledge that Jesus really lived a century before the time written in the Gospel texts; because it would have been like a bomb exploding in their own faces; that knowledge was directly related to the knowledge that, in fact, according to the key prophecy found in the book of Daniel, that was exactly the precise time when the Messiah was supposed to appear. The Rabbis couldn't bring this embarrassing fact up, without it violently recoiling upon themselves; they would thereby only be providing evidence that Jesus really was the true Messiah, since he lived at precisely the right time, according to the chronology of the prophecy of the seventy weeks, as found in Daniel. This is also the key to why Daniel was demoted from *Nehevim* to *Kethuvim* within *TaNaKh*, and also why "Artaxerxes" was substituted for "Xerxes" in the Massoretic texts of Ezra and Nehemiah.[47] As we will see, the falsification inherent in

---

46   Ibid.
47   As opposed to what we find written in Josephus.

these texts provided a precedent and a pretext for the dislocation of Jesus from his original time in the Gospels and other New Testament texts.

Mead also offers evidence from some of his colleagues and associates, that, according to "occult" knowledge, Jesus lived approximately a century earlier than the commonly-accepted time.[48] He was referring to alleged psychic perceptions that led to these conclusions. Without dismissing the validity of psychic phenomena, I personally would exclude any such evidence in such an historical inquiry, simply due to the highly subjective nature of the evidence. In other words, I'm sure that although X number of people with genuine[49] psychic perception may agree that Jesus lived in the first century B.C., Y number of others will agree that he lived during the first century A.D. In the same way, any number of persons can claim (and have claimed) visions to support any number of conflicting doctrines, such as that Jesus survived the crucifixion, Jesus miraculously rose from the dead, or that this or that religious dogma is true or false, etc., etc., *ad nauseum, ad infinitum.* Therefore I would say that it is the better part of wisdom to exclude all such subjective sources of "knowledge" from any such historical inquiry as we are here undertaking.

Now that we are focussing on chronology proper I think it would be appropriate to debunk a popular dogma current in certain circles of Zionist Christianity vis-à-vis the so-called "times of the Gentiles". This is a myth propagated in certain Protestant circles of Bible prophecy that subscribe to the Dispensational Premillennialist interpretation of biblical prophecy. According to the common myth, the supposed "times of the Gentiles" spoken of by Jesus[50] began with the taking of Jerusalem by Nebuchadnezzar in 606 B.C.[51] and supposed to be used to calculate the time when Jesus Christ will return, based upon obscure prophecies and methods of such calculations. In other words, it is assumed that "the times of the Gentiles" began with the invasion of Jerusalem by Nebuchadnezzar, and that it would be absolutely uninterrupted until the Messiah would come in glory to establish the kingdom of God

---

48   Mead., op. cit., pgs. 18-27.

49   Or purported.

50   Luke 21:24.

51   Or 605 B.C.

on earth, etc.[52] However, this entire scheme of Bible prophecy can be completely debunked by the fact that the Jews were not always under Gentile domination from the time of Nebuchadnezzar on. The Jews had their own completely independent kingdom from 142 B.C. to 63 B.C., when the Romans invaded Judaea. So this completely demolishes the supposed prophetic scheme based upon such an interpretation of the so-called "times of the Gentiles". It's too bad so many Christians are so fanatical in their religious beliefs that they remain ignorant of the actual history of the Jewish people.

Mead also overlooks the possibility that the Jews could have had any reason to alter the chronology in respect to Jesus. He glosses over this, without really even giving it any due consideration. And, since he is also blithely oblivious to the prophecy of the seventy weeks of Daniel, and how it directly impinges upon the question under consideration, he fails to appreciate exactly why the Rabbis would not have been in a position to argue against any chronological doctoring on the part of the Christians. But even without a knowledge of this very important part of the relevant evidence, Mead still is rather obtuse and fatuous in not appreciating that the Rabbis were actually granted a gift of sorts by the Christians[53] that they could later use, and certainly did use and still use, down to the present day: the convenient disclaimer of any responsibility in the death of Jesus. They could just blame it all on the Romans. Today we here the constant refrain, from both Jews and their apologists, that the Romans were solely responsible for the crucifixion of Jesus. It doesn't matter that such a claim flies in the face of what is clearly recorded in the Gospel accounts; critical scholarship has granted an implicit *imprimatur* to the theory that Jesus was crucified as a political criminal by the Romans, and the Jews are merely incidental to the story. This is obviously a blatant form of revisionism, but nobody ever takes the Jews to task for it. And the same scholarship now also insists that the New Testament authors always bent over backwards to prevent any blame being placed upon the

---

52   Or until Israel became a nation in 1948, or until the six-day war of 1967, when Jerusalem was liberated from Arab occupation, etc., etc., *ad nauseum, ad infinitum.*

53   I.e., assuming that the Evangelists really did alter the time, as claimed herein.

Romans, and to always portray the Romans in a positive light. Aside from the fact that the claim is outrageously and provably false,[54] the likely truth of the case is that the Evangelists wanted to implicate the Romans in the murder of Jesus. In fact, this was probably one of the primary motivations for the chronological dislocation.

So we have two reasons why the Jews would have acquiesced in any chronological falsification engaged in by the Christians vis-à-vis Jesus; first, the Jews could not point back to the Hasmonean date without an implicit and automatic association with the perceived legitimacy of Christ's messianic claims vis-à-vis the famed prophecy of the seventy weeks, found in Daniel; secondly, by acquiescing to the new date, the Jews now received a potential disclaimer (or partial disclaimer, at any rate) in respect to the murder of Jesus, by placing the blame entirely on the Romans. In fact, the Jews would have been the ones who would have had a much stronger motive to place Jesus in Roman rather than Hasmonean times. They would thereby be able to discredit any alleged claim to the fulfillment of the prophecy, and thus undermine the Messianic status of Jesus in the eyes of the Christians and Jews, and also by having a scapegoat in the Romans for the death of Jesus. But the early Jewish sources place Jesus in the days of the Hasmoneans, rather than the Romans. If anything, the Christians would have had more reason to place Jesus back in Hasmonean times, rather than Roman times; first, to bolster the Messianic claims respecting Jesus vis-à-vis the prophecy of the seventy weeks; and secondly, by placing the entire blame for the murder of Jesus on the Jews. But this is the very reverse of the actual situation that we encounter. These circumstances converge to support the Hasmonean date, rather than the Roman date, as the true date for Jesus. In fact, I dare say that the circumstantial evidence is actually overwhelmingly strong, once one understands and appreciates the issues involved.

One possible counterargument is that the Christians would not have been so easily willing to sacrifice such an important part of the evidence in favour of the Messianic claims respecting Jesus, as having lived at precisely the right time to fulfill an ancient prophecy. Therefore, the

54 Luke 13:1.

argument goes, Jesus probably really did live in the first century A.D., as we've always been told. This is admittedly a valid and reasonable argument, but it is neither unanswerable nor is it necessarily sufficiently strong to overturn all the evidence in favour of our thesis. Once we understand the rationale for the chronological dislocation by the Evangelists, this line of argument is muted[55] to a considerable degree. We will explore the possible motivations for a chronological dislocation in the following chapter.

---

55   Not to say mooted.

PSEUDOCHRONOLOGY

We will now inquire into possible motivations on the part of the Evangelists to chronologically dislocate Jesus from his original time. It should be clearly understood that, in spite of whatever seemingly strong evidence we may have already presented in favour of our thesis herein, unless we can provide a reasonably convincing argument as to why Jesus would have been dislocated from Hasmonean times in the Gospels, then our thesis rests upon a shaky foundation. We will first examine what Mead himself had to say along these lines, and I dare say that his argument was woefully inadequate.

"When it was further questioned: But why did the writer who put together this marvellous story place it at a date which you say was not the real date of Jesus? - the explanation suggested was somewhat as follows. The evangelical writer put the story at a date between himself and what we consider the actual historical date, most probably because he desired to avoid controversy and criticism; he did not desire that the public, and especially those inimical to his own tradition, should be put on the track of the actual date, so that the memory of one who was regarded in the tradition of his school as the beloved Teacher, *par excellence*, should escape being bandied about in the arena of vulgar curiosity and violent theological controversy. Although his affection induced him to weave many sayings and perhaps some doings of the Master into his work, he especially did not wish to have it mistaken for the actual historical account of the life of the real Jeschu. This was the main reason; but the Pilate date was also determined by the fact that there seems to have been some Jewish semi-prophet who created a little disturbance in a very small way, and who was in consequence brought before Pilate on a charge of sedition. The writer may have thus also taken some few facts from this incident and woven it into the main story; but he never had the slightest idea that anyone would take the story in any sense except that in which he intended it."[1]

I dare say that the above passage is a spectacular pyrotechnic display of Mead's ineptitude, naiveté, and an unrivalled example of insipid inanity. First of all it strikes me as absurdly sentimental; such syrupy sentimentalism overshadows and clouds his judgment on more than one occasion. Then Mead assumes that one person could have made such a sweeping decision. This is almost guaranteed to not be the case; otherwise, would we not have diverse Gospel accounts of Jesus, some placing him in the Roman era, and others placing him in Hasmonean times? Mead also seems to sidestep responsibility for such an absurd and insipid explanation by saying "the explanation suggested was somewhat as follows", as if to imply that it was not his explanation at all, but one suggested by some unnamed third party. Perhaps Mead sensed how weak and inadequate his supposed "explanation" was. Then he as much as undermines the whole of his central thesis by postulating a so-called "semi-prophet" (What is a "semi-prophet" anyway? [Mead's term]) living in the days of Pontius Pilate, who nevertheless managed to "create a little disturbance in a very small way" and who thus was brought before Pilate on a charge of sedition. But then why would this hypothetical proto-evangelist have confused this man with his great Teacher, who lived back in Hasmonean times? Mead fails to explain this. His "explanation" actually raises more objections than it answers. Mead also supposes that such a document could be anything other than among the most controversial of documents ever written. And, as if that wasn't enough, Mead then supposes that this person "would never have the slightest idea that anyone would take the story in any sense except

---

1   Mead., op. cit., pgs. 422-423.

that in which he intended it." Can anyone really be that naïve? Can the depths of naiveté really be so very deep? And, pray tell, exactly what sense would this hypothetical proto-evangelist have intended his story to be interpreted? Such a hopelessly mongrelized document could mean anything, presumably. Since Mead could come up with nothing better than this, (and virtually conceding the historical existence of Jesus in the days of Pontius Pilate, at least as a "semi prophet" {whatever that means}), then it is no wonder that his book did not create "shockwaves" throughout Christendom, rattling it to its very foundations (as the advertising blurbs on numerous dime-a-dozen Grail books claim for such books), but instead has been relegated to a dark obscurity. This is most unfortunate, however, since we have already seen that there is at least some very significant evidence suggesting that Jesus may have lived in the first century B.C. But in all fairness to Mead, although he did not present as complete a case for his thesis as we would have wished, he at least paved the way for future study, by at least bringing forward what evidence he did know of to the attention of the general public. The full evidence was not beyond his intelligence, but it was beyond his diligence. And, without a knowledge of the crucial evidence from the prophecy of the seventy weeks of Daniel, and also the admittedly obscure but highly relevant evidence respecting the books of Ezra and Nehemiah, and how *Artaxerxes* was substituted for *Xerxes* in those documents, he lacked a key part of the evidence, which would have led him to a better explanation. Indeed, it is possible that there may be other evidence that I am unaware of, but which may come to light through some other person in the future, who will be able to present an even stronger case that Jesus may have lived in Hasmonean times.

But to tackle the question of why the Evangelists would have changed the date of Christ's nativity, we first have to address the question of the dating of the Gospels. But even before we do that, it should be implicitly understood that any such decision, assuming the correctness of our thesis, must have been absolutely unanimous on the part of the Evangelists, or proto-evangelists. Otherwise the entire scheme would have been fruitless from the start. And in that case we would expect a profusion of Gospels placing Jesus in two or more different time periods, which is not the case.

The issue of the dating of the New Testament texts will also come up later in our study, but we need to at least briefly broach the topic here, particularly in respect to the Gospels. There is not a unanimous consensus among biblical scholars respecting exactly when the Gospels were first written. There is instead a general range of prospective dates, from approximately 40 A.D. to as late as 180 A.D. However the evidence from the *Diatessaron* suggests that only the four canonical Gospels were accepted (or even extant) at the time it was composed, which is generally said to originate from 160 to 175 A.D. The *Diatessaron* was an early "harmony of the Gospels" that took most of the material from each of the four Gospels and wove them together into one consecutive narrative. Therefore all four Gospels had to have been written before the writing of the *Diatessaron,* and only the four standard Gospels would have been considered authoritative.[2] Some people may be displeased with me for writing these things, but this is what the evidence supports. As far as the earlier range on the spectrum of dates, it seems very doubtful to me that any of the Gospels were written quite so early. In fact, it seems unlikely that any of the Gospels were written any earlier than 70 A.D. And they may very well have been written somewhat later than that date. The earliest dated fragment of any Gospel text is the famed *Rylands* fragment from the Gospel of John, dated by scholars to between 125 A.D. and 150 A.D. More recently, there has been an attempt to date a papyrus fragment of Matthew's Gospel to A.D. 66, by Carsten Peter Thiede and Matthew d'Ancona, on a palaeographic basis.[3] Naturally we expect those of a more fundamentalist religious persuasion to take a position that the Gospels and other New Testament texts were written

---

2   Or were even extant at the time. Most of the much-touted Gospels we here so much of today, such as the Gospel of Thomas, the Gospel of Philip, the Gospel of Mary (Magdalene), the Gospel of Judas (Iscariot) probably dated from the third century or later. The same also holds true of other texts, such as the Infancy Gospels, the Proto-evangelium of James, the Gospel of Nicodemus, the Gospel of Peter, etc.

3   See *The Jesus Papyrus.*, by Carsten Peter Thiede & Matthew d'Ancona. ISBN 1857999584. Their theory & dating remain controversial, however.

at a very early time. Some have even claimed that all the New Testament documents were written before 70 A.D. By contrast, it seems more likely to me that all the New Testament documents postdate 70 A.D., rather than otherwise. Conservative Bible scholars have always consistently clung tenaciously to the earliest possible dating for the New Testament texts, while critical scholars have tended to favour later dates. Although it is true that the general consensus of critical biblical scholars has shifted somewhat from very late dates, which were *en vogue* in the 19th century, to slightly earlier dates, their estimates, their methods, and their rationale has remained distinct from that of the conservative school. Critical Bible scholars have striven for scientific objectivity, rather than subordinating their specialty to the requirements of theological "correctness". It is not at all unreasonable to suppose that the Gospels were written in the late first century, or even the early second century.

There is at least one verse in the Gospel of John that suggests that it was possibly written at a fairly late date.

"I am come in my Father's name, and ye receive me not; if another shall come in his own name, him ye will receive." (John 5:43)

Christian fundamentalists assume that Jesus is here speaking of the antichrist, etc. But it is plausible that the reference to one coming "in his own name" was to the notorious false Messiah Simeon Bar Kochbah, whose name meant "Son of the Star"; if so, then we have circumstantial evidence that the Gospel of John was not written until 135 A.D. or later. In fact, I suspect that all the Gospels were probably written after this date. In any case, the Gospels were written fairly late in the game, even assuming Jesus lived in the days of Herod and Pilate. Of course if we assume that the thesis herein is correct, then the Gospels were written long after the original time. But why would the evangelists have placed Jesus in a time far later than the original, assuming our thesis is correct?

We have already mentioned one possible motive: to implicate the Romans in the murder of Jesus. If the Gospels were not written either until late in the first century, or in the early to middle of the second century, then by that time Christians had already come under the merciless Roman lash. As such, it would have been desirable to, if at all possible, somehow implicate them in the murder of Jesus. In a mystical sense this idea may have been justified in the minds of some early believers, on the basis of mystical union with Christ, and as composing the mystical body of Christ. This concept is frequently found in the Pauline epistles, and is also implicit in John's Gospel. But such a reason would be inadequate to justify a wholesale historical falsification. This may have been merely one subsidiary reason, but it was not the real reason at all. The real reason had to do with the perceived requirements of messianic prophecy. And once again they were based upon the book of Daniel. But now attention was focussed on other portions of Daniel.

If the thesis herein is correct, then Jesus having already lived at just the right time to fulfill the prophecy of the seventy weeks would already have served whatever necessary purpose had been required; those who now embraced the new movement, whether they were converts, or children who had been born into families that had accepted the messianic status of Jesus, needed a message that more fully corresponded to their current reality. In Roman times, this would have been reflected in the need to portray the Romans in the darkest possible colours. Therefore if there were any way for them to be implicated, even symbolically, in the murder of Jesus, then so much the better. But once again, times had changed, together with perceptions of the world and the supposed fulfillment of prophecy.

Ever since the Roman conquest of Judaea, the Romans were perceived as being the dreaded fourth beast/kingdom of Daniel's prophecies, in which times God would establish an everlasting kingdom. We ought to look at some of the prophecies of Daniel to understand what was said therein. In the second chapter of Daniel, King Nebuchadnezzar dreams a dream, which he cannot remember. He calls all the wise men of Babylon to discover his dream, and its interpretation. Since the wise men answer the king saying that it is impossible to discover the king's dream without divine intervention, the king orders the execution of all the wise men. Daniel and his three companions were counted among the wise men, and so their lives were also endangered. When Daniel learns of the king's decree, he asks the captain of the guard for time to discover the dream and its interpretation. So this is granted. Of course God reveals the dream and its interpretation to Daniel, who in turn reveals it to the king.[4] Daniel recounts the king's dream as follows:

29 As for thee, O king, thy thoughts came *into thy mind* upon thy bed, what should come to pass hereafter: and he that revealeth secrets maketh known to thee what shall come to pass.

30 But as for me, this secret is not revealed to me for *any* wisdom that I have more than any living, but for *their* sakes that shall make known the interpretation to the king, and that thou mightest know the thoughts of thy heart.

31 Thou, O king, sawest, and behold a great image. This great image, whose brightness *was* excellent, stood before thee; and the form thereof *was* terrible.

32 This image's head *was* of fine gold, his breast and his arms of silver, his belly and his thighs of brass,

33 his legs of iron, his feet part of iron and part of clay.

34 Thou sawest till that a stone was cut out without hands, which smote the image upon his feet *that were* of iron and clay, and brake them to pieces.

35 Then was the iron, the clay, the brass, the silver, and the gold, broken to pieces together, and became like the chaff of the summer threshingfloors; and the wind carried them away, that no place was found for them: and the stone that smote the image became a great mountain, and filled the whole earth.

36 This is the dream; and we will tell the interpretation thereof before the king.

37 Thou, O king, *art* a king of kings: for the God of heaven hath given thee a kingdom, power, and strength, and glory.

38 And wheresover the children of men dwell, the beasts of the field and

---

4   Daniel 2.

the fowls of the heaven hath he given into thine hand, and hath made thee ruler over them all.

39 And after thee shall arise another kingdom inferior to thee, and another third kingdom of brass, which shall bear rule over all the earth.

40 And the fourth kingdom shall be strong as iron: forasmuch as iron breaketh in pieces and subdueth all *things*: and as iron that breaketh all these, shall it break in pieces and bruise.

41 And whereas thou sawest the feet and toes, part of potters' clay, and part of iron, the kingdom shall be divided; but there shall be in it of the strength of the iron, forasmuch as thou sawest the iron mixed with miry clay.

42 And *as* the toes of the feet *were* part of iron, and part of clay, *so* the kingdom shall be partly strong, and partly broken.

43 And whereas thou sawest iron mixed with miry clay, they shall mingle themselves with the seed of men: but they shall not cleave to one another, even as iron is not mixed with clay.

44 And in the days of these kings shall the God of heaven set up a kingdom which shall never be destroyed: and the kingdom shall not be left to other people, *but* it shall break in pieces and consume all these kingdoms, and it shall stand for ever.

45 Forasmuch as thou sawest that the stone was cut out of the mountain without hands, and that it brake in pieces the iron, the brass, the clay, the silver, and the gold; the great God hath made known to the king what shall come to pass hereafter: and the dream is certain, and the interpretation thereof sure. (Daniel 2:29-45)

Ever since the Roman conquest of Judaea in the first century B.C., the Roman empire came to be regarded as the dreaded fourth kingdom of the prophecy in the eyes of the Jews. As such, it was expected and hoped that, now that the dreaded fourth kingdom/fourth beast was revealed, God would send the Son of man to deliver them, and establish his kingdom on earth. We should also look at the parallel in the seventh chapter of Daniel:

2 Daniel spake and said, I saw in my vision by night, and, behold, the four winds of the heaven stove upon the great sea.

3 And four great beasts came up from the sea, diverse from one another.

4 The first was like a lion, and had eagle's wings; I beheld till the wings thereof were plucked, and it was lifted up from the earth, and made *to* stand upon the feet *of it* as a man, and a man's heart was given to it.

5 And behold another beast, a second, like a bear; and it raised itself up on one side, and *it had* three ribs in the mouth *of it* between the teeth of it; and they said thus unto it, Arise, devour much flesh.

6 After this I beheld, and lo another, like a leopard, which had upon the back of it four wings of a fowl; the beast also had four heads; and dominion was given to it.

7 After this I saw in the night visions, and behold a fourth beast, dreadful and terrible, and exceedingly strong; and it had great iron teeth: it devoured and brake in pieces, and stomped *on* the residue with the feet of it: and it *was* diverse from all the beasts that *were* before it; and it had ten horns.

8 I considered the horns, and, behold, there came up among them another little horn, before whom there were three of the first horns plucked up by the roots: and behold, in this horn *were* eyes like the eyes of *a* man, and a mouth speaking great things.

9 I beheld till the thrones were cast down, and the Ancient of days did sit, whose garment *was* white as snow, and the hair of his head like the pure wool: his throne *was like* the fiery flame, *and* his wheels *as* burning fire.

10 A fiery stream issued and came forth from before him: thousand thousands ministered unto him, and ten thousand times ten thousand stood before him: the judgment was set, and the books were opened.

11 I beheld then, because of the voice of the great words which the horn spake: I beheld till the beast was slain, and his body destroyed, and given to the burning flame.

12 As concerning the rest of the beasts, they had their dominion taken away: yet their lives were prolonged for a season and time.

13 I saw in the night visions, and, behold, *one* like a son of man came with the clouds of heaven, and came to the Ancient of days, and they brought him near before him.

14 And there was given him dominion, and glory, and a kingdom, that all people, nations, and languages, should serve him: his dominion *is* an everlasting dominion, which shall not pass away, and his kingdom shall not be destroyed.

15 I Daniel was grieved in my spirit in the midst of *my* body, and the visions of my head troubled me.

16 I came near unto one of them that stood by, and asked him the truth of all this. So he told me, and made me know the interpretation of the things.

17 These great beasts, which are four, *are* four kings, *which* shall arise out of the earth.

18 But the saints of the most High shall take the kingdom, and possess the kingdom forever, ever for ever and ever.

19 Then I would know the truth of the fourth beast, which was diverse from all the others, exceedingly dreadful, whose teeth *were* iron, and his nails brass; *even that beast which* devoured, brake in pieces, and stomped *on* the residue with his feet.

20 And of the ten horns that *were* in his head, and *of* the other which came up, before whom three fell; even *of* that horn that had eyes, and a mouth that spake very great things, whose look *was* more stout than his fellows.

21 I beheld, and the same horn made war with the saints, and prevailed against them;

22 until the Ancient of days came, and judgment was given to the saints of the most High; and the time came that the saints possessed the kingdom.

23 Thus he said; The fourth beast shall be the fourth kingdom upon earth, which shall be diverse from all kingdoms, and shall devour the whole earth, and shall tread it down, and break it in pieces.

24 And the ten horns out of this kingdom *are* ten kings *that* shall arise; and another shall rise after them; and he shall be diverse from the first, and he shall subdue three kings.

25 And he shall speak *great* words against the most High, and shall wear out the saints of the most High, and think to change times and laws; and they shall be given into his hand until a time and times and the dividing of time.

26 But the judgment shall sit, and they shall take away his dominion, to consume and to destroy it unto the end.

27 And the kingdom and dominion, and the greatness of the kingdom under the whole heaven, shall be given to the people of the saints of the most High, whose kingdom is an everlasting kingdom, and all dominions shall serve and obey him. (Daniel 7:2-27)

So we can see that the seventh chapter of Daniel corresponds to the second chapter, and the four kingdoms are also symbolized by four beasts. In the days of the Roman occupation of Judaea, the Roman empire was looked upon as the dreaded fourth beast/fourth kingdom of the prophecies of Daniel in the eyes of the Jews. But the Jews also acquired hope from this interpretation; since the prophecies foretold that God would establish his kingdom during that time, destroying all the earlier kingdoms, then the people hoped that God would bring an end to the dominion of the Romans. And since the prophecy of Daniel 7 mentioned "one like unto a son of man" as being granted an eternal dominion, this prophecy was interpreted as a messianic prophecy, and it was hoped that through a great Messianic Deliverer God would grant his people devliverance from Roman dominion, and grant his people independence once again. This explains the rampant messianic pretenders who multiplied like rabbits in the days of the Roman occupation. But now the disciples of Jesus would have been confronted by a seeming lack of fulfillment of prophecy: Jesus had lived before the time of the fourth beast/kingdom, when the prophecies of Daniel foretold that God would establish an everlasting kingdom through his Messiah, the Son of man. Now it was not enough for Jesus to have lived at the right time to "fulfill" the prophecy of the seventy weeks; now it became necessary to show that Jesus also fulfilled these other messianic prophecies as well; otherwise some other, latter-day messianic pretender could become preferred by prospective converts to a messianic movement within Judaism. Of course since the kingdom of God was not established in any detectable way during that time, it became necessary to reinterpret these prophecies in a spiritual sense, as meaning an invisible, mystical kingdom of God "within" the believer, until such time as God decides to send Jesus back, of course. But what was required was that Jesus had to have come at just the right time to fulfill these other prophecies as well; therefore it was expedient to "prove" that Jesus had lived during the time of Roman occupation. One thing that helped facilitate the falsification was the fact that the other Jews had rejected the legacy of Jesus, and his messianic claims (and the ongoing claims of his disciples) had become a source of embarrassment to the Jews, especially the Rabbis. Therefore the only people who had an interest in preserving the legacy of Jesus were those who also had a vested interest in perpetuating the legitimacy of his messianic status. Therefore if it had been agreed, by some *kahal* of these proto-Christians, that from that time it would be taught[5] that Jesus had indeed come in the days of the fourth beast/fourth kingdom, namely, the Roman empire,[6] then the other Jews, who did not believe in the messianic status of Jesus, would have had no reason or grounds to object, and apparently[7] there were no written documents to disprove the new teaching, since the Rabbis

---

5   First orally, and then in written texts.

6   Meaning, in practical terms, in the days of the Roman occupation of Judaea.

7   And luckily, for the revisionists.

no doubt had done everything possible to eradicate the memory of Jesus from the people. This convergence of circumstances[8] would thereby facilitate the art of the proto-evangelical revisionists. In fact, this scenario seems particularly plausible if we further suppose two things: first, that the followers of Jesus during the time of the revision were all Jewish; and second, that during the time in question they taught either primarily or exclusively by oral, rather than written, transmission of their tradition. Both of these circumstances are also reasonably likely as well. I will not go so far as to say that these conditions were necessary, but they would more conveniently facilitate any chronological revision on the part of the disciples. I dare say that this explanation and this scenario are both more reasonable and more probable than that proposed by Mead in his work. And this prophetic rationale is also not in opposition to the desire to implicate the Romans in the murder of Jesus. Therefore both explanations may have a reasonable degree of plausibility. Together they create at least a reasonable basis to consider the legitimacy of the evidence presented so far, as well as additional evidence, yet to be presented, that Jesus lived back in Hasmonean times.

So the picture that emerges is one in which Jewish disciples of Jesus perpetuate his legacy generation after generation by oral transmission, and remain a very close-knit group, being outcasts within Jewish society. Any outreach to Gentiles is minimal to nonexistent. The message would be shared in Hebrew, Greek, and Syriac, languages fairly commonly spoken by Jews in the Near East of those times. But at some point after the Roman conquest of Judaea (and Egypt, where many Greek-speaking Jews lived) there eventually was perceived a desire to place Jesus within the days of the "fourth kingdom/fourth beast" of Daniel's prophecies, namely the Roman empire. One additional benefit would be the implication of the Romans in the murder of Jesus. At some point, a decision is made by a *kahal* of these messianic Jews or proto-Christians to place Jesus in the days of the Romans, to thus "prove" that he fulfilled these prophecies of Daniel. This act would have been facilitated by the circumstance that no earlier, written texts would have been extant to contradict the new teaching. So now generations of these people would be

---

8   An eminently plausible convergence of circumstances, I might add.

brought up being taught that Jesus was born in the days of the Romans, and died under Roman rule.

In anticipation of one possible objection that some persons may make, by saying that, even if the above seems plausible, Why wouldn't the teachers have sought to place Jesus at least closer in time to the days of the Hasmoneans, rather than so long afterwards? The answer is to be found in what we discovered about the books of Ezra and Nehemiah. In other words, since these books of Ezra, and Nehemiah facilitated claims made by latter-day messianic pretenders that they had a rightful claim to the fulfillment of the prophecy of the seventy weeks, by virtue of removing the *terminus a quo* of the prophecy from the time of the decree of Cyrus, and replacing it with a *terminus a quo* originating from a supposed decree by Artaxerxes,[9] then there would be a desire to exploit this situation, and thus to "jump" Jesus from the border of the Hasmonean/Roman eras, and place him sufficiently "late" to have come (as an adult) at just the right time, in terms of chronology. And an examination of the chronology in question proves that they succeeded fairly well in doing just this. Of course Christians will claim it is an instance of genuinely fulfilled prophecy, but they conveniently overlook the numerous *imperfections* in the overall scheme of their religion.

So if we accept provisionally the scenario outlined immediately above, the decision by the messianic *kahal* occurred sometime during the Roman occupation of Judaea, but before there were any[10] Gentile converts to the new movement, and therefore also some time[11] before the first Greek Gospels were written. Also the specificity of the Gospels[12] in placing Jesus under the procuratorship of Pontius Pilate indicates that those texts apparently postdate the Massoretic texts of Ezra and Nehemiah.[13]

---

9   Even though according to earlier records Nehemiah lived in the days of Xerxes, the father of Artaxerxes. Furthermore since the texts of Ezra and Nehemiah read simply "Artaxerxes" rather than specifying Artaxerxes Longimanus, it may have been hoped and exploited by some Jews that it was supposed to be the later Artaxerxes Mnemon who was intended in those texts.

10   Or at least not many.

11   Although it is uncertain and debatable how long a time.

12   Particularly of Luke and Matthew, but the others as a matter of course.

13   Which must have been written some time after 46 B.C., according to the

So apparently the followers of Jesus exploited the texts of Ezra and Nehemiah, even though they knew those texts to be forgeries; they instead made them serve their own purposes. And of course the other Jews would have been in no position to protest against this, since in doing so they would have to expose the forgery. Likewise those Jews who rejected Jesus were in no position to protest against any chronological innovation in the teachings of the early proto-Christians, even assuming they knew of them.[14] Therefore an oral form of the *Toldoth Jeschu* may even predate the writing of the Greek Gospels. The *Toldoth Jeschu* may have first circulated as an oral tradition in response to an oral tradition circulated by the disciples of Jesus. The difference is that the Jews[15] did not alter the original chronology. The same general form of the *Toldoth* was presumably retained in the earliest written copies as well. In the meantime, the proto-Christian Jews had already made a secret chronological alteration in the transmission of their tradition, so that when the first texts were written, they reflected the new chronology. This is at least a reasonable possibility. Whether or not these were the actual events that transpired is unknown, and ultimately a matter of interpretation. We still have a considerable amount of evidence to consider. But if indeed this scenario, or some similar scenario, is what took place, then we would only expect that all subsequent Christian documents to reflect the new chronology, which would then have become standard. Thus of course all of the New Testament documents, as well as all the texts of the New Testament Apocrypha, would all uniformly uphold the new chronology. We have so far found only one sole exception on the Christian side of the evidence. I dare say that the explanations I have offered for possible motives on the part of proto-Christians to alter the chronology with respect to Jesus, and the scenario I have depicted are far more reasonable and probable than what Mead had to say on the subject. In any case we have clear indications of what would have been a sufficient motivation to dislocate Jesus from his original time, and,

arguments above. So even any Dead Sea Scroll fragments cannot prove that either Ezra or Nehemiah are older than this, as many scrolls were written later than this.

14   Remember the Rabbis had forbidden the Jews from reading any books by the *Minim*, or heretics.

15   I.e., the normative Jews, who rejected Jesus.

coupled with the evidence that Jesus may in fact have lived approximately a century earlier than the commonly-accepted time, we have a fairly strong case that this is what happened. I would hasten to add, however, that there may have been other possible motives that I have not discerned, but which may come to light through the research of another person, just as there may be still more hidden evidence unknown to myself that Jesus really lived in the first century B.C., rather than the first century A.D., as we have always been led to believe. Furthermore if the general scenario outlined above is true, then we would have to grant that, according to the disciples of Jesus, the decision to dislocate Jesus chronologically must have been considered "worth it" in evangelical-propagandistic terms, to promote their messianic faith, and was also sufficiently justified in the sense of feeling that the original message, character, and legacy of Jesus would still be kept intact, albeit placed within a new timeframe. The decision to sacrifice the original timeframe was well-calculated, inasmuch as everyone who would have been sufficiently motivated by such evidence *at the time* had already joined the movement, and now, after the new tactic of substituting a new, implicit *terminus a quo* to the prophecy, it was not as if all claim to the original fulfillment of the prophecy of the seventy weeks was being relinquished, but rather reinterpreted in a new, more comprehensive framework. In a sense, the decision was a stroke of genius. Any sacrifice of truth was justified in the minds of the disciples as being in the service of a greater truth. In fact, this same kind of rationale could account for the Gospel stories of Jesus eating and drinking with the apostles after his passion, which stories all contradict one another.[16]

Tertullian, writing in the very late second century, makes an off-hand comment that seems to allude to a story found in the *Toldoth Jeschu*. He speaks derisively of "the gardener" who removed the body of Jesus "that his lettuces might not be disturbed by the crowds of visitors" to the tomb.[17] Apparently this refers to a variant of the *Toldoth*, in which the gardener removed the body of *Jeschu* from the tomb to protect the lettuces growing in the garden from visitors to the tomb. This proves that at least an oral form of the *Toldoth* was in circulation among the Jews as

---

16   And therefore cannot all be true.
17   Tertullian, quoted in Mead., op. cit., pgs. 132-133.

early as the late second century. This is reasonably strong evidence that everything presented above is likely to be true.

The reader may still have reservations due to non-Christian sources that allegedly confirm the traditional timeframe for Christ. But upon investigation, it soon becomes apparent that these sources are of questionable validity or they don't really prove the traditional date for Christ. We have already mentioned the infamous *Testimony Flavium*, and dismissed it as a likely Christian forgery. There are in fact scarce few examples. I will deal with the few that I know of herein.

There is a brief passage in the *Annals* of Tacitus that speaks thus of Christ:

"Nero, in order to stifle the rumour {that he himself had set Rome on fire}, ascribed it to those people who were hated for their wicked practices, and called by the vulgar *Christians*; these he punished exquisitely. The author of this name was *Christ*, who in the reign of Tiberias, was brought to punishment {crucified} by the procurator Pontius Pilate."

But this brief "testimony" is summarily disposed of by the Rev. Robert Taylor as a blatant forgery. Mead also likewise disposes of the passage.[18] The fact that the sole manuscript of the *Annals* containing this brief passage was in the possession of one Poggio Bracciolini, who brought it to light in 1429, casts such a dark cloud of suspicion upon its provenance, antiquity, and authenticity that no reasonable person would lend it the slightest credence, especially when mountains of contrary evidence of an impeccable and undisputed character militate against its supposed veracity. Mead also rightly points out that the absence of any mention of the province of Pontius Pilate's procuratorship confirms how bogus the passage is.

The next passage is, by contrast, almost certainly genuine. But the precise purport of the passage is open to interpretation. It is a very brief passage found in Suetonius' *Lives of the Twelve Caesars*. It describes an action taken by Claudius, and his expulsion of Jews from Rome.

---

18   Mead., ibid., pgs. 53-57.

"Because the Jews at Rome caused continuous disturbances at the instigation of *Chrestus,* he expelled them from the city."

(Suetonius, *Lives of the Caesars; Claudius; section 25, paragraph 3*)

This event occurred in approximately 45 A.D., according to the standard chronology. If this reference to Chrestus is interpreted as applying literally to Jesus himself, then of course this places Jesus in the middle of the first century A.D., but also alive after the passion, in a completely non-supernatural context. Therefore Christians have always interpreted it to refer to disputes between Jews and early Jewish Christians. There is also a passage in the biblical book of Acts that corresponds to the above passage, but it is strangely and suspiciously silent in respect to the *reason* why Claudius expelled all the Jews from Rome:

After these things Paul departed from Athens, and came to Corinth,

2 and found a certain Jew named Aquila, born in Pontus, recently come from Italy, with his wife Priscilla, because Claudius had commanded all Jews to depart from Rome. (Acts 18:1-2)

Although the verse from Acts confirms what we find in Suetonius, the strange thing is we are not told why Claudius had commanded the Jews to leave Rome. We would normally have expected there to be more, rather than less, information about this in such a text. But I suspect that one reason is that, the context would belie the supposedly large number of Gentile converts to Christianity who supposedly existed at the time in question. In other words, even as late as the reign of Claudius, the messianic movement centered around Jesus was still very much a Jewish affair. It was Jews who were probably fighting among themselves that caused such disturbances in Rome. After all, Claudius only expelled Jews from Rome, not any Gentiles. This implies that there were no Gentile converts to the messianic movement as yet. The author of *Acts* apparently did not want this embarrassing fact brought to light, since it was in stark contrast to the historical revisionism we find rampant throughout that text, to the effect that there were large numbers of Gentile converts to the new messianic movement at that time. This appears to be the real reason for the strange silence of Acts 18:2 as to why exactly Claudius had expelled all Jews from Rome. I suppose a person subscribing to the traditional chronology vis-à-vis Jesus could argue that the real reason was that the fact that Jesus was still alive in the flesh at the time was evidence against the alleged miraculous resurrection of Christ, and therefore the presence of Christ in Rome became suppressed. However we must remember that Suetonius was a Roman writing from a Roman perspective; in thus speaking of *Chrestus* he may have been speaking in a very broad sense, implying followers of the movement, rather than Christ himself. In fact, Suetonius provides no further data on this *Chrestus,* whom, if we were to suppose was the real, personal instigator of such tumultuous disturbances, would have been dealt with quite harshly and summarily by the Romans. Therefore the very fact that such a distinctive personal judgment is not recounted is at least circumstantial evidence that the reference to *Chrestus* was general, rather than highly specific, and that it indicates no more than that, at Rome, there were disturbances instigated by messianic Jews, which led to the expulsion of all Jews from Rome. Therefore I feel that my interpretation is more justified.

Other than these few non-Christian sources, there remains only certain passages in Josephus concerning John the Baptist and James the Just. But I will deal with these in the respective chapters under those headings.

One other point that may be worth mentioning has to do with the book of Enoch. The book of Enoch, which was written in the reign of Herod I,[19] contains many Messianic passages, and no doubt the book was written in part at least to keep Messianic hopes alive in the minds of the Jews. The book exalts the Messiah to a celestial, superhuman, pre-existent status, proving (contrary to what some famous Grail authors have insisted) that at least some Jews held a Messianic *eschatology* more akin to what is found in Christianity than in contemporary Judaism.

---

19   I.e., the current form of the book. Most critical biblical scholars take a composite view of authorship in respect to the book of Enoch. If composite authorship is valid, (a point I do not necessarily concede) then portions of *Enoch* may predate the reign of Herod I. But the text as it has come down to us (i.e., the *Ethiopic* text) originates from a point no earlier than the reign of Herod I. Fragments of the work were found among the Dead Sea Scrolls, and according to one source, a complete scroll of *Enoch* in Hebrew or Syriac was secreted away in a private collection. The book of Enoch really deserves a book in itself.

No doubt the book was written to keep the Messianic hope alive in the aftermath of what must have appeared to be bitter failures of expected prophetic fulfillments. Although the book was not sufficiently popular to attain universal canonicity, it did attain canonical status among some Jews and early Christians, and was accepted as sacred Scripture by both Ethiopian Jews and Ethiopian Christians. These facts are evidence that the work originated as a distinctively Jewish work. My point here has to do specifically with the *eschatology* of the book. Towards the end of the book, there is an extended parable depicting the history of Israel as sheep, and the culmination of the parable seems to depict the birth of the Messiah some time around the reign of Herod I. Possibly the author of Matthew used this as the basis for his story of the nativity of Christ in the days of Herod. Of course this would have been some time after the decision by the messianic *kahal* to adopt the new chronology for Jesus, assuming the theory herein is correct. And presumably also this decision would have been sufficiently long after the time in question[20] to provide a degree of plausibility to the new account. A great national trauma, such as the burning of the temple by Rome, would also have sufficed to create enough of an upheaval among the Jews, both physically and emotionally, to provide cover for the new chronology. In fact, it is just barely possible that the decision may have occurred in the aftermath of the Bar Kochbah uprising. But I would not insist on this, as the evidence of exactly when the first Greek Gospels were written is ambiguous, and some of them (or even all of them) may have been written before this time. However I dare say that the position of Carsten Peter Thiede and Matthew d'Ancona vis-à-vis the Gospel of Matthew is unrealistic and unwarranted by the evidence. Fundamentalist apologists like Josh McDowell make an absurd false pretence that their position respecting New Testament authorship is supported by the evidence, and it is simply not true. In fact, McDowell seems blithely oblivious to the fact that, in terms of evidence, *internal* evidence from any given document can only prove that the document in question was written *no earlier than* the time indicated by such *internal evidence*; this is the exact opposite direction from what he would have wanted, or what he pretends, to be the case. In other words, it is relatively easy for a person to write a document as

---

20   I.e., after the time of Pontius Pilate, etc.

if it had been written a century before; and back in the second century, there were no scientific laboratories specializing in forensic evidence that could have proven that a document was really more recent that it pretended to be. Therefore the Gospels and other New Testament texts could very well have originated in the second century, rather than the first. And in this case, there would have been a definite motive on the part of the writers of such texts to make it appear as if such documents actually were older than they really were. It would have lent credence to the message being advocated. Christians will always suspect the motives of non-Christians, but will not in the least suspect motives on the part of the supposedly pristine origins of their religion. This is a strange combination of unwarranted blind trust and unwarranted paranoid suspicion, which produces a skewed view of the world. They need to wake up and smell the coffee.

CRUCIFIXION

No less than 17 times the New Testament tells us that Jesus was crucified.[1] Yet the *Toldoth* does not say that Jesus was crucified in the traditional sense. Instead, it says that he was hanged from a giant cabbage-stalk. It says that the Rabbis wanted to hang him from a tree, but no tree would hold him, because every tree that they tried to hang him from broke, or the branches of the tree broke. So they could not hang him from any tree, because, according to the Toldoth, Jeschu had spoken the letters of the *Shem* over every tree, since he knew his enemies would seek to hang him from a tree. Finally they found a giant cabbage-stalk from which to hang him.[2] This is a strange discrepancy from the Gospel story as it is narrated in the New Testament, yet it could possibly lead to some obscure but relevant evidence in favour of our central thesis. But first we ought to address the question of crucifixion in a general sense, since according to some sources, the Jews did not practice or even know of the custom of crucifixion, before the time of the Roman occupation of Judaea.

Michael Baigent, in writing of the apostle Paul, in his latest tome, writes:

---

1   Mt 27:31-44; 28:5; Mk 15:13-37; 16:6; Lk 23:21-49; 24:7,20; Jn 19:15-42; Acts 2:22-23,36; 4:10; Romans 6:6; 1 Corinthians 1:20; 2:14; Hebrews 6:6; 12:2; Revelation 11:8.
2   Possibly this absurd detail to the story was another attempt to mock Jesus and his disciples.

"One move was to openly blame the Jews for the death of Jesus, thereby absolving the Romans. This was a difficult bit of spin, since the Jews never indulged in crucifixion [sic], quite apart from the fact that this type of execution was specifically used as a punishment for political crimes. But he managed it nevertheless."[3] As usual, Michael Baigent is glaringly wrong, on several points. In support of his allegation, apparently that the Jews supposedly knew nothing of crucifixion before the Roman era of Judaean occupation, he has a footnote in his work citing a work by S.G.F. Brandon, known as *Jesus and the Zealots*. He also cites his own earlier work, *Jesus Papers*. However we can easily and superabundantly prove that he is wrong here about his allegation that the Jews knew nothing of crucifixion before their conquest by the Romans. And as far as "absolving the Romans", we have already seen, from evidence presented above, that one of the primary reasons for placing Jesus in the Roman era was to *implicate* the Romans in the death of Jesus. Furthermore anyone who reads the Gospels can clearly see that, according to those texts, it was only at the instigation of the scribes and Pharisees that Jesus was even brought before Pilate. Even taking a highly critical view of the Gospel texts, the probability of the case suggests that Jesus would likely have crossed paths with the religious leaders of his people before being brought before the Roman overlords, assuming he lived in Roman times. Finally, Baigent blames everything on Paul, which is completely unrealistic. In fact, I will present evidence in the following chapter that the Pauline corpus likely postdated the Gospels, rather than the reverse, which is almost otherwise universally accepted as fact. Baigent is also mistaken in ascribing such boundless powers to Paul, since he could not have single-handedly placed the "blame" for the murder of Jesus on the Jews *per se*, since it is not only in the Pauline corpus that we find such "blame", but rather throughout the New Testament, much of which is otherwise at odds with the Pauline corpus on other points.

But to proceed with our proof that the Jews did know of crucifixion before the Roman era, we will cite several sources. Michael Wise, Martin Abegg, Jr., and Edward Cook, in their introduction to their translation of

---

3   Baigent, Michael., *RACING TOWARD ARMAGEDDON.* (New York: Harper Collins. © 2009 by Michael Baigent. http://www.harpercollins.com. HarperCollins Publishers, 10 East 53rd Street, New York, NY 10022.); pg. 123.

the Dead Sea Scrolls, write the following: "It so happens that Alexander did crucify eight hundred men for the crime of siding with the Greek king Demetrius III and inviting him to invade Judea."[4] So these Scroll scholars, who are well acquainted with the Bible and cognate topics and history, have no problem with the Jews having known of crucifixion before the Roman era, since Alexander Jannaeus himself had eight hundred Pharisees crucified. G.R.S. Mead, for his part, also wrote of this same notorious event, and thus wrote explicitly that Alexander Jannaeus, otherwise known as King Jannai, crucified eight hundred Pharisees.[5] But the most unanswerable evidence, and the primary evidence, upon which both Mead and these scroll scholars have based their pronouncements, comes from the writings of Josephus himself. Josephus writes in quite graphic and descriptive terms of exactly what Alexander Jannaeus did to his enemies, despite the fact that they were his own countrymen:

"Now as Alexander fled to the mountains, six thousand of the Jews hereupon came together (from Demetrius) to him out of pity at the change of his fortune; upon which Demetrius was afraid, and retired out of the country; after which the Jews fought against Alexander, and being beaten were slain in great numbers in the several battles which they had, and when he had shut up the most powerful of them in the city Bethome, he besieged them therein; and when he had taken the city, and gotten the men into his power, he brought them to Jerusalem, and did one of the most barbarous actions in the world to them; for as he was feasting with his concubines, in the sight of all the city, he ordered about eight hundred of them to be crucified; and while they were *still* living, he ordered the throats of their children and wives cut before their eyes. This was indeed by way of revenge for the injuries they had done him; which punishment yet was of an inhuman nature, though we suppose that he had been ever so much distressed, as indeed he had been, by his wars with them, for he had by this means come to the last degree of hazard, both of his life and his kingdom, while they were not satisfied by themselves only to fight against him, but introduced foreigners also for the same purpose; nay, at

---

4   Wise, Abegg & Cook., op. cit., pg. 27.
5   Mead., op. cit., pg. 139.

length they reduced him to that degree of necessity, that he was forced to deliver back to the king of Arabia the land of Moab and Gilead, which he had subdued, and the places that were in them, that they might not join with them in the war against him, as they had done ten thousand other things that tended to affront and reproach him. However, this barbarity seems to have been without any necessity, on which account he bare the name of a Thracian among the Jews; whereupon the soldiers that had fought against him, being about eight thousand in number, ran away by night, and continued fugitives all the time that Alexander lived; who being now freed from any further disturbance from them, reigned the rest of his time in the utmost tranquility."[6]

So according to Josephus himself, a Jewish historian of the first century, crucifixion was both known and practiced by Jews before the time of the Roman occupation of Judaea. Josephus uses the very same Greek root-word that we also find in the Greek New Testament, and also in his *Vita, section 75*, where he speaks of three former acquaintances of his who were being crucified by the Romans. Josephus tells us that he intervened with Titus on behalf of the three men, and they were all taken down alive from the crosses. Two of the men subsequently died as a result of the physical trauma, but one man fully recovered.[7] The very same Greek root-word, *stauroo*, is the word also used in the Greek New Testament. The same Greek root-word, *stauros*, is also translated as "cross" 28 times.[8] The very same Greek root-word is used in both cases. Some have claimed that the Greek word in question, *stauros*, denotes no more than a single upright pole or stake. While technically this may be true, we ought to take the complete evidence into consideration. The Greek terms *stauros* and *stauroo* correspond to the Latin terms *crux* and *crucifigatur*, respectively.[9] The latter term is the word from which we get *crucify, crucified,* and *crucifixion.* To "crucify" literally means to

---

6   Jos. Ant. 13.14.2.
7   This account makes it reasonably plausible that Jesus may have survived the crucifixion. But this is only one theory among several viable alternatives.
8   Mt 10:38; 16:24; 27:32,40,42; Mk 8:34; 10:21; 15:21,30,32; Lk 9:23; 14:27; 23:26; Jn 19:17,19,25,31; 1 Corinthians 1:17,18; Galatians 5:11; 6:12,14; Ephesians 2:16; Philippians 2:8; 3:18; Colossians 1:20; 2:14; Hebrews 12:2.
9   BIBLIA SACRA VULGATA., op. cit., pgs. 1541, 1571, etc.

"crossify"; it is the same root-word in Latin as the noun, which is also the case in Greek. Furthermore, in the Greek New Testament, in the John 20:25, where it speaks of the wounds from the nails, we have in the Greek the word *helon*, which is indeed the proper plural form of the Greek word in question.[10] Therefore Jesus must have been crucified upon a traditional cross, as commonly pictured; otherwise the Romans would only have had to use a single nail to penetrate both hands, on a single upright stake or pole. But of course this is somewhat different from what is depicted in the Toldoth. G.R.S. Mead made an interesting comment on this discrepancy: "The hanging is admitted, but not the crucifixion (of which both Talmud and Toldoth know nothing), and it is interesting in this connection to remember that "hanging" is also preserved in Christian tradition as an equivalent to crucifixion."[11] Those who are less familiar with the New Testament may not be sure of exactly what Mead is referring to, but in fact it leads to what may be some highly obscure but relevant evidence supporting our central theory. Despite the standard references to crucifixion in the New Testament, there are a small handful of verses that are slightly deviant.[12] The verses in question I have always found to be rather strange, and almost even "out of place", since they seemed to say something different from what most of the relevant verses of the New Testament said about the death of Jesus. These verses speak of Jesus as having been slain and hanged on a tree. We should take a look at the verses in question:

"The God of our fathers raised up Jesus, whom ye slew and hanged on a tree." (Acts 5:30, KJV)

"And we are witnesses of all things which he did both in the land of the Jews, and in Jerusalem; whom they slew and hanged on a tree"

(Acts 10:39, KJV)

"And when they had fulfilled all that was written of him, they took *him* down from the tree, and laid *him* in a sepulchre." (Acts 13:29, KJV)

---

10   Nestle-Aland., op.cit., pg. 316.

11   Mead., op. cit., pg. 179.

12   Acts 5:30; 10:39; 13:29; Galatians 3:13; 1 Peter 2:24.

"Christ hath redeemed us from the curse of the law, being made a curse for us: for it is written, Cursed *is* every one that hangeth on a tree"

(Galatians 3:13, KJV)

"Who his own self bare our sins in his own body on the tree, that we, being dead to sins, should live unto righteousness: by whose stripes ye were healed." (1 Peter 2:24, KJV)

So these five verses give a slightly different picture of the death of Jesus. And we can also be sure that this was not due to any caprice of the translators; the underlying Greek words, *xulou* and *xulon,* denote "tree" in Greek; so we are seeing what is written in the underlying original Greek texts.[13] Furthermore, in the first two examples from the book of Acts, the texts say "whom ye slew and hanged from a tree" and "whom they slew and hanged from a tree", which implies at least that Jesus was first killed, and then hanged from a tree afterwards. Experts in Greek grammar and syntax may assure me that this interpretation is not required by Greek syntax, and they may be correct; but without wishing to appear overly contentious, I will simply point out that, the King James translators, who must at least have been competent Greek scholars, have thus translated the verses in question, which, in the English translation, imply at least this meaning. Christians may rationalize these verses away by saying that the wood from the cross must have come from a tree, and therefore, to speak of Jesus being "hanged on a tree" is merely another way of speaking of traditional Roman crucifixion. But if each of the relevant verses in the New Testament had spoken of Jesus being thus "hanged on a tree" rather than crucified on a cross, we would picture the event differently. Christian art would also have reflected this belief, by depicting Jesus hanging from a tree, rather than a cross. But my real question is, do we have here, in these few verses, a hint, a clue, or a remnant of a tradition, that Jesus may have come to his demise somewhat differently from what we have traditionally been told? If so, this may provide oblique evidence that Jesus may have lived back in Hasmonean times, rather than in the Roman era, as traditionally supposed. Thus we see that even small details, which formerly seemed so mysterious, can fit into a pattern of evidence that suggests an alternate, earlier chronology for Jesus.

13   Nestle-Aland., op. cit., pgs. 334, 352, 359, 497, 602.

PAUL

For those who are more familiar with the New Testament I can imagine the lingering reservations that must remain towards my thesis, and exactly what those reservations are based upon. One obvious problem with the theory would be the question of the apostle Paul, who presumably lived in the middle of the first century A.D., not B.C. If Paul was a real, historic figure, who actually lived in the first century A.D., then that single fact would single-handedly demolish the theory advocated herein. At least I'm laying my cards honestly on the table here. The way that Mead dealt with Paul was entirely inadequate. Mead makes the insipid, inane, fatuous, absurd and ridiculous assertion that Paul's reference to James as "the brother of the Lord"[1] and also to the other "brothers of the Lord"[2] was not to bloodkin of the Messiah, but that the expression "brother of the Lord" was merely a title.[3] Such a "solution" is merely laughable in its sheer stupidity and inanity. I will not insult the intelligence of the reader with any such absurdities.

Those who have read the Toldoth Jeschu above, together with my notes and commentary, will recall that therein I made the observation that the mere existence of Paul was not necessarily fatal to the thesis advocated

---

1   Galatians 1:19.
2   1 Corinthians 9:5.
3   Mead., op. cit., pgs. 228-229.

herein; however what I left unstated was that, just as Jesus himself lived approximately a century before the commonly-accepted time, then, Paul himself, if he existed, must also have lived about a century before the canonical time in the New Testament. Of course this is remotely possible, with the *proviso* that, assuming the Pauline corpus is essentially genuine, those epistles were chronologically doctored to bring them into conformity with the "new" chronology for Jesus, which we find in the Greek Gospels. Although this is just barely possible, it seems much less probable than the possibility that Paul never existed as a real, historical person, but was a completely invented figure. A critical scrutiny of the New Testament will uphold this postulate. In fact, I am much more convinced that Paul never existed than I am that Jesus himself lived in the first century B.C., despite the strong evidence that has already been presented in favour of that postulate.

Some writers have written that Jesus himself never existed. Of course that is a distinct possibility, although I feel that there is a historical subtext to the Gospels, or at least to the Synoptic Gospels, that point to an actual, historical Jesus. But the case with Paul is different. The irony is that some of the writers advocating a phantom Jesus theory nevertheless allow Paul to be real. But as we have seen above, there is a definite logical contingency in place, in two verses of the Pauline corpus, such that, if Paul existed, then Jesus himself necessarily also existed. Otherwise how could Paul claim to have met face-to-face with a man who was himself "the Lord's brother"? And how could Paul have made reference to men who were, by common consent, "brothers of the Lord" and were also contemporaries with him? So if Paul existed, Jesus definitely existed. But observe that this logical contingency does not flow in the opposite direction: Jesus may have been real, while Paul was a *chimera*. And the evidence bears this out.

It is actually fairly easy to prove from Scripture that Paul never existed as a real person, once you know what to look for. First we need to know what Scripture says about Paul, about when and where he lived, and also what Paul himself[4] allegedly wrote in his own epistles.

---

4   Paul himself. Speaking in a hypothetical "As if" vein for the sake of euphony.

Paul had been known as Saul, who persecuted the early Christians.[5] Paul could also speak Greek.[6] Presumably Paul was both fluent and literate in Greek, Hebrew and Syriac, since he was highly educated and was taught by the prestigious Rabbi Gamaliel in Jerusalem.[7] Paul was not one of the original twelve apostles, nor with any of the original seventy disciples. He persecuted the early Christians until his own miraculous vision.[8] The three accounts of the vision of Paul on the road to Damascus all contradict each other, thus making the accounts less credible in and of themselves. The book of Acts was allegedly written by the Evangelist Luke. But I personally doubt this very much. Although most critical Bible scholars may not have made a point of this, there is at least one reason to strongly suspect that the author of the Gospel of Luke is not the same man who wrote the book of Acts. I only mention this because it is directly pertinent to our theme. It is not surprising to me that Bible scholars have not noticed this; critical biblical scholars generally ignore the kinds of considerations that lead to such doubts, since they apparently cannot see the forest for the trees; and conservative Bible scholars, if they do notice this discrepancy at all, will no doubt "piously" remain silent on the embarrassing issue. The "style" of Greek may be similar,[9] but there is a rather glaring discrepancy between the two different (and mutually exclusive) soteriologies presented in *Luke* and *Acts*. Luke, just as Matthew and Mark, presents Jesus as insisting upon obedience to the commandments for salvation.[10] By contrast, in the book of Acts, the new message is that faith in Jesus Christ is all that is essential for salvation.[11] This latter, *sectarian* interpretation of Christ's message is in accord with the Pauline-Johannine soteriological scheme.[12] This contrasts sharply with the earlier, Synoptic scheme of salvation,

---

5   Acts 8:1-4; 9:1-8; 22:1-11; 26:9-18; 1 Corinthians 15:9.

6   Acts 21:37.

7   Acts 22:3.

8   Acts 9:1-8; 22:1-11; 26:9-18.

9   Supposedly a more elegant, proper, sophisticated Greek than found in Matthew and Mark.

10   Luke 18:18-20 cf Mt 19:16-19; Mk 10:17-19.

11   Acts 16:30-31.

12   Ephesians 2:8-9; Galatians 2:16; Colossians 1:14; Romans 5:1-11; 6:23; 8:1; 10:9-10; John 3:16; 6:29; 10:27-29; 11:25-26.

based upon works apart from faith.[13] In fact, one can make a rather clear distinction between two distinct "halves" of the New Testament; i.e., those books that uphold salvation by works,[14] and those that teach the contrary, sectarian Johannine-Pauline scheme of salvation by faith apart from works.[15] I am trusting that it is fairly evident, not to say reasonably clear, that the salvation by works scheme is the older, original, scheme, that was subsequently replaced by a completely *sectarian* scheme of salvation by faith apart from works, rather than vice-versa. At least in critical-historical terms this seems to be a fairly safe assumption. In fact, the teaching of salvation through faith *and* works, which we find in James,[16] seems to be a *synthesis* between two more starkly contrasted teachings of salvation by faith apart from works[17] on the one hand, and salvation by works apart from faith,[18] on the other. So everything that we learn about Paul, whether ostensibly from himself, or from his trusted colleague Luke, comes from the latter "half" of the great divide found in New Testament Scripture. Paul also claimed to have been an Israelite, an "Hebrew of the Hebrews", of the tribe of Benjamin, and therefore a Jew.[19] So if we find something within the Pauline corpus that belies the supposedly Hebrew ethnicity of Paul then we at least have grounds for suspecting that Paul lied about it, assuming he even existed. And there are no less than three passages that give the lie to the tale that Paul was a Jew, an Israelite, or a Hebrew. When I first discovered some of these passages, I at first thought that Paul simply lied about being Jewish, for

---

13   Matthew 25:31-46.

14   Matthew, Mark, Luke, Revelation, Jude, James, 1 & 2 Peter. Mark 16:16 is an anomalous exception, but this may be due to the probability that another hand wrote the last twelve verses of Mark. If anything, the discrepancy vis-à-vis salvation proves the critical scholars right on this score. But see discussion on dispensationalism.

15   John, 1 John, 2 John, 3 John, Romans, 1 Corinthians, 2 Corinthians, Galatians, Ephesians, Philippians, Colossians, 1 Thessalonians, 2 Thessalonians, I Timothy, 2 Timothy, Titus, Philemon, Hebrews & Acts. (the Johannine & Pauline corpii & the book of Acts.).

16   James 2:14-26.

17   Ephesians 2:8-9.

18   Matthew 25:31-46.

19   Philippians 3:4-5; 2 Corinthians 11:22; Romans 9:3-4; 11:1; Galatians 2:15.

whatever reason. But the truth is that the evidence is more congruent with the assumption that Paul himself was an invented character, and that his various epistles were written by Greeks. In fact, the names of the men who wrote the epistles of Paul can be found in deluxe editions of the King James Bible, as well as in the Greek New Testament. In fact one of Paul's epistles was evidently written by a woman.[20]

But before we get lost in a maze of convoluted data, we need to first establish that Paul lied. In fact, some may point to certain contradictions between what Paul himself (allegedly) wrote in Galatians, and what is narrated in the book of Acts, and from this, surmise that, either Paul lied or the author of Acts lied, but that the historicity of Paul is more well-founded due to the nature of the contradiction. But the "contradiction" in question is not necessarily a contradiction at all, and even if it is, it still fits into the overall pattern that proves that Paul was merely an invented figure. We need to consider all of the evidence *holistically*, once we have made ourselves familiar with it.

If indeed Paul was an invented character, and all the epistles attributed to Paul were really written by Greeks rather than Jews, then it is easy to see where a Greek writer might inadvertently "slip up" in a few places, and let loose a statement that reveals the author is really a Gentile, rather than a Jew. Of course the alternate theory would be that Paul was real, but he lied about being Jewish, that he might gain Jewish converts to his version of the gospel. There is a story that presumably originates with the Rabbis to the effect that Paul was really a Greek who was enamoured of the daughter of the high priest. In an effort to win her hand in marriage, Paul submitted to circumcision. Despite this, the woman scorned him anyway (or the high priest would not grant the marriage). As a result, Paul, inflamed with undying rage, preached against circumcision relentlessly, and ultimately only used the new messianic movement as a vehicle to promote his own teaching against circumcision and Judaism. It is a fascinating story, but almost certainly not true, since Paul almost certainly never existed. The fact that this tale originates with the Rabbis also casts it into grave suspicion; after all, the Toldoth presents a completely different rationale for Paul's motivation;

---

20   I.e., Romans, which was written by Phoebe. Colophon to Romans.

in that text he is an agent of the Rabbis, seeking to secretly sabotage Christianity. Therefore these two mutually exclusive Jewish traditions respecting Paul cancel each other out.

But we ought to examine the three passages that belie the Hebrew ethnicity of Paul. In Romans, we read the following:

24 Even us, whom he hath called, not of the Jews only, but also of the Gentiles? (Romans 9:24, KJV)

Why would a man who is a Jew write of "us, whom he hath called, not of the Jews only, but also of the Gentiles?"? Presumably a Jewish man would not write any such thing. But this verse in itself is somewhat equivocal; let us compare it with two other passages, however.

13 Christ hath redeemed us from the curse of the law, being made a curse for us: for it is written, Cursed is every one that hangeth on a tree:

14 That the blessing of Abraham might come on the Gentiles through Jesus Christ; that **we** might receive the promise of the Spirit through the faith. (Galatians 3:13-14; emphasis added)

13 And you, being dead in your sins and the uncircumcision of your flesh, hath he quickened together with him, having forgiven you all trespasses;

14 Blotting out the handwriting of ordinances that was against **us**, which was contrary to **us**, and took it out of the way, nailing it to his cross

(Colossians 2:13-14, KJV; emphasis added)

Why would a man who was a Jew have written such things? Obviously a man who was Jewish would not have accidentally slipped up and admitted that he was really a Gentile, as we see in these two passages. Paul includes himself among the Gentiles in these two passages; together with the third one from Romans, we have a definite pattern. Either Paul was a notorious liar, and not even clever enough to be consistent in his lies as to not get caught, or he was merely an invented character altogether.

One reason why Paul may have been invented[21] was to "lock in" the story of the resurrection. Without Paul, we only have records based upon what we are told is testimony by the original twelve apostles that Jesus rose from the dead, and appeared alive to them, after the time of his passion.[22] People taking a critical view of the Gospel texts, or even of an earlier, oral form of the Gospel story, could easily counter the claims being made with charges that the disciples simply secretly reburied the body of Jesus elsewhere, or that he may have survived the crucifixion, or even that he had never been crucified. In other words, the claims were emanating from only one source; but with the story of Paul, we have an outsider who also agrees with the essential claims of Christ's resurrection. Paul, who as Saul had so grievously persecuted the meek Christians, who, after his miraculous vision, now proclaimed the Messianic status of Jesus. Thus if the incredible story of Paul could ever become accepted as historical verity, the disciples would have a "lock" against any rationalistic arguments explaining the "resurrection" from a natural[23] standpoint. Paul could also become a vehicle for the promotion of the new, sectarian version of the salvation doctrine, as found in the Johannine literature. Note also that these two reasons are not mutually exclusive, but rather complementary; they may both be true.

Some may be disappointed that I am so easily sacrificing Paul, a character rich in potential psychological analysis. But as clever as the story of Paul was, it contains the seeds of its own unravelling. We will quickly see this. In fact, we have already seen that there is a fatal crack in the edifice of lies that has thus been constructed. If Paul was real he had to have been either a Jew or a Gentile. If he was a Gentile who lied and said he was a Jew when he wasn't, then anything he wrote is suspect on those grounds alone. If the Pauline literature is spurious then it also lacks authority. Critical Bible scholars have long been arguing over which of the Pauline epistles are genuine, and which are pseudepigraphal. But of course it is taken for granted that Paul himself existed. If Paul never existed, then all of the Pauline corpus is spurious by definition. Mead quotes from a critical biblical scholar of his time who held the position

---

21 I.e., assuming he was. I do not want to be accused of begging the question.

22 I.e., the four Gospel accounts.

23 As opposed to supernatural.

that none of the Pauline epistles were genuine.[24] Unfortunately, the scholar in question[25] merely pontificates, without giving any reasons for repudiating the Pauline authorship of the Pauline corpus. But it is at least worth noting that at least some critical biblical scholars were of the opinion that the entire Pauline corpus was bogus. The implications of this are rather far-reaching, however. The reason why is because the alleged historicity of Paul is inextricably bound up with the authenticity of the Pauline corpus, or at least of the authenticity of some genuine "core" of that corpus. Without even this for an anchor, the case for the historicity of Paul vanishes like a puff of smoke. Stated otherwise, the single greatest piece of evidence that Paul actually existed is the Pauline corpus, under the assumption that that corpus of writing is authentic.[26] Van Manen did not deny the historicity of Paul, but he may as well have; without any genuine Pauline corpus to fall back on, there is really no evidence that Paul ever lived. In other words, without the authenticity of the Pauline corpus as a historical anchor, the historicity of Paul vanishes like a puff of smoke. But I do not pretend to have yet proven my case that Paul never existed, or even that the Pauline corpus is entirely spurious. But to prove the latter is virtually sufficient to prove the former. But we will now proceed to the proof.

The Pauline epistles were written by ten different people, who are thus named in the New Testament: Phoebe, Stephanus, Fortunatus, Achaicus, Timotheus,[27] Titus, Lucas,[28] Tychicus, Epaphroditus, and Onesimus. The person who wrote the Petrine epistles was Silvanus. These names can be found at the end of the epistles of Paul, in the respective colophons of the various epistles.[29] These names can also be read in the *Subscriptio* sections to these epistles in the King James Bible, and possibly in some other Bibles as well. In some cases, there may have

---

24 Mead., op. cit., pg. 38.

25 Van Manen.

26 Or at least that some few of the epistles attributed to Paul were truly written by him. Most contemporary critical Bible scholars probably hold to a "hybrid" view, holding some of the Pauline epistles as genuine, and others as spurious.

27 Timothy.

28 Luke.

29 Nestle-Aland., op. cit., pgs. 440, 472, 492, 514, 522, 531, 562, 587.

been a valid reason for other men to have written the epistles in question (assuming Paul was real and he dictated the epistles in question), but as we will see, this rationale will not stand for the entire corpus. Christians may eagerly cite the example of the famous "prison epistles", written (or dictated) by Paul when he was bound by the Romans.[30] To justify this, we are expected to picture Paul as so constantly bound by the Romans that he was not free to write anything for himself, but was instead permitted to at least dictate letters to men who would write down what he said. This is at least possible. But without desiring to be contentious, I will say that the comfortable manner of Paul's arrest, and the privileged treatment he routinely received from the Romans, as narrated in the book of Acts, leads me to suspect the image of Paul being so closely bound at any time that he could not write on his own behalf. Perhaps experts in early Roman history will prove me wrong, and provide evidence that no prisoner was ever permitted to write anything on his own behalf. On the other hand, perhaps they will vindicate me by finding an example of prisoners who were granted such liberal treatment. But even granting the concession that this explanation may account for the prison epistles of Paul, it does not suffice for the others. There are only four prison epistles: Ephesians, which was written by Tychicus; Philippians, which was written by Epaphroditus; Colossians, which was written by Tychicus and Onesimus; and Philemon, which was written by Onesimus. Surprisingly in the last case, Onesimus, a runaway slave, was nevertheless literate, which we would not commonly expect of a slave. So the colophons to the prison epistles may thus be accounted for by recourse to this plausible explanation. But what of the several others, which are still nevertheless ascribed to other authors? To be fair, I suppose one could include Hebrews as a prison epistle; it was written by Timothy. So one could say it was dictated by Paul to Timothy, since Paul was still bound. Fine. But why was Romans written by Phoebe? Why was first Corinthians written by Stephanus, Fortunatus, Achaicus, and Timotheus? Why was second Corinthians written by Titus and Lucas? Paul was not bound by the Romans during the time these epistles were supposedly written by him. Furthermore,

---

30   The famous prison epistles being Ephesians, Philippians, Colossians, and Philemon.

Galatians was written, supposedly by Paul, from Rome. Would Paul not still have been under arrest? Well it is possible that it may have been written after he got a favourable sentence from Caesar, since Paul was apparently brought before Nero twice.[31] Nevertheless the problem remains for the Corinthian epistles, and for Romans. Why would Paul, a highly educated man, have merely dictated letters, rather than writing them himself? He was no doubt both fluent and quite literate in Greek, so writing would have been no obstacle to him. Christians may carp that the men[32] who thus "wrote" these epistles were merely acting in the role of secretaries, taking down *verbatim* what Paul dictated. They will no doubt scoff at what is written here, and declaim against what they will no doubt construe as an absurd argument, by the mere fact of the rather obvious nature of the colophons with the inherent argument being that said colophons would not have been included in any text of the New Testament if there were anything injurious to the Christian faith in them. In other words, the evidence is too obvious and "hidden in plain sight" as it were. But that is merely a matter of them begging the question with their endless excuses and unwarranted assumptions. I would argue on the contrary, that such blind faith being chiefly what is inculcated in such writings[33] it was considered "safe" to include such colophons, to maintain a true record of who were the original authors of said epistles. Furthermore, if such colophons are truly so innocent and safe, why then do so many Bibles exclude them? True they can be found in the King James Bible, but most modern English translations do not include them. In fact, I have a Russian Bible that excludes them, and a modern Greek Bible that excludes them, and my critical edition of the Latin Vulgate[34] also excludes them. So these supposedly "innocent" colophons are suspiciously absent from many Bibles, even though they were written in ancient Greek scrolls and codices of the New Testament.

All the names of the persons mentioned in the colophons as the writers of the epistles are Greek, and presumably they were Greek. This would

---

31   2 Timothy, colophon; cf Nestle-Aland., op. cit., pg. 556.
32   And one woman, Phoebe, who wrote the epistle to the Romans in the name of Paul.
33   I.e., the Pauline corpus in particular and the New Testament in general.
34   BIBLIA SACRA VULGATA., op. cit.

more easily account for the occasional "slips" where the author admits to being a Gentile, rather than a Jew. A Jewish man who was both fluent and literate in Hebrew and Greek would no doubt have taken great pride in writing his own epistles. If he was Jewish, he would not have "slipped" by inadvertently admitting that he was not. But if the people who wrote these epistles were Greek, then that would account for the occasional "slips" we have seen along those lines. So this is evidence that is at least congenial to the idea that Paul was merely an invented character. But the picture should come into clearer focus as we learn more.

One serious problem with Paul is that, although he supposedly was taught in Jerusalem by the prestigious Rabbi Gamaliel,[35] he seems to not so much as even heard of Jesus, until the time that Peter and John and the other apostles were preaching the resurrection in Jerusalem. How could this be? The Gospels themselves lead us to believe that Jesus was travelling all throughout Judaea, Samaria, and Galilee, routinely performing the most amazing miracles that anyone had ever seen, and yet Paul, who supposedly lived right in Jerusalem, which Jesus must have visited at least three times during his ministry, never so much as even heard of him, much less had seen him perform any miracle. This is a gigantic problem for the assumption that Paul was a real, historical person. It creates too much of a credibility gap to extend the huge "benefit of the doubt" to the increasingly dubious proposition that Paul was a genuine historical person. Christians will no doubt come up with endless excuses for this case, (as they always do) by saying such things as, Paul must have returned to Tarsus during those times when Jesus went down to Jerusalem to perform miracles. But would Paul, an educated man of the world, not have at least been sufficiently curious about the famous wonder-worker from Galilee that he would have made at least some effort to see him? The question answers itself. Once again, we have a very suspicious circumstance that is conveniently overlooked by Christians. Of course it must be admitted that this circumstance is also somewhat injurious to the historicity of Jesus, or at least of his miracles; and I suppose that, for some, the claims made for Jesus are so incredible that those who may have noticed this discrepancy before would thus opt for

---

35   Acts 22:3.

the historicity of Paul rather than Jesus.[36] Others have denied historicity to both Jesus and Paul.[37] But this rather glaring discrepancy in the New Testament belies the simple story of Saul/Paul.

Before I move on to my final pillar of proof that Paul was a phantom, I want to first briefly address potential counterarguments based upon a different discrepancy. The discrepancy has to do with Paul's own[38] account, found in Galatians, and what we read in the book of Acts, concerning his whereabouts immediately after his vision and conversion. Of course the discrepancy is an argument against fundamentalism *per se*, but we are not thus writing this with any such purpose.[39] Therefore if I point out that the "contradiction" is not necessarily a real contradiction I am not seeking to give aid & comfort to fundamentalists by any means, as should be readily apparent to anyone who has read thus far in my book. I am not claiming an absence of a contradiction; I merely claim that the contradiction is not necessarily as glaring as some have supposed. In Galatians, Paul[40] claims that immediately after his vision, he went to Arabia, and then returned to Damascus. Then, after three years he returned to Jerusalem to see Peter, and stayed with him fifteen days.[41] He also says that he saw no other apostles, except James "the Lord's brother"[42]. Then "Paul" protests that "before God" he "lies not", a strange protest coming from a man who supposedly was telling the truth. Why would an honest man make such a protest, unless there either already were claims that he was lying, or that "he" expected such claims to be made after "his" epistle was spread abroad? It only draws attention to

---

36   Since it is claimed that Jesus was/is the Son of God, he is inherently miraculous and supernatural.

37   Acharya S.

38   Once again I am speaking in an "As if" sense of the apostle Paul, as if he were a real person, both for the sake of euphony, convenience, and because I do not want to be accused of "begging the question" before my final proof is submitted.

39   Instead we take the position that fundamentalism has already been excluded, as having already been previously discredited, for a large number of compelling reasons.

40   See note 38, above.

41   Galatians 1:15-24 cp Acts 9:1-30.

42   Galatians 1:19 cp Acts 9:1-30.

the possibility that the man in question was lying. "Paul" also claims to have been "unknown by face" to the Christian churches in Judaea. Then "Paul" claims that fourteen years later he returned to Jerusalem with Barnabas and Titus.[43] Apparently this was to resolve a dispute about whether Gentile converts to the new movement had to be circumcised. But, as we have seen from Suetonius, it is doubtful that there were very many, if any, Gentile converts to the messianic movement during this time. Why else would Acts 18:2 be so suspiciously silent as to the reason that Claudius had expelled all Jews from Rome? Suetonius supplies the wanting evidence, by telling us that it was at the instigation of Chrestus that the Jews in Rome were causing so many disturbances that Claudius commanded them all to leave Rome. Thus the messianic movement was still very much a Jewish affair in the days of Claudius, despite what is written to the contrary in Acts. Of course Suetonius does supply us with a notice of Gentiles following the Christian movement in the days of Nero, which was fairly shortly after the time of Claudius; Nero succeeded Claudius. We learn that Titus was a Greek.[44] Nevertheless he was allowed to remain uncircumcised.[45] Of course all this leads to the famous[46] passage where Paul rebukes Peter for dissembling and withdrawing from fellowship with Gentile Christians, at the arrival of James' disciples.[47] The very fact that this passage[48] was allowed to remain untouched in the Canon, as well as the notorious presence of 2 Peter 3:15-16, in which "Peter" openly acknowledges the divine inspiration of "Paul" in "his" epistles, only testifies to the overwhelmingly strong position that the Pauline faction held within the latter days[49] of the nascent[50] Christian movement. In fact, this Greek element came

---

43   Galatians 2:1. Remember that Titus is one of the men who wrote 2 Corinthians.

44   Galatians 2:3.

45   Ibid.

46   Or rather, infamous, passage, among Roman Catholics.

47   Galatians 2:11-21.

48   Or even the whole epistle to the Galatians.

49   Comparatively speaking, especially if we view the movement as originating in the first century B.C., rather than A.D.

50   Without wishing to sound like an immediate contradiction of the foregoing, the Christian movement was thus still "nascent" in a comparative sense; compared to later orthodoxy.

to predominate over the earlier, Jewish aspect of the movement, due to the larger number of Greek adherents over time. The more ethnically and culturally Jewish adherents of the messianic movement eventually became eclipsed by the large number of Greek converts to the new faith. This would especially have been the case after the destruction of the Jerusalem temple in 70 A.D. And this same tendency would only have become more pronounced after the bloody aftermath of the abortive Bar Kochbah uprising. This marginalization of the Jewish element[51] of the movement may have been due in part to the influx of large numbers of Greek converts, who initially brought greater prestige to the movement. It may have come about partially by Roman persecution of Jews, regardless of religious persuasion. But it seems that, to some degree, the eclipse of the "Jewish" aspects of the movement was due to the apparent victory of the Pauline-Johannine faction within the movement, who quickly and ruthlessly imposed their own dogma upon the entire movement as if it were a trademark.© There are no complete surviving texts of the *Ebionim*, whom we may look upon as likely candidates of exemplars of the original, Jewish element of the proto-Christian messianic movement. Of course there is always the possibility that certain Jews latched on to the messianic movement from without, and sought to thus interpret Jesus Christ's teachings in a manner more congenial to their own religious persuasion.[52] The chaotic upheavals of those times, and the unfortunate loss of so many ancient texts, makes it that much more difficult to reconstruct the probable past.

The statement above respecting the Johannine-Pauline faction must be qualified somewhat, by saying that ultimately a pseudo-Petrine faction ultimately won out, which subsumed the two mutually antagonistic factions, but that, the Synoptic tradition, which clearly seems to be the

---

51   Presumably the original element, ostensibly. But see the notes above respecting Galilee of the Gentiles.

52   Therefore certain texts, like the Gospel of the Hebrews, the Gospel of the Nazarenes, and the Gospel of the Ebionites, may be more "Jewish" than even Jesus and the original twelve apostles. It is uncertain how much the historical Jesus may have been influenced by Platonism & Gnosticism. Texts like the Toldoth likely give us an exaggeratedly "Jewish" Jesus, named Jeschu. The same is equally true of the Talmud.

most primitive element within the New Testament tradition, was made subservient to the sectarian interpretation, which was naturally more congenial to ecclesiastical control. This is at least the general picture that emerges from a critical-historical review of the material.

There is also a crisis created by a couple of verses in the Pauline corpus, that also point to one of two mutually exclusive concessions: either Paul truly performed miracles, or he never wrote the epistles ascribed to him, in which case, he may very well never have existed. From a *holistic* perspective the latter option seems far more reasonable. The verses in question are Romans 15:19 & 2 Corinthians 12:12, where "Paul" himself claims to have performed miracles and signs,[53] and in the latter instance he specifically calls the Corinthians as witnesses to "his" miracles.[54] Either Paul was a real man, who really performed miracles, or was able to so impose himself[55] upon the Corinthians as to convince them that he had performed miracles before their very eyes, or these epistles are notoriously spurious productions, made to seem older than they really are, and brought forward in the wake of Roman devastation, as being genuine exemplars of a legendary man. The claim to miracles was evidently made in conformity with "Evangelical" tradition; namely, what we find written in the book of Acts.[56] But it would be absurd to concede the miraculous in the case of Paul, while denying it in the case of Jesus. The evidence instead militates against the alleged historicity of Paul. In one sense, we can be thankful for such verses as Romans 15:19 and 2 Corinthians 12:12, since they essentially create an "all-or-nothing" crisis in terms of legitimacy for the Pauline corpus; there are no possible half-measures. Critical Bible scholars routinely sidestep these issues like expert politicians during an election campaign. Either we concede the miraculous in the New Testament, or we must seriously challenge (if not jettison) the historicity of Paul.

---

53   We would remind the reader of Mark 8:12, where Jesus himself explicitly says that his generation would not be granted a sign. If either Jesus, Peter, Paul, or any of the apostles performed signs, this is a contradiction.

54   But according to the respective colophons, Romans was written by Phoebe, and 2 Corinthians was written by Titus & Lucas.

55   Either by hypnosis or some other means of illusion or trickery.

56   Acts 14:8-13; 15:12; 16:16-21; 19:11-12.

But my final pillar of proof is to be found in one of the pastoral epistles of Paul. These epistles did not come to light until the second century. In fact, most likely, the entire Pauline corpus was probably not even written until the early to mid-second century, if not later. Even those critical scholars who maintain the historicity of Paul and of at least a core of the Pauline corpus as genuine, generally reject the *pastorals* as *pseudepigrapha*. Nevertheless I will soon demolish the "hybrid" theory in respect to the Pauline corpus. One potentially legitimate reason why these pastoral epistles never saw the light of day until the second century may have been that they were addressed, not to churches, but to individuals. And not just to any individuals, but to clergy. This is at least what we ought to expect as the Christian response to any aspersions cast upon these epistles. I want to at least acknowledge a key point that might be brought up by those who would thus contend with my thesis, and subsidiary conclusions. But once we look at the complete picture, the case for the historicity of Paul vanishes like a puff of smoke.

In 2 Timothy 4:13, "Paul" writes: "The cloak that I left at Troas with Carpus, when thou comest, bring with thee, and the books, especially the parchments." The Greek word that is thus translated as "parchments" is *membranas*,[57] and denotes books made of sheepskin, rather than papyrus. The key point here is that sheepskin was not used for scrolls, but only for codices, which did not come into use until the second century. Therefore the epistle in question, based upon internal evidence, can originate no earlier than the second century. I realise that Christian fundamentalists are not likely to concede the point, and even those who do, such as critical biblical scholars, will only admit that I have only proven what they "knew" all along: that the pastoral epistles are forgeries. This does not in and of itself "prove" that the entire Pauline corpus is spurious. And while that point is technically true, there is a logical argument that topples any supposition that any "core" portion of that corpus is truly genuine. First of all we need to recall all of the evidence that we have presented herein against the alleged historicity of Paul. But the key point is precisely this: If we assume that Paul was a real, historical person, and that some "core" epistles from the Pauline corpus are genuine exemplars of his

---

57   Nestle-Aland., op. cit., pg. 555.

writings, then why would his genuine writings ever become confused with *pseudepigrapha* written in his name? If Paul was a real man, he would have been a living legend in the eyes of the early Christians; he would've been virtually a "rock star" in the Roman empire, with thousands of adoring disciples, believing that they owed eternal life to his teachings. If and when Paul was beheaded, as tradition maintains, then the writings of Paul would have remained canonical and clearly recognised as such; there would not have been the slightest possibility for spurious writings to ever become confused with genuine Pauline writings. In fact, notice the huge discrepancy between the canonical Pauline texts and those found in the New Testament Apocrypha. Such writings were attributed to Paul, of course; but they were always excluded from the "genuine," canonical texts. Why? Clearly because they were written either too late and/or because they were written by those outside the inner circle of the Pauline school, who alone were in a position to thus write in Paul's name.[58] The very same argument applies in the case of the Apostle Peter; critical biblical scholars have strangely admitted first Peter as genuine, but reject second Peter as pseudepigraphal. But Peter, even more than Paul, would've been a "rock star" among the earliest believers; as soon as he died,[59] news of his martyrdom would have spread like wildfire throughout the Roman empire, among the Christians; thereafter it would have been impossible for anyone to thus impose their own production as Peter's own. In other words, the "hybrid" theory vis-à-vis historicity falls apart due to its own internal inconsistency. The spuriousness of 2 Timothy is therefore an argument of the spuriousness of the entire Pauline corpus. And, without the authenticity of the Pauline corpus to support it, the alleged historicity of Paul vanishes like a puff of smoke. Therefore "Paul" is no obstacle or objection against the thesis presented herein.

It is well worth noting that there are only six Pauline epistles not ascribed to contrary authorship in the respective colophons; namely, Galatians, 1 Thessalonians, 2 Thessalonians, 1 Timothy, 2 Timothy, and Titus. But note well that even in these six colophons, Paul is not named as the author; it is merely implicitly assumed that he is. In the case of Galatians,

---

58   Since they knew that Paul was a mere phantom, having created him.
59   Assuming he was historical, rather than chimerical.

we can readily see the necessity for the absence of any other person being named as the author, since "Paul" therein wrote "You see how large a letter I have written unto you with mine own hand."[60] Therefore "Paul" himself _had_ to have been the implicit author; the colophon merely indicates that the letter was written from Rome.[61] Galatians is certainly the boldest of the Pauline epistles. Whoever really wrote it must have been in a position of privilege within the Pauline faction. The pastorals are implicitly attributed to Paul; indeed Titus and Timothy are ascribed authorship to some of Paul's epistles. Critical biblical scholars have been debating over the true authorship of Hebrews for a long time; some say the real author was Apollos, some say Aquila; some say Barnabas; but the colophon says it was written by Timothy in Italy. The unspoken implication is that it had been dictated by Paul himself.

It is remarkable that Romans, possibly the most distinctive and definitive epistle of the Pauline corpus, was written by a woman.[62] In the King James, the true authorship of the epistle is somewhat obscured by words supplied by the translators; in the King James, the colophon reads as follows: "Written to the Romans from Corinthus, *and sent* by Phoebe servant of the church at Cenchrea." But the two words *and sent* are in italics, which means that they are absent from the original Greek. In other words, the colophon really reads: "Written to the Romans from Korinthus, by Phoebe, a deaconess of the church at Kenchraea." The latter is a more literal translation from the Greek. This position is in stark contrast to the *misogynistic* dogma found in some of the other Pauline epistles.[63] This is further confirming proof that the Pauline corpus was not written by a single, solitary man, but rather by a school, or rather a faction, within the proto-Christian messianic movement that gained ascendancy over the original wisdom tradition found in the Synoptic Gospels. So we can see from this that even within the Pauline faction there were differences of dogma and interpretation.

It is also worth noting that I have noticed something distinctive about

---

60   Galatians 6:11.
61   Nestle-Aland., *NOVUM TESTAMENTUM GRAECE.*, op. cit., pg. 503.
62   Phoebe. Cf Nestle-Aland., pg. 440.
63   1 Corinthians 14:34-35; 1 Timothy 2:11-15.

the Thessalonian epistles, as distinct from the remainder of the Pauline corpus. The two Thessalonian epistles seem to depict a very carnal, corporeal concept of the resurrection, whereas by contrast the rest of the Pauline canon strongly upholds a spiritual interpretation of the resurrection.[64] This may also indicate a difference of authorship. But despite the subtle nuances, or sometimes more glaring differences over doctrine and practice, there seems to be a general organic unity to the Pauline corpus, that ultimately gives it its distinctive character.

Of course in the scheme envisioned here, the four Gospels and the book of Acts predate the Pauline corpus, rather than vice-versa, as in most schemes of New Testament analysis. In other words, once the Paul character had been created in the book of Acts, then the figure of Paul became a vehicle by which to "flesh out" the new, sectarian scheme of salvation by faith apart from works. The innovation was not without opposition from those upholding a more ethical version of the gospel. Eventually the need for both faith and works became emphasized,[65] and as time passed, there came to be a greater emphasis upon the sacraments as necessary for salvation. This gave greater power to the clergy.

The four Gospels thus remain the primary and most essential of Christian documents, and always will be. The Gospel of John was the first challenge to the Synoptic orthodoxy of salvation through works. The book of Acts followed, written by pseudo-Luke;[66] then the characters of John and Paul became literary vehicles for the sectarian faction of the movement to articulate their soteriology. This innovation was responded to by the Petrine epistles, and the epistles of James and Jude.[67] Notably even 2 Peter 3:15-16, which openly acknowledges the Pauline epistles as sacred Scripture, cleverly co-opts the Pauline corpus into a "works" based salvation scheme. The legacy of the pseudo-Petrine faction is primarily carried on by the Papacy. The Apokalypse was also written to counteract the Johannine-Pauline salvation scheme. We will have more to say of this

---

64   1 Thessalonians 4:13-18; 5:1-10; 2 Thessalonians 2:1-10 cp 1 Corinthians 15:44-55; Hebrews 12:23; Philippians 1:23; 3:20-21; 2 Corinthians 5:1-8.

65   James 2:14-26; 1 John 3:14-19; 2 Peter 2:20-22; 3:15-16.

66   See discussion above respecting the authorship of Acts.

67   Judas in the Greek. Not Iscariot.

in the section on Nicodemus. In one sense, doctrinal differences between Catholics and Protestants can be traced directly back to differences held by the original factions of the proto-Christian messianic movement. But of course this was centuries after the New Testament Canon had been standardized in the West. The selection of books for the Canon seems to me to be more a matter of compromise than of conspiracy. There was a desire to be sufficiently inclusive of all the earliest branches of Christianity,[68] but to limit the Canon to the oldest extant texts. And there can be no reasonable doubt that the Canonical New Testament is the earliest exemplar of any extant Christian writing. Gnostic texts, as well as the New Testament Apocrypha, postdate the New Testament by a century or more, in my view. This also appears to be true for even such texts as the Gospel of Peter, the Gospel of the Nazarenes, the Gospel of the Hebrews, and the Gospel of the Ebionites. However it is possible, if not probable, that the Gospel of the Ebionites may contain an early genuine saying of Jesus. This possibility will be explored in greater detail in the chapter on James the Just.

But as I have tended to favour a later dating for the New Testament documents, then the relative dating of the other texts likewise must be reevaluated; they are all almost certainly pseudepigraphal, and are of significantly later origin than commonly supposed, even by critical biblical scholars. I am surprised and frankly disappointed over the unwarranted attention granted to such texts as the Gospel of Thomas, which I do not find particularly impressive at all. A text like the Gospel of Thomas has no real historical value at all. It can also be clearly proven from internal evidence that the Gospel of Philip postdates all four canonical Gospels. The character of Gospels like the Gospel of Mary {Magdalene} and the Gospel of Judas {Iscariot} prove that they are relatively late compositions. Besides, the *Diatessaron* proves that only the four Canonical Gospels were regarded as authoritative in the latter half of the second century. Even if any of these other gospels had already been extant at that early time,[69] they were not in the least bit regarded at the time, as not so much as one verse from any of them can be found in the *Diatessaron*. So the

---

68   Except *Ebionism* and *Gnosticism*.
69   A possibility that I distinctly doubt.

evidence from the *Diatessaron* belies the much-touted assumption of an "early" text of the Gospel of Thomas. However the *Diatessaron* does not prove that the four Gospels were written in the first century. It merely proves that in the latter half of the second century only the four canonical Gospels were regarded as authoritative.

Some few other texts remained sufficiently popular and respected as to attain canonicity among the Ethiopian Christians. The texts in question are the epistle of Barnabas, and the Shepherd of Hermas. Another text, presumably of Ethiopian origin, called *Sinodos,* is claimed to contain the secret teachings of Jesus Christ. The Coptic Orthodox Church has a secret book of Mark as part of their New Testament Canon. The Syrian Orthodox Church accepts all the books of the New Testament except Jude, 2 Peter, 2 John, 3 John, and Revelation. But all the other Orthodox churches accept the same New Testament Canon as held by both Catholics and Protestants.

In the course of my research I have come across a claim of a discovery proving that the Gospels originated in the first century. I am referring to the Washington Codex.[70] The codex itself apparently dates to the fourth century, or possibly as early as the very late second century. The claim unfortunately is being made by one Lee Woodard, a fundamentalist Christian minister. Therefore the claim is accompanied by a vested interest. Contrary sources indicated the codex in question originated in the fourth or even the fifth century. The artwork alone seems to date from at least the fourth century, if not later. Nevertheless Mr. Woodard claims to have discovered a secret system of Aramaic alphanumeric notation in the texts, "proving" a first-century origin for the texts in question. I must admit that I find his material somewhat intriguing. But even if Mr. Woodard is correct in thus "proving" some secret system of notation in such texts, by palaeographic analysis, this in itself does not prove the *actual* origin of those texts at such an early date; second-century forgers were likely clever enough to provide certain "secret" marks on texts alleged to be older than they were. Thus Mr. Woodard, together with men like Carsten Peter Thiede & Matthew d'Ancona, are "preaching to the choir" while critical biblical scholars and other

---

70   http://www.washington-codex.org.

skeptics remain decidedly unimpressed. Furthermore the very fact that the Gospels are bound together in codex form proves that it can date to no earlier than the second century. But just to show what a good sport I am, I am willing here to make a huge concession: It is just barely possible, that in the Washington Codex, we may very well have a genuine exemplar of a late second-century Gospel Codex. Mr. Woodard seems to be under the woeful misimpression that the notorious hypothetical text known as "Q" is the single source of Christian apostasy. Mr. Woodard fatuously disregards that such problems as contradictions, errors, anachronisms, barbarisms, suspicious omissions, discrepancies, imperfections, as well as grave uncertainty respecting the Canon, text, and interpretation of Scripture might account for such apostasy. "Q" may be as much of a fantasy as Mr. Woodard alleges, but that in no way vindicates the authenticity of the four Gospels. The issues involved in New Testament textual criticism are subtle and complex, and for the most part are beyond the scope of our inquiry. But I trust that what I have proposed herein is at least reasonable within a critical-historical analysis of the New Testament. Finally, returning once again to Paul, Paul is not mentioned in the Koran. Likewise Josephus is completely silent respecting Paul. There is not even a forged passage in Josephus about Paul. Paul, the man who supposedly "turned the world upside-down" is not so much as even mentioned in all of the writings of Josephus, who was such a meticulous historian. Although admittedly there are limits to the argument from silence, in this case, and in conjunction with all of the other evidence against the alleged historicity of Paul, this is the final nail in the coffin of that chimera.

John the Baptist

John the Baptist obviously must be addressed, or rather, the question of John the Baptist, vis-à-vis historicity, and how the question impinges upon our current chronological theory of Jesus. Stated succinctly, if we hold to the postulate that the original, historical Jesus lived in the first century B.C., rather than the commonly-accepted time, then there are three fundamental possibilities respecting John the Baptist: 1. John the Baptist, like the apostle Paul, is also a completely fictional character; 2. He was a real person, but, being a contemporary with Jesus, he also lived a century earlier than the commonly-accepted time; or, 3. Jesus and John were both real men but were not in fact contemporaries. Any one of these three theories would at least allow for Jesus to have lived a century earlier than the commonly-accepted time. And I further believe that all three of the above theories have a sufficient degree of plausibility that the person (or figure) of John the Baptist does not pose a serious challenge to the chronological theory presented herein.

John the Baptist left behind no written documents, whereas by contrast, the Pauline corpus was attributed to the invented character Paul.[1] Nevertheless it is difficult to say whether or not there is more or less evidence in favour of the historicity of John the Baptist than the case with

---

1   I trust that the previous chapter on Paul was sufficient to demolish any pretence to Pauline historicity; therefore my point is proven and I am not begging the question.

Paul. John at least has the distinct advantage of being a character within the Gospels, which are clearly the "core" documents of Christianity. He is also mentioned in the book of Acts. In the Gospels, John holds the privileged position of being the Herald of the Messiah. John it is who baptizes Jesus, to "fulfill all righteousness" according to Christ.[2] Therefore John the Baptist is important to the Gospel scheme. But outside of the New Testament itself there are only two sources of reference to John the Baptist: a brief passage in Josephus, and in the traditions of the Mandaeans, who venerate John the Baptist as a true prophet. As far as I know, the Mandaeans do not precisely date the time of John the Baptist; but Josephus places him within the reign of Herod II who had John killed.[3] We ought to take a look at the passage in question.

"2. Now, some of the Jews thought that the destruction of Herod's army came from God, and that very justly, as a punishment for what he did against John, that was called the Baptist; for Herod slew him, who was a good man, and commanded the Jews to exercise virtue, both as to righteousness towards one another, and piety towards God, and so to come to baptism; for that the washing [with water] would be acceptable to him, if they made use of it, not in order to the putting away [or the remission] of some sins [only], but for the purification of the body; supposing still that the soul was thoroughly purified beforehand by righteousness. Now, when [many] others came in crowds about him, for they were greatly moved [or pleased] by hearing his words, Herod, who feared lest the great influence John had over the people might put it into his power and inclination to raise a rebellion (for they seemed ready to do anything he should advise), thought it best, by putting him to death, to prevent any mischief he might cause, and not bring himself into difficulties, by sparing a man who might make him repent of it when it should be too late. Accordingly he [John] was sent [as] a prisoner, out of Herod's suspicious temper, to Macherus, the castle I before mentioned, and was there put to death. Now the Jews had an opinion that the destruction of this army was sent as a punishment upon Herod, and a mark of God's displeasure against him." (*Jos. Ant. 18.5.2; 116-119*)

---

2   Mt 3:15.
3   Jos. Ant. 18.5.2.

This is an interesting passage, and, if allowed to be genuine, it would at least prove a historical John the Baptist. However not all scholars esteem the passage in question as genuine. Once again, there is no corresponding passage in Josephus' *War*. Acharya S. evidently negates the passage, since she esteems both Jesus and John the Baptist as fictional characters. Be that as it may, it is at least possible that the passage is indeed genuine. However, if so, and we further concede that Jesus and John were contemporaries, as maintained in the canonical Gospels, then this would definitely place Jesus in the first century, rather than earlier, as I herein contend. On the other hand, the passage may be genuine, albeit Jesus and John were neither contemporaries nor cousins, as we read in the Gospels. The placement of the passage about John the Baptist in Josephus occurs after the infamous *Testimoniun Flavium*, which speaks of Jesus; this fact suggests in fact that the account from Josephus may be genuine, since in the Gospels, Jesus does not rise to prominence until after the martyrdom of John. Therefore it seems unlikely that a Christian scribe would have interpolated a forged passage about John the Baptist *after* rather than *before* the passage about Jesus Christ. Taking this view of the matter, John may have been a genuine person who acted in the role of a latter-day prophet whom the proto-Christian Messianic movement wanted to somehow co-opt into their new message about Jesus. In other words, it may have been as late as the early second century when the Jesus movement deliberately incorporated John the Baptist into the traditions respecting Jesus; in fact, an association with a pious prophet such as John the Baptist may even have been one more motive in the chronological dislocation of Jesus from his original time. Now Jesus can be not only heralded by John, he can even be his cousin! The association with John and his martyrdom also evokes one more tantalizing motive for the men of the messianic *kahal* to chronologically transplant Jesus from the time of the Hasmoneans to the days of the Herods: to implicate the Herods in the death of the Messiah. In fact, this greatly strengthens the case that Jesus may have originally lived in the first century B.C., but was chronologically dislocated and shifted to the first century A.D.; implicating the infamous Herods, who also murdered John the Baptist, as well as implicating the Romans, while still keeping the blame upon the hated Pharisees (religious rivals to the messianic movement); this, together with the prophetic-eschatological-chronological reasons already stated vis-à-vis the book of Daniel.

In Matthew we read of the infamous slaughter of the innocents.[4] The story is almost certainly based upon what we read in Josephus respecting the murder of Aristobulus by Herod I.[5] This Aristobulus was much later than Aristobulus the brother of Alexander Jannaeus; but nevertheless was from the same Hasmonean line of high priest-kings. Herod had married Mariamne, a daughter of the same priestly stock. This was no doubt in an effort to thus "legitimize" his pretensions to royalty in Judaea. We can clearly see that the Matthew story is a literary parallel with what is found in Josephus; the lamentation of the women spoken of so profusely in Josephus[6] becomes in Matthew the supposed "fulfillment" of Jeremiah's prophecy of weeping and lamentation in Rama and how Rachel could not be comforted for the loss of her children.[7] Herod I wanted no rival from the Hasmonean family to thwart his royal pretensions. Therefore Herod also murdered Hyrcanus, who was the sole remaining scion of the Hasmonean line.[8] However in a sense our research has thus created a circle: Aristobulus and Hyrcanus were brothers, and were both sons of Alexandra-Salome, in whose reign the Toldoth places Jeschu (Jesus). It is just barely possible that Jesus himself was from the same Hasmonean family. Thus he would have been not Davidic, but Levitical, royalty. In the next chapter we will see that there is at least some obscure, oblique evidence that Jesus and his brother James were in fact Levites. If Jesus was not merely a Levite, but an Aaronite as well, then he may also have been a descendant of the Hasmoneans. As such, he would have had somewhat of a legitimate basis for an assumption of messianic royalty.

The Jews never forgave Herod I for the murder of the last line of Hasmonean high priests. The entire bloody Herod family became cursed in the eyes of the Jews. This hatred of the Herods would most likely have been shared by the followers of Jesus. As such, and especially if

---

4   Mt 2:16.
5   Jos. Ant. 15.3.3.
6   Jos. Ant. 15.3.4.
7   Mt 2:17-18 cf Jeremiah 31:15.
8   Jos. Ant. 15.6.1-4.

Jesus was another murdered Hasmonean, there would have been an outstanding motive to somehow implicate the Herods in the murder of Jesus. Therefore there would have been at least a triple motive to dislocate Jesus into a new time: to lay claim to Jesus being the Messiah by virtue of coming in the days of the "fourth kingdom" and "fourth beast" of Daniel, to establish an everlasting kingdom; to implicate the Romans in the death of Jesus; to implicate the Herods in the death of Jesus. And, if John the Baptist was really a first-century prophet, then a fourth reason would be to link the legacy of Jesus with that of John the Baptist, and thus seek to coax converts from among the disciples of John.

Another interesting literary parallel also strikes me: in Josephus, we read of the last two brothers from the Hasmonean dynasty slain by Herod I; in the New Testament, Jesus and John, two cousins, are also both slain at the behest of Herod II. Of course in the case of Jesus, Herod was only partially responsible for his condemnation; the rest of the blame being shared by Pilate and Caiaphas. But even in this circumstance greater bloodguilt is attributed both to Herod and Caiaphas; in Matthew[9] we have the account of Pilate washing his hands and declaring his innocence of the blood of Jesus, while the Jews respond by saying "His blood be on us, and on our children". The Gospel of Peter must originally have had the same story, since the opening verse of the surviving fragment reads: "But of the Jews none washed his hands, neither Herod nor any one of his judges. And when they had refused to wash them, Pilate rose up. And then Herod the king commandeth that the Lord be taken, saying to them, What things soever I commanded you to do unto him, do." We can clearly see from this that the Gospel of Peter much more strongly places the greater burden of guilt upon Herod, rather than Pilate, as we find in most of the canonical Gospels. The literary borrowings from Josephus and Suetonius suggest a second century origin for the Gospels. Aristobulus and Hyrcanus, who were slain at the behest of Herod I, were the last anointed high priests from the beloved Hasmonean line; this evokes the image of the two anointed ones, or two Messiahs, spoken of in Jewish tradition, and even in Scripture.[10] There is at least a slight,

---

9   Mt 27:24.
10   Zechariah 4:11-14 cf Revelation 11:3-13.

but definitely recognizable, hint of a literary parallel to John the Baptist and Jesus Christ in the New Testament. Cousins according to Luke's account, John the Baptist and Jesus are two anointed ones or Messiahs, although of course Jesus is the central, redeeming Messiah. We also learn from Luke's Gospel that Jesus may have been a Levite. We will see more evidence in favour of this in the following chapter, and also when we study evidence from the Talmud. But Luke's Gospel actually provides the earliest and strongest evidence that Jesus was not of the tribe of Judah, as so many contrary Scriptures claim, but rather was of the priestly tribe of Levi.

According to Luke, Zechariah the father of John the Baptist was a priest of the course of Abijah, and his wife Elizabeth was of the daughters of Aaron, the first high priest.[11] Elizabeth was the kinswoman of Mary.[12] This indirectly confirms that Mary must also have been a Levite, and so also was Joseph. Because according to Numbers 36, God commanded the Israelites through Moses to only marry within their ancestral tribe, that the inheritances be not removed from one tribe to another. Therefore as Zechariah and Elizabeth (and presumably also Mary and Joseph) were "righteous before God, walking in all the commandments and ordinances of the Lord blamelessly"[13] they must also have obeyed the injunction against intermarrying between different tribes. Therefore they were all Levites. Of course a fundamentalist would completely disregard all this, and seek to quickly sweep it all under the rug, and find theoretical loopholes in the commandment to "prove" that Jesus could be both of the tribe of Levi and Judah, etc., and will usher in the fact that Luke provides a royal genealogy for Jesus, tracing him back to King David of the tribe of Judah. But the fact that the genealogy found in Luke completely contradicts the one in Matthew will of course not be mentioned by our pious brethren. The evidence favours Levitical descent for Jesus, precisely because it clashes with the normative Messianic claims respecting Davidic descent for Jesus in the New Testament. Curiously,

---

11 Luke 1:5.
12 Luke 1:36. The Greek word in question is *syngenis*; Nestle-Aland., op. cit., pg. 152.
13 Luke 1:6.

Jesus himself seems to disavow Davidic descent.[14] A Levitical descent for Jesus would seem to be part of a hidden historical subtext to the Gospels. Perhaps Luke's use of the Greek *syngenis* rather than *adelphe (sister)* was a clue or a hint that Jesus and John were not contemporaries, but were nevertheless cognate. And this consanguinity between Jesus and John was also linked by a common martyrdom at the hands of a usurper, the son of a usurper, in the Gospels. So there may have been political motives to dislocate Jesus from his own original time, and thus to place the blame upon the Herods. Therefore in a strange and unexpected way, John the Baptist provides some oblique evidence in favour of our thesis; or at least, the probable historicity of John the Baptist is not an obstacle to our thesis. Our thesis has somewhat of an advantage in the sense that, not only do several independent sources of evidence converge together in an unsolicited way to confirm our postulate, but individual variables and branches of evidence are also governed by severability clauses, inasmuch as dubious nonessentials are unnecessary to support the prime postulate. Finally, John the Baptist does seem more substantial than the chimera Paul, since, the brief passage found in Josephus seems genuine; there is no mention of Herod's birthday, nor of Salome's dance, nor any of the intrigue found in the Gospels. We would have expected a Christian scribe to have included such lurid details, had the passage been merely a Christian interpolation. Therefore the third of the three fundamental options mentioned at the outset of the chapter seems most likely. This would also account for the curious fact that in the Gospels, John "still" has his own disciples, even after he has already supposedly identified Jesus as the Lamb of God and the Son of God.[15]

---

14   Mark 12:35-37 cf Matthew 22:41-46; Luke 20:41-44.
15   Mt 9:14 cp Jn 1:29-36.

James the Just

J ames the Just has gotten more attention recently, due to some scholarly works written on him.[1] He is not all that prominent in the New Testament, but this may be due to the fact that James did not attain legendary status until after the time when those documents were supposed to have been written, or rather, the times that they claim to narrate. Nevertheless James is an important foil within the Pauline corpus,[2] and was supposedly an important figure within early church history. We must address the question of the historicity of James, and also how this impinges upon our central thesis.

The greatest claim to fame of James the Just, other than his legendary piety towards God, is that he was the brother of Jesus Christ.[3] But we must proceed with great caution, since several years ago an ossuary was discovered that at the time was claimed to be that of James, due to an inscription that experts later proved was a forgery.[4] Therefore we ought not to necessarily take the historicity of James for granted. On the other

---

1   Most notably by Robert Eisenman.
2   Most notably in Galatians.
3   Galatians 1:19 cf Mt 13:55; Mk 6:3.
4   The ossuary had me fooled, I must confess. The inscription read "James, son of Joseph, brother of Jesus" in Aramaic (Syriac) script. Israeli experts determined that the clause "brother of Jesus" was a recent forgery by an unscrupulous antiquities dealer.

hand, if Jesus really lived in the first century B.C., then so did his brother James, assuming he existed. Conversely, if it can be proved that James lived in the first century A.D., then Jesus himself must also have lived at that time. Therefore James represents somewhat of a potential challenge to the theory under consideration, but not necessarily an insurmountable obstacle. In fact, a study of James may lead to some obscure confirming evidence in favour of our theory.

There is a brief passage in Josephus respecting James the brother of Jesus that must be taken into account. Once again, there is an absence of scholarly consensus regarding the authenticity of the passage in question. Acharya S. disregards the passage as spurious, since she esteems James as a mere chimera; after all, if Jesus never existed, then the brothers and sisters of Jesus also never existed. But the passage at least seems to have more credibility than the infamous *Testimonium Flavium*, which is almost universally discredited by scholars, historians and literary critics. The very brevity of the *Testimonium Flavium* is one very strong argument against its authenticity; if Josephus were to write of Jesus, he should have written far more than a mere few sentences, forming a very small paragraph, which is almost parenthetical to the context in which it appears. By contrast, James would not necessarily merit quite so much attention. Nevertheless the passage, if genuine, would be a challenge to the thesis advocated herein, although not absolutely fatal. We ought to examine the passage in question:

"Festus was now dead, and Albinus was but upon the road [to Jerusalem]; so he assembled the Sanhedrin of judges, and brought before them the brother of Jesus, who was called Christ, whose name was James; and some others: and when he had formed an accusation against them as breakers of the law, he delivered them to be stoned" (*Jos. Ant. 20.9.1; 200*).

There seems not to be so much vocal criticism of this latter passage, compared with the *Testimonium Flavium*. Nevertheless it places James the brother of Jesus well within the latter half of the first century A.D., which would require Jesus to have also lived in the same century. Therefore there are three possibilities: Either Jesus really did live in the first century

A.D. after all, despite all the seemingly strong evidence to the contrary presented herein so far; or the passage really is merely a Christian interpolation; or, the passage is mostly genuine, but the phrase "the brother of Jesus, who was called Christ" was a Christian interpolation. In the last instance, a historical James the Just, noted for his piety, became linked with Jesus by the messianic *kahal*, by having the honor of becoming the brother of Jesus, after the decision to chronologically transplant Jesus to the days of the Herods and the Roman occupation of Judaea. That would be a situation akin to what we postulated of John the Baptist above. It is also possible that some later Christian scribe inserted the phrase into an otherwise genuine passage. In other words, possibly a real man known as "James the Just" who lived in the late first century A.D. was associated with Jesus posthumously, by a claim of being the brother of Jesus.[5] This is one possible resolution to the passage from Josephus.[6] However, I believe it is reasonable to suppose that James lived in the first century B.C., just as Jesus himself did.[7] In fact, in terms of chronological markers, there are far more linking Jesus himself with the first century A.D. than those thus linking James his brother. Therefore if all[8] such chronological markers can be disregarded on the basis of contrary evidence, then the far fewer instances in the case of James are far less formidable.

The very fact that the Messiah is said to have brothers and sisters in the New Testament is somewhat remarkable, and therefore those passages seem more likely to reflect an underlying historical subtext, rather than complete invention. In fact, the siblings of Christ became an embarrassment to later orthodoxy, which sought to exalt Mary as a

---

5   Obviously this claim was made *after* the chronological dislocation of Jesus from Hasmonean times, assuming such was the case.

6   Since the Josephus passage so clearly places James in the late first century A.D.

7   I am here speaking in an "As if" sense; I do not want to be accused of begging the question, nor do I want to weaken my case by overstating it.

8   In the case of Jesus, these markers all come from the New Testament itself, aside from the highly controversial *Testimony Flavium*, and the very brief passage from Suetonius that we examined earlier (Claudius 25).

"perpetual virgin" and therefore invented spurious gospels to supposedly account for the brothers[9] of Jesus.

The curious traditions respecting James the brother of Jesus are so unusual in some respects as to almost guarantee their authenticity. Perhaps that is going too far; but my point is, that inasmuch as any tradition incorporates novel, unusual, and unexpected material, the more likely it is to be genuine, rather than merely invented. It is clear from the New Testament itself that James very strongly upheld the Mosaic law. We can recall words attributed to Jesus in Scripture that also very strongly uphold the divine authority of *TaNaKh*.[10] As such, James was very much in line with views attributed to Jesus himself. Due to the surrounding context, the statement attributed to Christ in John, "Scripture cannot be broken" is particularly pungent. But as we have already seen, the Gospel of John innovated by presenting a doctrine of salvation the exact antipodes from what is found in the Synoptics. This new doctrine of salvation was also taught in the Johannine epistles, the Pauline epistles, and the book of Acts. However the Gospel of John is distinctively different inasmuch as Jesus himself is the one teaching the new doctrine, which is anachronistic to the dispensational scheme of soteriology otherwise implicit throughout the New Testament. In other words, even Mark 16:16, where Jesus says "Whoever believes and is baptized shall be saved; whoever disbelieves shall be damned" can be reconciled with Mark 10:19, where Jesus quotes the commandments, in response to what must be done to obtain eternal life. In a dispensational scheme, a Christian apologist could say that, after Jesus had been crucified, the righteousness of the law had been fulfilled, and therefore belief in Christ became the new criterion for salvation. This would be a credible line of argument except for the rather embarrassing fact that, in the Gospel of John, Jesus himself is preaching this new message of salvation, <u>before</u> he is crucified. Therefore in a real sense the Gospel of John is far more radical than the Pauline corpus or the book of Acts. I suppose that a Christian "true believer" could rationalize the discrepancy

---

9 I.e., they were children of Joseph from an earlier marriage; Joseph being an elderly widower; etc. See the Protevangelion of James & other texts of the New Testament Apocrypha.

10 Mt 5:17-18; Jn 10:35.

by saying that, Jesus had the right to proclaim the new message, since he knew he would follow through with his sacrifice, etc. In the Synoptic Gospels, Jesus consistently upholds observance of the commandments as requirements for salvation. James is squarely in this Synoptic tradition.

The epistle of James in the New Testament is commonly attributed to James the brother of Christ, at least by Protestant expositors. Even many Catholic expositors would concede that the epistle may have been written by the notable James the Just, who (according to Catholicism) may have been a cousin, half-brother, or step-brother of Christ. Of course it is also possible that the epistle was written by James the son of Alphaeus, who was one of the twelve Apostles.[11] It is notable that James Alphaeus had a brother named Judas, and the author of Jude[12] also claimed to be the brother of James.[13] But of course Jesus also had a brother named Judas.[14] Therefore it is uncertain whether or not James was supposedly written by James the brother of Jesus, or James ben Alphaeus the Apostle. James the brother of John had been slain by Herod II.[15] So the epistle of James is rarely, if ever, attributed to him. Of course some Protestant expositors have tried to claim an early date for the epistle of James, to avoid the obvious *polemics* against the Pauline teaching of salvation by faith apart from works. But it seems fairly evident that the *polemics* are quite real, and were waged, not by James against Paul, but rather by two rival factions within the Messianic movement. The Jamesian faction eventually became eclipsed by the Pauline faction; although both became subordinated to a pseudo-Petrine faction that sought to reconcile the various factions and traditions, and present a united front to the Roman empire. Curiously however, there is nothing in either James or Judas[16] that functions as a chronological marker. The only thing that could so function are in fact the *polemics* found within both epistles, directed against the Pauline-Johanine faction vis-à-vis salvation. Therefore these

---

11 Mt 10:2-4; Mk 3:14-19; Lk 6:13-16.
12 Judas. Ioudas in Greek (pronounced YOU-das).
13 Jude 1.
14 Mt 13:55; Mk 6:3.
15 Acts 12:1-2.
16 Jude.

epistles are almost certainly pseudepigraphal, in my scheme.[17] They almost certainly date from the second century. However I will say that, I do not feel that a significantly earlier date of origin for the New Testament texts is necessarily fatal to my theory. In fact, my theory may be able to account for a very early origin of the Gospels, if such should prove to be the case. I will discuss this in greater detail later.

We ought to consider Christian traditions about James the Just. The most complete account I have found so far occurs in Foxe's Book of Martyrs, and is as follows:

"Of James, the brother of the Lord, thus we read: James, took in hand to govern the Church with the apostles, being counted of all men, from the time of our Lord, to be a just and perfect man. He drank no wine nor any strong drink, neither did he eat any animal food; the razor never came upon his head. To him only was it lawful to enter into the holy place, for he was not clothed with woolen, but with linen only; and he used to enter into the temple alone, and there, falling upon his knees, ask remission for the people; so that his knees, by oft kneeling (for worshipping God, and craving forgiveness for the people), lost the sense of feeling, being benumbed and hardened like the knees of a camel. He was, for the excellency of his just life, called 'The Just', and, 'the safeguard of the people'.

When many therefore of their chief men did believe, there was a tumult made of the Jews, Scribes and Pharisees, saying; There is danger, lest all the people should look for this Jesus, as though he were Christ [the Messiah]. Therefore they gathered themselves together, and said to James, 'We beseech thee restrain the people, for they believe in Jesus, as though he were Christ; we pray thee persuade all them which come unto the feast of the Passover to think rightly of Jesus; for we all give heed to thee, and all the people do testify of thee that thou art just, and that thou dost not accept the person of any man. Therefore persuade the people that they be not deceived about Jesus, for all the people and we ourselves are ready to obey thee. Therefore stand upon the pinnacle of the Temple,

---

17   Otherwise we would have to surrender our central thesis and acknowledge Jesus having lived in the first century A.D.

that thou mayest be seen above, and that thy words may be heard of [by] all the people; for all the tribes with many Gentiles are come together for the Passover. And thus the forenamed Scribes and Pharisees did set James upon the battlements of the temple, and they cried unto him, and said, 'Thou just man, whom we all ought to obey, this people is going astray after Jesus which is [was] crucified.' And he answered with a loud voice, 'Why do you ask me of Jesus the Son of Man? He sitteth on the right hand of the Most High, and shall come in the clouds of heaven. Whereupon many were persuaded and glorified God, upon this witness of James, and said, 'Hosannah to the Son of David.' Then the Scribes and Pharisees said among themselves, 'We have done evil, that we have caused such a testimony of [to] Jesus; let us go up, and throw him down, that others, being moved with fear, may deny that faith.' And they cried out, saying, 'Oh, oh, this just man also is seduced.' Therefore they went up to throw down the just man. Yet he was not killed by the fall, but, turning, fell upon his knees, saying, 'O Lord God, Father, I beseech thee to forgive them, for they know not what they do.' And they said among themselves, 'Let us stone the just man, James;' and they took him to smite him with stones. But while they were smiting him with stones, a priest said to them, 'Leave off, what do ye? The just man prayeth for you.' And one of those who were present, a fuller, took an instrument, wherewith they did use to beat and purge cloth, and smote the just man on his head; and so he finished his testimony. And they buried him in the same place."[18]

If we read the above account carefully, we can see that it differs somewhat from the passage from Josephus. True in both passages there is a stoning of James; but there are many more details in the above passage, including James having been thrown down from the pinnacle of the temple, and being beaten with a fuller's club, until he died. But one distinct difference also is the fact that, aside from the implicit assumption respecting the date of Christ, there are no chronological markers from the above passage. In other words, the events in question could have as easily transpired in the first century B.C. as the first century A.D. But that is not all that

---

18   Foxe, John., *FOXE'S BOOK OF MARTYRS.*; 1500's; 1600's. (W. Grinton Berry, editor. Spire. 1998; 2004: Baker Publishing Group); pgs. 9-11.

is curious from the above passage. We read that James wore linen, just like the high priest in the temple. It also says that he drank no wine or liquor. We also read that James ate no "animal food" presumably indicating vegetarianism.[19] The *Ebionim* were strict vegetarians. This was apparently directly related to their objections against animal sacrifices. But note also that it says that James never allowed a razor to pass over his head. This evokes the vow of a Nazarite.[20] But most curious of all, to my mind, is the phrase "to him only was it lawful to enter the holy place", which implies that James acted in the role of high priest. There are two possible reactions to this. One is that, it is a garbled tradition, cobbled together by some ignorant Gentile who had badly digested the *Torah* and wanted to impose a fable about James, based upon his imperfect knowledge. The other is that, there may be something genuine here, although we must approach the material with caution. James could not have acted as high priest unless he was of the tribe of Levi.[21] We have already seen some evidence that Jesus was really a Levite, rather than a Jew.[22] In fact, the Gospel of Luke predates any of the other sources

---

19 Cf Romans 14:2.

20 Numbers 6:1-21.

21 And if James was a Levite, so was Jesus.

22 Although today the term "Jew" is used in a broader sense, originally it denoted a person descended from the tribe of Judah. Thus the etymology. In fact, even Josephus concurs with this interpretation of the word: "So the Jews prepared for the work: that is the name they are called by from the day that they came up from Babylon, <u>which is taken from the tribe of Judah, which came first to these places, and thence both they and the country gained that appellation.</u>" (*Jos. Ant. 11.5.7; 173*). In fact, throughout *TaNaKh*, in the original Hebrew there is a distinction evident in descriptive terms; in Esther 8:17, where it says in the King James Version "And in every province, and in every city, withersoever the king's commandment and his decree came, the Jews (*Yehudim*) had joy and gladness, a feast and a good day. And many people of the land became Jews (*Yahadim*); for the fear of the Jews (*Yehudim*) fell upon them." As one can see, in the underlying Hebrew, two distinctly different Hebrew words are used; therefore one cannot become a Jew (*Yehudiy*) in the primary sense; one can instead join the community (*Yahad*); this latter term being found in the famous Damascus Document. Thus the term "Jew" as originally used, and as confirmed by the etymological derivation, denotes a person descended from the tribe of Judah; but the term has come to be used as an umbrella term to include Levites, Benjaminites, the remnants of the other tribes of Israel who remained faithful to the Jerusalem cultus after the division of the

confirming the Levitical descent of Christ. But this tradition respecting James inadvertently confirms Levitical descent for James, and hence for Jesus, at least in an oblique way, and therefore has some degree of evidential value.

However, we are not told explicitly that James acted as high priest in the Jerusalem temple; which, had it been the case, Christian tradition could hardly have overlooked it completely. But what is incongruous in the passage is a clue to a deeper mystery, which may lend even greater credence to our thesis. The incongruity being the apparent vegetarianism of James, coupled with what seems otherwise descriptive of a man acting in the role of high priest. James could not have thus fulfilled that role in the Jerusalem temple, since blood sacrifices were offered there up until the very day that the Romans conquered the city and burned the temple down. Therefore if James ever acted in the role of high priest, it was not at the Jerusalem temple.

What is not very well known is that there was another Jewish temple in the first century B.C., in Egypt. It was built by Jews in Leontopolis. Josephus wrote of this temple.[23] Taking everything that Josephus wrote about this temple in context, it appears that it was first built some time subsequent to the conquest of Jerusalem by the tyrant Antiochus Epiphanes, who abolished the sacrifices for three years. Apparently the fact that sacrifices had ceased being offered in the Jerusalem temple became a precedent for blood sacrifices being offered elsewhere. Otherwise it would have been a violation of the *Torah*, since the Israelites were admonished to only offer sacrifices "where God has chosen to place his name"[24] and nowhere else. But after the sacrifices were restored to the Jerusalem temple, then if sacrifices were still offered in the temple in Leontopolis, then this would have been a grievous violation of Deuteronomic law. Therefore we can safely conclude that sacrifices ceased at the Egyptian temple after the death of Antiochus. As such, the temple in Leontopolis would have been an ideal place for the Ebionites to worship. There would be no blood

---

kingdom, and ultimately to all converts to Judaism, and their descendants. But a Jew proper denotes a descendant of Judah.

23   Jos. Ant. 13.3.1-3; War 1.1.1. & 7.10.3-4.

24   Deuteronomy 12:4-6,11,21; 14:23-24; 16:2,5-6,11.

sacrifices offered, and so no moral violation of their creed. I submit that, if James ever acted as a high priest, it was at this temple in Leontopolis, Egypt. This accords with his vegetarianism, and his being allowed to enter into the holy place, wearing only linen garments. This is also congenial to James and Jesus both being of the priestly tribe of Levi, rather than the tribe of Judah. And all of this evidence converges in an unsolicited way to support the underlying thesis that Jesus lived in Hasmonean times. It is true that the temple in Leontopolis was still standing until shortly after the fall of Masada. But when we study evidence from the Talmud, we will see that, according to at least one Talmudic source, Jeschu was "near to those in power" and thus probably cognate to the Hasmonean dynasty. We also have a surviving fragment from the Gospel of the Ebionites, in which Jesus makes a statement clearly in opposition to the offering of animal sacrifices:

"I have come to abolish the sacrifices. And if you do not cease making sacrifice, God's wrath will not cease afflicting you."

This is quite a radical statement, but it may very well be genuine. In fact, I think it is the most trustworthy statement ever attributed to Jesus, despite the fact that it is absent from any of the four Canonical Gospels.[25] We need to recall the verse from Daniel's prophecy that says "in the midst of the week he shall cause sacrifice and oblation to cease"[26] and the possible relationship to *Ebionism*. If we assume that Jesus lived in Hasmonean times, there would have been no reason for Jesus or anyone else to suspect that the reference to "he" in the verse in question was to anyone other than the Messiah. We have already discussed this somewhat in the section on Daniel's prophecy of the seventy weeks, but we need to keep this in mind. Even if Jesus himself was not an Ebionite, if he wanted to fulfill messianic prophecy, then he "knew" that the Messiah would cause sacrifice and oblation to cease for three years and six months. In fact, Josephus apparently made the mistake of at first supposing that this prophecy was fulfilled by Antiochus Epiphanes; in his *War of the Jews*, he wrote that Antiochus had stopped the sacrifices

---

25   The Gospel of the Ebionites may in fact have predated any of the four Canonical Gospels.
26   Daniel 9:27.

in the temple for three years and six months,[27] which is corrected in his *Antiquities of the Jews* to three years precisely.[28] A person reading the prophecy of the seventy weeks in Daniel without any theological preconceptions will readily see that it is none other than the Messiah himself who abolishes sacrifice and oblation. The question is whether or not the verse in Daniel gave rise to *Ebionism*, or was it possibly a product of *Ebionism?* It is impossible to tell for sure. But there are at least a few Gospel passages that place Jesus as being somewhat sympathetic to the attitudes of the *Ebionim*, respecting blood sacrifices.[29] There are quite a few passages within *TaNaKh* expressing agreement or at least sympathy with the Ebionite view of blood sacrifices.[30] Nevertheless the normative view is in accord with the priestly tradition of blood sacrifices.

Mead speaks of a number of different religious groups in Palestine, from the first century B.C., to the third century C.E. One of these were the Nazoraions, called by him "Nazoraei" and "Nasaraei". Tellingly, one of these groups of Nasaraei existed <u>before</u> the commonly-accepted time of Jesus Christ. In a section where he is discussing the writings of Epiphanius, Mead writes the following:

"There was, he says, a sect of the Nasaraei before Christ ("Haer" xxix. 6); these he has already described (Haer.," xviii. 1-3), calling them, however, Nazaraei. He treats of these in connection with the Daily Baptists, who, like the Essenes and allied communities, baptized or washed themselves in water every day; they were Jews, and lived in the same districts as the Essenes. They observed the law of circumcision, the Sabbath and the appointed feasts, and especially reverenced the ancient patriarchs and sages of Israel, including Moses; they however, rejected the canonical Pentateuch, and said that the real Law was different from the one in public circulation. They apparently also rejected all the prophets after Moses. Moreover, they refused to have anything to do with the blood sacrifices

---

27   Jos. War. 1.1.1.

28   Jos. Ant. 12.7.6. Cf 1 Maccabees 1:54; 4:52-54.

29   Mt 9:13; 12:7 cf Hosea 6:6; Mk 12:22-24; Jn 4:19-26.

30   Jeremiah 7:22; Isaiah 1:11-15; 1 Samuel 15:22; Psalms 40:6-8; 50:7-15; 51:16-17; 107:22; 116:17; Proverbs 15:8; 21:3,27; Ecclesiastes 5:1; Hosea 6:6; Micah 6:6-8; Daniel 9:27.

of the Temple and abstained from eating flesh. They contended that the books which laid down the rules of these sacrifices were inventions of later times, and that their true ancestors from Adam to Moses did not perform such bloody rites; all the accounts of such sacrifice in the popular scripture were later inventions of scribes who were ignorant of the true doctrine. These Nazars, then, were an extreme school of those dissentient mystics whose sayings had from about 150 B.C. crept into the books which subsequently became canonical, such sayings as: "The sacrifices of God are a broken spirit"; "Sacrifice and offering Thou didst not desire." This spiritual protest against the grossness of blood-offerings was also a characteristic of the Essenes; and there can be little doubt but that there must have been a very close connection between the ideals of these pre-Christian schools of mystic and humanitarian Judaism and the earliest Christians."[31]

The fact that there were such Nazoraions or Ebionites who objected to blood sacrifices *before* the alleged time of Christ is also congenial to our thesis; this also dovetails nicely with what we read of James acting in the role of high priest, yet being a vegetarian, and also with evidence that Jesus and James were Levites. If we picture James as acting as high priest at the temple in Leontopolis, then all of this data fits together quite well: Leontopolis was a place where *Ebionim* could worship God without animal sacrifices; James and Jesus were Levites (and possibly cognate to the Hasmonean dynasty); James was a vegetarian; and this movement predates the time commonly accorded to Christ. The very fact that so many diverse sources of information can converge together to support our thesis is a strong argument in favour of it, in my view.

In Egypt there were many Greek-speaking Jews living in Alexandria. In fact, critical biblical scholars suspect that the large Greek-speaking Jewish population of Alexandria was the real motive behind the translation of the Hebrew Scriptures into Greek. The Pentateuch was translated into Greek in the third century B.C., in the days of Ptolemy Philadephus, according to the Letter of Aristeas. We find, not only in Jewish tradition, but also even within the Gospel of Matthew, a link between Jesus and

---

31   Mead., op. cit., pgs. 345-346.

Egypt.[32] Albeit Jesus was merely an infant in the story from Matthew, perhaps this may hint at a more intimate acquaintance with that land. Possibly both Jesus and James worshipped at the temple in Leontopolis; perhaps Jesus himself had acted as high priest there, before his death, and was later succeeded by his brother James. In fact, what I suspect is that Jesus and his family may have been native Egyptian Jews. Maybe this is the great forbidden secret of Christ's origin; not that he was a Canaanite or a Galilean Gentile, but that he and his family were really Greek-speaking Egyptian Levites. The Jewish Scriptures had been translated into Greek by the first century B.C., so this would have been no obstacle to Jesus in seeking messianic glory. In fact, if Greek was the first language of Christ and his family, then this may account for what otherwise would appear to be quite strange: Greek originals of the Gospels. Of course in our view there is a huge gap of approximately two centuries between the real time of Jesus and the composition of the Gospels. And the discrepancy is usually accounted for by saying that by the time the Gospels were written, there were more Greek-speaking adherents to the Christian faith than those who spoke Hebrew or Syriac. But if Jesus and his family were Greek-speaking Levites then Greek originals of the Synoptic Gospels is not so glaring of a discrepancy. I am not going quite so far as to say that the entire Jesus drama took place in Egypt; but it is at least possible that his family may have been native Egyptian Jews.[33] As such, it would have been natural for them to speak Greek. However bright and educated men like Jesus may also have spoken Hebrew.[34] This is at least one possible interpretation of the evidence. This would also be congenial to Greek originals of the Gospels, without requiring large numbers of Greeks as adherents to the religion at an early stage. In fact, the alleged Galilean provenance of Jesus may have been merely a literary device, or perhaps an oral tradition, with the intent to furnish

---

32   Mt 2:13-15.

33   Jews. Here I am using the term in a more general sense, as those who practice Judaism, or some form of it, as a religion.

34   Hebrew. Hebrew was the common postexilic tongue of the Jews; Syriac, otherwise known as Aramaic or Chaldee, was not commonly spoken in Palestine, contrary to common misconceptions on the matter. Jesus did not speak Syriac. Neither did the Apostles. Jews living in Syria would have spoken Syriac. Palestinian Jews spoke Hebrew, at least until the third century.

Jesus with gratuitous messianic credentials, just as his supposed birth in Bethlehem also did, by fulfilling messianic prophecy.[35] For all we really know, Jesus and his family may very well have been native Egyptian Jews. On the other hand, we ought not to reject outright everything in the Gospels that claims to be a fulfillment of messianic prophecy. We should be suspicious, but we should not be surprised if some details are accurate, and that certain events and circumstances at least had the appearance of the fulfillment of biblical prophecy. Otherwise on what basis would Jesus have claimed Messianic legitimacy? In fact, if we take a critical-historical look at the Galilean provenance of Jesus, then there emerges a circumstance that is illuminating, and even more pungent, assuming the thesis herein is correct. John Hyrcanus, the father of Aristobulus, Antigonus, and Alexander Jannaeus, had conquered southern Syria, as well as Samaria and Idumea, and forced the inhabitants to embrace Judaism.[36] Galilee is included in this general area, lying between southern Syria and Samaria. If the family of Jesus were really native Galileans, then they were not ethnically Jewish, and may also have secretly hated Judaism. Perhaps this was one reason why they adopted a "heretical" version of Judaism like *Ebionism*, assuming such was the case. But this also casts the Messianic aspirations of Jesus in a new light. Perhaps both the ethnic identity and also the heretical interpretation of Judaism advocated by Jesus is at the core of his rejection by the Pharisees, and also the underlying philosophical differences between the Old and New Testaments as well. Furthermore Jesus could easily have travelled to Alexandria from Galilee, either in the first century B.C. or the first century A.D. In Alexandria he would have been exposed to Greek philosophy, and even possibly to Buddhist missionaries. He could have imbibed the teachings of Stoicism, Cynicism, and Platonism. There are certainly traces of Cynicism in the Synoptic Gospels, and I dare say more than a hint of Platonism in the Gospel of John. One can also detect at least a slight hint of Stoicism in the New Testament, while both Stoics and Epicureans are mentioned.[37] Of course that was in Athens. But the

---

35   Isaiah 9:1-2 cp Mt 2:22; 4:15-16; Lk 1:26 cf Micah 5:2 cp Mt 2:1-6; Lk 2:1-7.
36   Jos. Ant. 13.9.1. The Herods were Idumeans.
37   Acts 17:18.

entire Near East was very much under the cultural sway of Hellenism, from the time of Alexander the Great on. Therefore whether Jesus was Galilean or Egyptian, he was no doubt quite familiar with the varieties of Greek philosophy, as well as the Jewish Scriptures and traditions.

Buddhist missionaries were also present in the Near East during those times. Quite possibly *Ebionism* was influenced by Buddhism. Both religions are opposed to animal sacrifices, or partaking of animal flesh. Unfortunately there is only the most fragmentary evidence of the *Ebionim* surviving. Even the Gnostics have a greater surviving legacy, especially after the discovery of the Nag Hammadi codices. It is uncertain whether or not Gnosticism was extant in the first century B.C., but there is no unambiguous evidence confirming such an early Gnosticism. Nevertheless there were a great variety of religious and philosophical ideas prevalent throughout the Near East in the first century B.C., and we ought to at least give Jesus the credit of being somewhat of an innovator.

G.R.S. Mead also quotes from Eusebius, who in turn quotes from Hegesippus, an account of James the brother of Jesus very similar to the one above:

"Eusebius tells us that in his day the "most accurate account" of this James was to be found in the fifth book of the Commentaries of Hegesippus, who, he says, "flourished nearest to the days of the Apostles"; modern scholarship, however, [sic] assigns the date of writing of Hegesippus's "Memoirs" to about 180 A.D. Eusebius then proceeds to quote from Hegesippus the story of the martyrdom of this James, the setting and tone of which is very Jewish. The most interesting part of the story, however, is the description of James himself, where we read: "He was holy from his mother's womb; drank no wine or strong drink, nor ate animal food; no razor came upon his head; he neither oiled himself nor used the bath; he alone was permitted to enter the holy places, for he never wore wool, but [always] linen. And he used to go alone into the Temple, and was found on his knees, interceding for the people, so that his knees grew hard like a camel's, because of his kneeling in prayer to God, begging forgiveness for the people. Indeed, on account of his exceeding great righteousness he was called 'the righteous' and Olbias, which means in Greek 'defence of the people' and 'righteousness.'" Here we have the picture of a rigid ascetic, a Chassid, an Essene, a Therapeut, a Nazir, for from his mother's womb he was vowed to holiness. It is, however, difficult to understand what is meant by the sentence which I have translated, "he alone was permitted to enter the holy places"- generally rendered the "Holy of Holies," or the "Sanctuary." It is, of course, impossible to believe that James could have been permitted to enter the Holy of Holies of the Temple at Jerusalem, which no one but the high priest, and he only on a certain day in the year, could enter."[38]

In answer to Mead's perplexity I have proposed the temple in Egypt as a possible solution. And this solution does seem to dovetail nicely with some of the other evidence which we will hereafter examine, respecting traditions of Jesus in Egypt. Indeed, as stated above, the temple in Leontopolis would have been an ideal place for *Ebionim* or *Notzrim*[39] to observe their form of worship without blood sacrifices. Notice also that the reference to Olbias meaning <u>in Greek</u> "defence of the people" and "righteousness", which further supports the idea of Egyptian provenance for both James and Jesus.[40] Notice also that Mead refers to James as a "Chassid"; he is right in this, against the erroneous assumptions of some lesser scholars.

Respecting the temple in Egypt, some clarification is desirable. Certain careless people have paraded their ignorance as knowledge on the Internet, as so often happens, and spread their own misinformation about this temple, and have unjustly accused Josephus of errors and contradictions in respect to this. But if one carefully reads and examines everything that Josephus wrote about this temple, one can see that he was both internally consistent, and also consistent with all other known facts of the case. In fact, the erroneous website is none other than the

38   Mead., op. cit., pgs. 224-225.
39   Notzrim. The Hebrew form of Nazoraion, otherwise also called Naza-renes, Nazaraeans, Nazarei, Nasarei, Nazars, Nasraye, etc., and are seemingly identical to the Ebionites. In Arabic countries Christians are called Nazraye, or some variant thereof.
40   Since Greek was the common tongue of Egyptian Jews, as well as the many Greeks living in Alexandria. By contrast, Greek was <u>not</u> commonly spoken by Palestinian Jews. Cf Acts 21:37.

Jewish Encyclopedia, found @ www.jewishencyclopedia.com. I will not apologize for pointing out errors, from wherever they emanate. Josephus is accused of using spurious letters, or thus composing them, due to "his assertion that a central sanctuary is necessary because a multiplicity of temples causes dissension among the Jews [sic] evidences [sic] imperfect knowledge of Jewish religious life [sic]". Perhaps it ought not to surprise me that a Jewish encyclopedia thus distorts the writings of Josephus, and most unjustly accuses him of forging epistles and contradicting valid accounts.[41] But anyone who actually reads the letters in question can clearly see that Josephus was not speaking of divisions among Jews,[42] but of the native Egyptians themselves. Furthermore it is fatuous to assume, much less pontificate, upon the supposed unity of Jews, either in Egypt, or elsewhere, during those times. There were many different sects of Jews during that time, and during the reign of Alexander Jannaeus, some Jews had even invited a foreigner to invade Judaea, to oppose their hated monarch. Therefore any unity among Jews during those times was likely against common enemies. What we read in the online Jewish Encyclopedia is nothing less than a shameless revisionism in which we are expected to believe in some monolithic unity of Judaism in the period in question. Nothing could be further from the truth.

In the interest of truth, fairness, and justice, and to set the record straight, I will reproduce the relevant portions from Josephus below:

"1. But then the son of Onias the high priest, who was of the same name with his father, and who fled to King Ptolemy, who was called Philometor, lived now at Alexandria, as we have said already. When this Onias saw that Judea was oppressed by the Macedonians and their kings, out of a desire to purchase to himself a memorial and eternal fame, he resolved to send to King Ptolemy and Queen Cleopatra, to ask leave of them that he might build a temple in Egypt like to that at Jerusalem, and might ordain Levites and priests out of their own stock. The chief reason why he was desirous so to do, was, that he relied upon the prophet Isaiah, who lived

---

41   Since the Jews still despise Josephus as a notorious traitor, and will never take his side, unless it is against the New Testament. Then and only then does Josephus become a trustworthy historian in the eyes of the Jews.

42   Even Egyptian Jews.

about six hundred years before, and foretold that there certainly was to be a temple built to Almighty God in Egypt by a man that was a Jew. Onias was elevated with this prediction, and wrote the following epistle to Ptolemy and Cleopatra: "Having done many and great things for you in the affairs of the war, by the assistance of God, and that in Celesyria and Phoenicia, I came at length with the Jews to Leontopolis, and to other places of your nation where I found that the greatest part of your people had temples in an improper manner, and that on this account they bore ill will one against another, which happens to the Egyptians by reason of the multitude of their temples, and the difference of opinions about divine worship. Now I found a very fit place in a castle that hath its name from the country Diana; this place is full of materials of several sorts, and replenished with sacred animals: I desire, therefore, that you will grant me leave to purge this holy place which belongs to no master, and is fallen down, and to build there a temple to Almighty God, after the pattern of that in Jerusalem, and of the same dimensions, that may be for the benefit of thyself, and thy wife and children, that those Jews who dwell in Egypt may have a place whither they may come and meet together in mutual harmony one with another, and be subservient to thy advantages; for the prophet Isaiah foretold, that "there shall be an altar in Egypt to the Lord God" and many other such things did he prophesy relating to that place." (Josephus, *Antiquities of the Jews, 13.3.1*)

Note well that here Onias does not ascribe schism to the Jews in Egypt, but rather to the native Egyptians themselves, contrary to what the online Jewish Encyclopedia claimed. Therefore we must be careful when we read such ancient documents, to see what they really say. I personally would rather go direct to the source, and see what is written in such ancient texts, rather than trust modern interpreters to accurately relay the information. The Jewish Encyclopedia is a disgrace. I will never retract that statement, nor ever apologize for it. We should also examine the following section from Josephus, to see the context of the above portion.

"2. And this was what Onias wrote to King Ptolemy. Now anyone may observe his piety, and that of his sister and wife Cleopatra, by that epistle which they wrote in answer to it; for they laid the blame and the transgression of the law upon the head of Onias. And this was their reply: "King Ptolemy and Queen Cleopatra to Onias, send greeting. We have read thy petition, wherein thou desirest leave to be given to thee to purge that temple which is fallen down at Leontopolis, in the Nomus of Heliopolis, and is named from the country Bubastis; on which account we cannot but wonder that it should be pleasing to God to have a temple erected in a place so unclean, and so full of sacred animals. But since thou sayest that Isaiah the prophet foretold this long ago, we give thee leave to do it, if it may be done according to your law, and so that we may not appear to have at all offended God herein."" (*Jos. Ant.* 13.3.2)

The Jewish Encyclopedia scoffs at this letter as spurious, because the "pagan king" protests that the proposed building is contrary to the Jewish law, and only relents due to the reference to the prophecy of Isaiah. As such, these letters are both ascribed to a "Hellenistic Jew". While it is admittedly strange that Josephus would ascribe piety to a king who was married to his own sister, and therefore in grievous violation of the Levitical prohibition against fraternal incest,[43] albeit it was an ancient royal custom of the Egyptians, yet Ptolemy and Cleopatra were not illiterate savages, as the article implies; the Jewish Scriptures had been translated into Greek, and were probably known to educated Egyptians, such as the king and queen. It would have been a matter of wise diplomacy for King Ptolemy to allow a vacant, abandoned temple to be rebuilt, as here requested by Onias, to secure the loyalty of his Jewish subjects, against Syrian aggression. Furthermore it is not beyond the realm of possibility that Ptolemy and Cleopatra may have thought of themselves as obedient to God, despite their cultural differences with the Jews. But of course we see from the Jewish Encyclopedia a scrupulous and intolerant narrowness of construction of what it means to be "Jewish", whether in ancient times or modern. The article also speaks of sacrifices at the Leontopolis temple, without even mentioning the Deuteronomic prohibition against blood sacrifices outside of the one place chosen by God to place his name. This naturally obscures the point made about the *Ebionim*, whether intentionally or not. The article then charges the Septuagint with changing the phrase "city of destruction" in Isaiah

---

43   Leviticus 18:9.

19:18 to "city of righteousness", when in fact it was the Jews, who in the Massoretic text, changed the original reading from "City of the Sun" to "city of destruction". This is a well-attested instance of Massoretic tampering with the original text, and critical editions usually concede the point; the variant is even found in the margins of the Massoretic text.[44] Finally, the article says that according to Josephus, the temple existed for 343 years, although the "general opinion" is that this must be corrected to 243 years. True it is that Josephus named the temple as standing for 343 years;[45] and at first this tripped me up too, since the temple was closed shortly after the fall of Masada in approximately 74 A.D., which would have placed the construction of the temple way back in 269 B.C., which obviously was long before the time of Antiochus Epiphanes. The solution to the apparent discrepancy is found by very carefully reading the two letters above; in both letters we see evidence that there had already been a structure in place, that had formerly been used as a temple. In the first letter, it is referred to as a "castle" and in the second as a "temple which is fallen down"; therefore when Josephus wrote that the temple had stood for 343 years, he evidently referred to the entire length of time that the structure had stood, even before it had become a Jewish temple. At least I am willing to extend the benefit of the doubt to Josephus, which the Jewish Encyclopedia is unwilling to do. The reference to "sacred animals" in both letters apparently referred to animals sacred to the Egyptians, which would have been an abomination to the Jews. From what Josephus wrote in *War 1.1.1.*, the Jewish temple was built, or rather rebuilt, upon what remained of a temple to Bubastis, shortly after the time when Antiochus had invaded Jerusalem and desecrated the altar there. So evidently the temple had first been built and dedicated to Bubastis about a century before this time. Therefore Josephus stands vindicated against the calumnies of his detractors.

Finally, we may as well read the final section on the temple from the *Antiquities:*

---

44   BIBLIA HEBRAICA STUTTGARTENSIA., op. cit., pg. 703. Cf BIB-
LIA SACRA VULGATA., op. cit., pg. 1115. Cp SEPTUAGINTA., op. cit., pg.
591. (vol. 2; duo volumina in uno).
45   Jos. War. 7.10.4.

"3. So Onias took the place, and built a temple, and an altar to God, like indeed to that in Jerusalem, but smaller and poorer. I do not think it proper for me now to describe its dimensions, or its vessels, which have been already described in my seventh book of the Wars of the Jews. However, Onias found other Jews like to himself, together with priests and Levites, that there performed divine service. But we have said enough about this temple." (*Jos. Ant. 13.3.3.*)

Once again it is worth stating that, even if blood sacrifices were initially offered at this temple, within three years time the sanctuary in Jerusalem would be cleansed, and therefore any further animal sacrifices would have been in violation of the Torah.[46] I am not saying that there were never any violations of the Torah, but if the Jews were truly scrupulous about observing the Torah, then the blood sacrifices would have ceased as soon as the altar in Jerusalem was cleansed. This would have allowed the temple in Leontopolis to become an ideal place for Ebionite Jews to worship. I cannot prove that this was the case; but nevertheless the circumstance seems reasonably plausible, given the available evidence. If there was in fact an ongoing dispute between two mutually antagonistic groups of Jews in Egypt, one of whom was in favour of blood sacrifices at the temple, and another in opposition, then if Jesus and his disciples were able "to cause sacrifice and oblation to cease" even in just the Leontopolis temple, this may have been sufficient to crown Jesus as the Anointed Prince of Daniel's prophecy in the eyes of his adoring followers. In this vein it is also worth noting that the incident of Jesus overturning the tables of the moneychangers in the Jerusalem temple[47] may have been an effort to interrupt the daily sacrifices there, and to bring those sacrifices to a definitive end. Jews like to portray the act as an affront to the Romans, but the reality is that the Romans would have been unaffected by such actions; it was the men who sold sacrificial animals who would've been most antagonized by such actions. Therefore we can clearly see this as an example of a confrontation between Ebionites and more traditional Jews. Or at least the circumstances lend themselves to such an interpretation. In respect to the question of sacrifices at the Leontopolis temple, I have

46   Deuteronomy 12:4-6,11,21; 14:23-24; 16:2,5-6,11.
47   Mt 21:12-13; Mk 11:15-17; Lk 19:45-46; Jn 2:13-17 cf Isaiah 56:7; Jeremiah 7:11.

at least some oblique evidence to support the opinion that the Jews were in fact very scrupulous about the Deuteronomic prohibition against unauthorized sacrifices. There was an earlier Jewish temple in Egypt, not mentioned by Josephus. This temple was in Elephantine. There are some surviving Aramaic papyri from the fifth century B.C., which are letters between the Jewish devotees at this Egyptian temple, and the temple in Jerusalem. There are three surviving letters, which, by the very nature of the correspondence, proves to my satisfaction that the Jerusalem Jews were very scrupulous about the Deuteronomic prohibition cited earlier. The first letter is a request to rebuild the temple to Yaho[48] after it had been all but destroyed; burnt offerings are proposed. But in the response from Jerusalem, the high priest answers the petition by only authorizing "meal offerings" rather than burnt offerings.[49] The final surviving letter acknowledges only "meal offerings" with the unstated understanding that burnt offerings were prohibited by the high priest. These letters can be found in *ANCIENT NEAR EASTERN TEXTS*, edited by James B. Pritchard.[50] Lest I be falsely accused of misinterpreting these texts, I will stipulate to the following: the editor of these texts speculated that the last letter was addressed to Arsames, but it seems much more likely to have been addressed to Bagoas, the governor of Judah. This is much more in accord with the second letter. Most likely, there had also been a letter sent from Bagoas to Yedoniah, prohibiting the offering of burnt offerings in the Elephantine temple, but this papyrus is no longer extant. So possibly the temple in Elephantine was rebuilt, but blood sacrifices were no longer offered there. If so, then it would have become an acceptable place for the *Ebionim* to worship.[51] I would gladly have reproduced the contents of these letters in full, but I would rather not be tedious to the reader, and I have not yet secured permission to quote from these letters from the publisher, which I am sure they would kindly grant. Furthermore Bagoas the governor of Judah, was probably also the high priest, as was a common custom in the postexilic period.

---

48 Yaho. A form of the Hebrew Name of God.

49 Burnt offerings would entail blood sacrifices of the animals in question.

50 Pritchard, James B. (editor), *ANCIENT NEAR EASTERN TEXTS*. (Princeton, New Jersey: Princeton University Press: 1950, 1955); pg. 492.

51 I.e., assuming they date back that far.

So James, rather than being an obstacle to our thesis, has instead become a source of confirmation and augmentation. We have seen that there are traditions of James acting in accordance with a high-priestly role, while abstaining from animal meat. From Josephus we have learned of a Jewish temple in Egypt, where presumably Ebionites, such as James probably was, could worship God in a sound conscience, since no bloody animal sacrifices were offered there. This evidence dovetails with a surviving fragment from the Gospel of the Ebionites, in which Jesus denounces animal sacrifices, and says he has come to abolish such sacrifices. This in turn is in accord with what we read of the Messiah the Prince in Daniel's prophecy of the seventy weeks.[52] This evidence is in further accord with unsolicited evidence that Jesus was really a Levite.[53] And, as we will see when we examine evidence from the *Talmud*, the tradition that Jesus was a Levite dovetails with a tradition that Jeschu was "close to those in power" at the time of the Hasmonean dynasty. All these diverse streams of evidence converge together to confirm our postulate, in an unexpected and unsolicited way. Furthermore all this evidence is congenial to a natural reading of Daniel's prophecy of the seventy weeks, namely that the *terminus a quo* of the prophecy was the famous decree of Cyrus, and also with the chronology of the *Toldoth Jeschu* and portions of the *Talmud* respecting Jesus. Is all this merely a huge coincidence? That seems too far-fetched. This evidence, as strong as it is, and as varied as the sources from which it comes, is too much to be so lightly dismissed. This is a genuine challenge to the standard chronology vis-à-vis Jesus Christ. And we also ought not to forget about what we learned about the substitution of Artaxerxes for Xerxes in the Massoretic texts of Ezra and Nehemiah; this further substantiates our thesis. And the evident chronological tampering in the Massoretic text of Esther only serves to complete the picture. This is too much to simply be ignored. This is an open challenge to the standard chronology for Christ. However, as strong as this evidence is, it is still possible to augment it somewhat. There is also a rather obscure passage that very tantalizingly suggests that, not only was Jesus a Levite, but he also sometimes officiated as a priest:

---

52   "In the midst of the week he shall cause the sacrifice and the oblation to cease"; Daniel 9:27.
53   Luke 1:5,36; Numbers 36.

"We have found Josephus, who hath written about the taking of Jerusalem (of whom Eusebius Pamphilii makes frequent mention in his Ecclesiastical History), saying openly in his Memoirs of the Captivity, that Jesus officiated in the temple with the priests. Thus have we found Josephus saying, a man of ancient times, and not very long after the apostles" *About A.D. 980. Suidas in voce Iesous.*

The quotation immediately above is from my edition of Josephus.[54] I was reluctant to even include it at all, but I chose to at least take some brief note of it, since it is part of the complete evidence. However the evidential value of the passage is certainly controversial, to say the least; the very fact that it is from as late as the tenth century is a potential argument against its validity. Yet notwithstanding this, if Suidas had a copy of Josephus that really contained a reference to *the* Jesus acting in the role of a priest, and Suidas was not mistaken in confusing some other priestly Jesus with *the* Jesus with whom we are concerned, then his evidence is very powerful and important. The problem is that Josephus mentions no less than five men named Jesus who acted as high priest at one time or another. Therefore it is quite possible, if not probable, that Suidas may have merely seized upon the name of Jesus, and automatically assumed that it was *the* Jesus; i.e., Jesus Christ. It is also just barely possible that Suidas may have been speaking, not of Jesus, but of James, the brother of Jesus, and that there has been a corruption in the text. If so, then his testimony may still be of some value, as establishing James as a Levite, or some old tradition of such. Of the five men named Jesus whom Josephus also says served as high priests, the first one lived back in the days of the judges, so we can exclude him. The other four all lived after the time commonly supposed in which Jesus lived, according to the New Testament. None of them lived in Hasmonean times. But then again we have stipulated of James, to say nothing of Jesus, that if he served as a high priest at all, it was definitely not at the Jerusalem temple; therefore he would not have been in the ordinary succession of high priests as enumerated by Josephus. Most likely James served as high priest in the temple in Leontopolis, Egypt. Possibly Jesus did as well. It is just barely possible that Suidas has merely reiterated a garbled version of

---

54   JOSEPHUS: THE COMPLETE WORKS., op. cit., pg. 982.

some genuine tradition respecting Jesus officiating as a priest in a temple; what Suidas would not have known was that if so, it was in Leontopolis in Egypt, and a full century before the time that Jesus supposedly lived. Whiston (the translator of Josephus) quotes from Suidas, but does not comment upon the novelty, strangeness, and uniqueness of what Suidas wrote. Indeed, in one sense it is amazing that such a weird testimony has survived the censorship of Christian scribes; this fact alone makes the brief passage at least worth taking note of. One ought to at least keep in mind the fact that any evidence suggesting that Jesus was really a Levite, rather than a descendant of David, however oblique, however controversial, and however seemingly tenuous, is still potentially as damaging as dynamite to the edifice of the pretended messianic scheme of the New Testament. Therefore the evidence, however arrived at, is worth at least some consideration.

Finally, there was an early edition of an apocryphal Gospel attributed to Matthew, concerning the birth of Mary, which taught that Mary was a daughter of Joachim, a priest of the tribe of Levi. No doubt this tradition was derived from the Gospel of Luke, but it is worth at least noting as part of the complete evidence. In fact, I will quote from the introduction to the Gospel of the Birth of Mary, found in *LOST BOOKS OF THE BIBLE AND THE FORGOTTEN BOOKS OF EDEN*: "The ancient copies differed from Jerome's, for from one of them the learned Faustus, a native of Britain, who became Bishop of Riez, in Provence, endeavoured to prove that Christ was not the Son of God till after his baptism; and that he was not of the house of David and tribe of Judah, because, according to the Gospel he cited, the Virgin herself was not of this tribe, but of the tribe of Levi; her father being a priest of the name Joachim. It was likewise from this Gospel that the sect of the Collyridians, established the worship and offering of manchet bread and cracknels, or fine wafers, as sacrifices to Mary, whom they imagined to have been born of a Virgin, as Christ is related in the Canonical Gospel to have been born of her."[55]

Once again I want to emphasize that this tradition is quite certainly

---

55   *LOST BOOKS OF THE BIBLE.*, (© 1926 by Alpha House, Inc., Thomas Nelson Publishers); pg. 17.

derived from the Gospel of Luke itself, lest I be accused of wanting to have my cake and eat it too. The reason why I make a point of saying this is because the Protevangelion of James is likewise attributed to James the brother of Jesus, and yet it is obviously spurious, and dates to no earlier than the third century at the very earliest.

But what we have learned herein of both James the Just and Jesus Christ is very pungent in terms of evidential value; we have seen multiple sources of tradition converging to confirm Levitical descent for Jesus and James. And the temple in Leontopolis, Egypt, which Josephus wrote about, seems to have been an ideal place where James could fulfill everything that is written of him: that he could act as high priest, while abstaining from animal flesh, and from offering blood sacrifices.[56] And furthermore all this evidence is congenial to our central postulate that Jesus (and James) lived a full century before the commonly-accepted time. I suspect that the temple in Leontopolis may have been the one referred to in Luke 24:53.

---

56 The priests at the Jerusalem temple were expected to partake of the sacrifices offered, in most instances. Therefore a vegetarian could not thus serve.

Nicodemus

Just as the historicity of Paul is questionable, so is also the biblical character of Nicodemus. Aside from the fairly obvious fact that the historicity of Nicodemus is necessarily logically contingent upon the historicity of *Christ*, so, just as in the case of Paul, there are still other reasons to suppose that, quite possibly, Nicodemus himself was merely an invented figure. First of all is the highly suspicious fact that, Nicodemus is only mentioned in the Gospel of John. No other book of the New Testament mentions him at all. Why would all three Synoptic Gospels remain completely silent about a man who supposedly helped Joseph of Arimathaea take Jesus down from the cross, and bury him? I suppose that one possible answer that may be offered was to protect him; if Nicodemus was still alive when the three Synoptic Gospels were written, but had died in the meantime, then and only then may it have become possible to disclose his loyalty to Jesus and set the record straight. Although this is just barely possible, it is not an entirely satisfying answer. Presumably it would have been socially acceptable for Nicodemus to assist in the burial of a fellow-Jew, however wayward or misguided; there should have been no social stigma attached to this. In fact, he ought to have been commended for his piety.

To illustrate my point, I will use an analogy between Nicodemus, who is only mentioned in the Gospel of John, and Zaccheus, who is only mentioned in the Gospel of Luke.[1] The difference is that Nicodemus is much more conspicuous by his absence from the three Synoptic Gospels than is Zaccheus by being omitted from Matthew, Mark, and John. This is brought out by the fact that all four Gospels mention Joseph of Arimathaea, and his role in burying Jesus.[2] But only John mentions Nicodemus. Why? The reason speculated on above is just barely possible, if one is inclined to so credit the Gospels. But this reason does not seem very satisfying. Even extremely early dates of composition for the Gospels would seem to still be too long after the event to justify such silence. Furthermore, even by being involved in any way in the burial of Jesus, Nicodemus would in a sense have been disclosing his loyalties to hostile parties, immediately. Therefore we can see how hollow the above explanation is. So the very silence of the Synoptics regarding Nicodemus leads to suspicion respecting his alleged historicity. There is even a sort of frailty to the story about Joseph of Arimathaea and Nicodemus together taking Jesus down from the cross, and burying him. Both men are said to have been *counsellors*, or *rulers*; meaning, they were members of the *Sanhedrin*.[3] As such, they were probably at least middle-aged, if not somewhat elderly. Therefore they probably still would have needed help from one or two younger, stronger, men, to take Jesus down from the cross. Furthermore the presence of Nicodemus as the helper of Joseph in the burial of Jesus almost appears as a belated afterthought; it is as if John, having invented this character, has him fill in a role that was useful but ultimately unnecessary.[4] Instead we need to go back to where Nicodemus is first introduced to us. He is thus introduced as a man who secretly came to Jesus by night, a ruler of the Jews, who marvels at the great wonders Jesus performed. This much-quoted third chapter of John is the first place where we read of the new, antinomian teaching of salvation. Therefore it is evident that Nicodemus is merely a foil for the new teaching. John's use of Nicodemus would be more believable if he had consistently presented the faith-based salvation dogma as an esotericism;

---

1   Luke 19:2-9.

2   Mt 27:57-60; Mk 15:42-46; Lk 23:50-53; Jn 19:38-42.

3   Mk 15:43; Lk 23:50-51; Jn 3:1.

4   For the very reason just stated: both men were too elderly to take a man down from a cross, without help from younger, stronger, men. Therefore Nicodemus in this role is utterly superfluous.

however he cannot contain himself, and foolishly has Jesus tell everyone and anyone who will listen to him that the key to salvation is to simply believe in him. The problem is, this teaching is diametrically opposed to that found in the three Synoptic Gospels. Not only that, but all credibility is lost by Jesus constantly preaching that eternal life is attained upon mere belief in him as the Son of God, since this proclamation, had it been made, would have precluded the necessity of any man asking Jesus, towards the very end of his ministry, "What must I do to inherit eternal life?" as we read in all three Synoptic Gospels. And the situation is rendered even more absurd by the fact that Jesus, in answering the man, gives him an answer[5] that is diametrically opposed to what is proclaimed throughout the Gospel of John, by none other than Jesus himself.[6] So Nicodemus is a very suspicious character.

Further confirmation of this suspicion comes from a comparison with the book of Revelation. Revelation, although purportedly written by John, is diametrically opposed to the Johanine doctrine of salvation through faith alone.[7] The way that this all relates to Nicodemus is that the Greek *Nikodemos* has the same essential meaning as the Greek *Nikolaos*, from which is derived *Nikolaitans*, whom the *Christ* of the *Apokalypse* says that he hates.[8] *Nikolaos* and *Nikodemos* both mean "victory over the people"; perhaps the author of the Apokalypse was using a code to convey the fact that his faction of the nascent *messianic* movement regarded the antinomian teaching as a false teaching, whereby the people or *laity* would be conquered, and led astray from the true, original teaching of loyalty to the *Torah*.

The Greek Dictionary found in Abingdon's Strong's Exhaustive Concordance to the Bible with Hebrew, Chaldee and Greek Dictionaries gives a rather misleading distinction between the meanings of *Nikodemos* and *Nikolaos*; in fact, the two names or words have the same meaning. *Demos* and *laos* are both Greek words having the meaning of *people*; *demos* obviously related to such words as *democracy, demographics, demonstration,*

---

5   Mt 19:16-19; Mk 10:17-19; Lk 18:18-20.
6   Jn 3:3-21; 6:29; 10:27-29; 11:25-26.
7   Revelation 20:12-13.
8   Revelation 2:6,15.

etc., while *laos* is related to the words *laity, layman, lay-minister, etc. Niko* means *victory* or *conquest*. What we seem to have is a rivalry by two different *messianic* movements, or possibly two different factions within a single *messianic* movement. From the available evidence, it appears that the dreaded teaching of the *Nikolaitans* was that of antinomianism, or the Pauline-Johanine doctrine of salvation by faith apart from works. In any case these facts create a suspicion at least that perhaps Nicodemus was an invented character, who was invented merely to introduce the new antinomian doctrine. Therefore *Nikodemos, Nikolaos,* and *Nikolaitans* were likely code-words to those who knew that Nicodemus was merely an invented figure, and that he was associated with the introduction of a hated *antinomian* doctrine into the messianic movement. This is further brought out by another contradiction, in which the Jesus of the Apocalypse rebukes two churches for having among them those who commit fornication, and eat food sacrificed to idols.[9] In the first instance, Christ refers back to Balaam[10] the false prophet, and in the second, to the wicked queen Jezebel.[11] Most likely, these were also codes; it seems unlikely that there would have been a woman claiming to be a prophetess, and calling herself by the name of the infamous Jezebel, and teaching Christians to commit fornication, and to eat food offered in sacrifice to idols. Although the Pauline corpus consistently condemns fornication,[12] nevertheless there is a comparatively lax attitude towards the question of "food offered to idols"[13] which creates at least the appearance of a discrepancy. Of course Christian apologists would be likely to point out that, since Paul consistently condemned fornication, adultery, and other forms of immorality, then he[14] could not have been the one intended in such rebukes. This in itself is a reasonable position; nevertheless, we can imagine that "Paul" merely represented a more moderate school of the antinomian teaching, and that there were others who abandoned all common concepts of morality. Indeed, it is known that some branches of *Gnosticism* advocated free love, as commonly understood today.

9   Revelation 2:14,20.

10   Numbers 22-24.

11   1 Kings 16:31; 18:4,13; 19:1-3; 21:5-25; 2 Kings 9:7-37.

12   Galatians 5:19-21; Ephesians 5:5; 1 Corinthians 6:9-10.

13   1 Corinthians 8; Romans 14:14.

14   Or those of his party.

My point about Nicodemus is that, based upon the available evidence, he was most likely a completely invented figure, just as was the apostle Paul. Nicodemus is also a key figure in the sense that he represented a code for the new, antinomian teaching. Of course Paul was also associated with the antinomian teaching as well, but Paul also served a dual purpose; through the story of Saul/Paul, the author of Acts was able to "lock in" the story of Christ's resurrection from the dead. After all, if an outsider, who had before been a persecutor of the movement, had a miraculous vision of the risen Christ, then who can argue with such perfect evidence as that? So Nicodemus was more than a merely incidental figure, unlike Zaccheus. Of course neither Zaccheus nor Nicodemus have specific chronological markers; they each only have the general chronological marker of being characters within Gospels that otherwise designate the time in question.[15] Of the four Gospels, Luke is the most specific in chronological terms.

There is an apocryphal text called the Gospel of Nicodemus, dating from the late third century. It is also otherwise known as the Acts of Pilate. Of course it follows the standard New Testament chronology. It is an interesting text, but less important than the Canonical Gospels, particularly for an historical inquiry. It refers back to other apocryphal works, and confirms the usage of the Greek Septuagint among early Christians.

I just want to briefly address the origin of the antinomian teaching among the early Christians. I suspect that the antinomian teaching itself may derive from an interpretation of Daniel's prophecy of the seventy weeks. Daniel predicted that from the time of the commandment to restore and rebuild Jerusalem, there would be seventy weeks (of years) until the inauguration of "everlasting righteousness"[16] which would coincide with the appearance of the Messiah, the Son of man.[17] The abolition of sacrifice and oblation was also decreed in the prophecy.[18]

---

15   Luke 1:5; 3:1-2; 13:1; 23; Jn 18-19.
16   Daniel 9:24.
17   Daniel 7:13-14; 9:24-27.
18   Daniel 9:27.

There would be no more sin offerings.[19] Therefore the coming of the Messiah was associated with the end of the ceremonial observance of the law, in the minds of at least some Jews. This ought not to surprise us; the coming of the Messiah was such a monumental and unprecedented event that great changes were only to be expected. Of course there were also other Scriptures that taught a seemingly perpetual sacrificial system in the Messianic kingdom.[20] So we can clearly see the possibility of two different and mutually opposed schools of interpretation to arise, even before the arrival of the Messiah. In more recent history, Sabbatai Zevi, a messianic figure of the seventeenth century, who gained many Jewish followers,[21] declared the abolition of ceremonial observances of the Torah, including observance of a *kosher* diet. Miracles were also attributed to Sabbatai Zevi, even in his own lifetime.[22] So the antinomian teaching is not necessarily all that foreign to the Jewish messianic movement; it is potentially implicit even within the messianic prophecy of Daniel. In fact, a person *could* argue that the Johanine version of Jesus is really closer to the original, while what is found in the Synoptics is a form of revisionism. Matthew and John are the two most mutually antagonistic Gospels, vis-à-vis salvation. In Matthew, there is not the slightest hint of dispensationalism; Jesus even admonishes his disciples to "pray that your flight be not in the winter, nor on the Sabbath"[23] an admonition that would be meaningless if Sabbath observance was expected to become obsolete.[24] By contrast, the clause about the Sabbath is absent from the parallel passage in the Gospel of Mark.[25] This implies, contrary to the opinions of most critical Bible scholars and their lap-dogs, that Mark postdates Matthew; the clause in question having been excluded from Mark. Mark also includes the Pauline-Johannine teaching in a post-passion declaration by Christ.[26] Although this could be construed as due to the work of another hand, an alternative interpretation is that Mark

---

19 Daniel 9:24.
20 Ezekiel 40-48. Cf Isaiah 66:21-23.
21 And who still has followers today.
22 So we ought not to be in awe of claims of miracles for Jesus Christ.
23 Mt 24:20.
24 Colossians 2:16.
25 Mk 13:18.
26 Mk 16:16.

implicitly incorporated the *dispensational* teaching in respect to salvation; namely, that after the passion of Christ, the law became null and void.[27] However in the Gospel of Matthew, where he admonishes his disciples to pray that their flight be not in the winter, nor on the Sabbath, he is clearly speaking prophetically of a time subsequent to his passion, and therefore the *dispensational teaching* vis-à-vis salvation does not apply in Matthew. Luke lends itself to the dispensational interpretation, while Mark also does, or was written (entire) with that intent, while John is the inversion of Matthew, inasmuch as therein Christ advocates the antinomian dogma even before his passion. Nevertheless all things considered, I still think that the Synoptics more closely correspond to a genuine, underlying historical subtext than the Gospel of John. Having said this, I do not want to dismiss the potential value of John altogether; even that Gospel has certain characteristics that suggest an underlying historical subtext. In fact, the entire New Testament must be taken into account in seeking to discover the truth about the historical Jesus. I have discovered characteristic passages scattered throughout the text of the New Testament that strongly suggest an underlying historical subtext. I refer to these passages as "fossil" passages. For example, the five verses examined above respecting Jesus being hanged on a tree I classify as "fossil" passages, since they deviate from the normative depiction of the crucifixion.

---

27   Romans 10:4.

THE SHEM

In the Toldoth, Jeschu is depicted as being able to perform miracles by means of the *Shem*. This has been supposed by some to refer to the *Tetragrammaton,* or four-letter divine Name of God; Mead himself seems to subscribe to this interpretation.[1] But this interpretation is untenable, for a couple of fairly obvious reasons. First of all, the four-letter Shem or Name of God occurs over 7,000 times on the Hebrew scrolls of *TaNaKh*. Any person reading such scrolls in the original Hebrew would easily be able to discern the Shem or Tetragrammaton from the multitudinous times it is used in those scrolls. Secondly, the relevant portion of the Toldoth, where the Shem is spoken of, as being some kind of great secret, mentions that the barking of dogs in the temple would cause a person to forget the letters of the Shem. Therefore it is absurd to suppose that the mere barking of dogs could make a person forget the sequence of four letters, two of which are the same. Therefore it is virtually certain that the reference to the "Shem" in the Toldoth Jeschu must instead be to the 72-letter divine Name of God, which was also said to be a great secret. This 72-letter Name of God is also otherwise known as the *Shemhamphorasch.* Mead briefly mentions this in his book, but doesn't seem to know much about it.[2] The Shemhamphorasch is spoken of in Jewish mysticism, and also in occultism and Satanism.

---

1 Mead., op. cit., pg. 262., note.
2 Ibid.

The attribution of miracles to Jeschu by means of the Shem is actually quite a huge concession on the part of Judaism. At least in theological terms this is potentially significant. Jesus said "the works that I do in my Father's name, they bear witness of me"[3] and also, "I have come in my Father's name, and you receive me not; if another shall come in his own name, him ye will receive."[4] Of course elsewhere in the New Testament, the scribes and Pharisees attributed the miracles of Jesus to Beelzebul.[5] By claiming that Jeschu performed miracles through the Shem, the Rabbis could create a pretext for how he could have "led astray" so many Israelites to believe in him as the Messiah. So they would not have to admit that here the devil somehow prevailed over God, but rather that a man misused divine power to lead the Jews astray. But of course the story exists within a seemingly magical context, in which the Shem, being the secret Name of God, is therefore divine and powerful, but it is neutral, and subject to use or misuse by men. This is a very magical concept. But this magical concept is common coin in Hasidic Judaism. We shall have a bit to say about Hasidic Judaism, albeit briefly, since it impinges upon our current subject-matter, and also because there appears to be somewhat of a discrepancy respecting the origins of this particular branch of Judaism.

According to some sources, Hasidic Judaism is a fairly recent phenomenon, emerging as recently as the eighteenth century: "Hasidism is a relatively young religious phenomenon, spanning the mid-eighteenth century to the present."[6] With all due respect to Mr. Mintz, he is wrong on this point. And this can definitely be proven from ancient texts. We have seen that Mead referred to James the Just as a "Chassid"[7] and he also refers to Simeon ben Azzai, who lived at the end of the first century and the beginning of the second, as a "Chassid".[8] It should be fairly evident that the term "Chassid" is essentially the same Hebrew root-word as

---

3   John 10:25.

4   John 5:43.

5   Matthew 12:24; Mark 3:22.

6   Mintz, Jerome R., *HASIDIC PEOPLE: A Place in the New World.* (1992: Harvard University Press; Cambridge, Massachusetts); pg. 9.

7   Mead., op. cit., pg. 225.

8   Ibid., pg. 153.

"Hasid", from which we get "Hasidic" Judaism. In fact, Hasidic Judaism originated as far back as the second century B.C. Indeed, even some critical biblical scholars of the 19th century postulated that the book of Daniel was written by a "Chasid". Of course in my theory James is a real brother of Jesus, and as such, would have lived in the first century B.C., if Jesus himself lived at that time, as advocated herein. In terms of this discrepancy between the information presented by Mr. Mead and that presented by Mr. Mintz, Mead is here provably correct. There is a document dating from the first century B.C., which proves that there were Hasidic Jews as early as the second century B.C. The document in question is the scroll of the first book of Maccabees. Therein it is written:

12 Then did there assemble unto Alcimus and Bacchides a company of scribes, to require justice.

13 Now the Assideans (Greek: *Asidaioi*[9]) were the first among the sons of Israel that sought peace from them:

14 For they said, A man that is a priest of the seed of Aaron has come with this army, and he will not do us evil.

15 So he spoke to them peaceably, and swore unto them, saying, We will procure the harm neither of you nor your friends.

16 Whereupon they believed him; howbeit he took of them sixty men, and killed them in one day (I Maccabees 7:12-16)

Clearly the Assideans (*Asidaioi* in Greek) are none other than Hassideans, or Chassids, otherwise also known as Hasids or Hasidic Jews; it is the very same root-word in each instance. The term Hasidic is linked to the idea of piety and purity. Those who claim a recent origin for Hasidic Judaism trace it back to Israel ben Eliezer, otherwise also known as the Baal Shem Tov (Master of the Good Name), who lived from 1700 to 1760, a pious healer and miracle worker who lived in the Ukrainian regions of Podolia and Volhynia.[10] Although he clearly was the most

---

9   SEPTUAGINTA., op. cit., pg. 1064. (vol. 1; duo volumina in uno).
10   Mintz., op. cit., pg. 9.

prominent leader of the contemporary expression of Hasidic Judaism, he nevertheless clearly had theological predecessors. But bearing the title of Baal Shem Tov evokes precisely the magical attitude towards the Shemhamphorasch found in the Toldoth Jeschu. Indeed, this is another form of evidence that Hasidic Judaism predates the 1700s. The very same attitude respecting the magical power of names is also shared by many Ethiopian Christians.[11] One possible reason for more contemporary Hasidic Jews to seek to disassociate themselves from the aforementioned Assideans is that, in the passage in Makkabees, they are not exactly cast in a very favourable light. One possible reason for this is that I Makkabees is most likely a Sadducean work; therefore it would portray their theological rivals in unfavourable terms. By contrast, II Makkabees is generally thought to be a Pharisaic work, and in that narrative the incident in question is omitted. But the Assideans are nevertheless also mentioned in II Makkabees, and in that book are not only presented in a favourable light, but are even identified with the hero of the epic:

6 Those of the Jews that be called Assideans (Greek: *Asidaioi*[12]), whose captain is Judas Maccabeus (Greek: *Makkabaios*[13]), nourish war, and are seditious, and will not let the realm be in peace. (II Maccabees 14:6)

Although this verse, taken in isolation, may appear to portray Judas Maccabaeus in an unfavourable light, the context proves the opposite. The context is that a renegade high priest named Alcimus who saw that Judas prevailed against the Greeks and Syrians, gave false counsel to King Demetrius, bribing him with a crown of gold and other gifts, and seeking to turn the king against Judas. So the context of this work, which is completely distinct from the other book of the Maccabees, presents the Assideans or Hasids in a favourable light. Possibly there was some degree of revisionism in II Maccabees, in the sense that the legacy of the Maccabees was co-opted by this religious movement, by claiming them as religious predecessors. On the other hand, the evidence is such that

11 See Budge, E.A. Wallis., *BANDLET OF RIGHTEOUSNESS: AN ETHIOPIAN BOOK OF THE DEAD.* (1929: London: LUZAC & CO. 46 Great Russell Street, W.C.); this is available @ www.kessinger.net.
12 SEPTUAGINTA., op. cit., pg. 1134. (vol. 1; duo volumina in uno).
13 Ibid.

there is a fairly strong presumption that historically Judas Maccabaeus and his brothers may very well have been Assideans, since it was John Hyrcanus who, according to Josephus, abandoned Pharisaic Judaism and embraced Sadducean Judaism.[14] Therefore if the Assideans were originally a branch sprung from Pharisaic Judaism (and all the relevant evidence seems to support this view), then the evidence from Josephus and the books of the Maccabees actually dovetail together nicely to confirm the supposition that the brothers Maccabee were indeed Assideans or Hasids. There is no reason to doubt the statement of II Maccabees 14:6 to that effect. As far as the passage from I Maccabees 7:12-16, it speaks only of one man from among the Assideans who became a traitor; this hardly proves that they were all bad; even Jesus had his Judas, and the American Revolutionaries their Benedict Arnold. Furthermore the Alcimus in both passages is apparently the same man; therefore the two accounts, rather than being mutually contradictory, seem instead to be complementary.

But men who are leaders among contemporary Hasidic Jews are called *Rebbes,* and are esteemed as healers and wonder-workers.[15] In this respect they are similar to the *Minim,* otherwise also known as *Notzrim* or *Ebionim.* Likewise, in the New Testament, Jesus and his disciples are alleged to have performed many miracles, especially miraculous healings.[16] Recall also that miracles were attributed to Sabbatai Zevi, even in his own lifetime.

In the Toldoth Jeschu, Jesus (Jeschu) is said to have performed his marvels by means of the Shem, the secret Name of God. As stated above, this could not have been the four-letter Divine Name, otherwise also known as the Tetragrammaton. Anyone reading one of the Hebrew Torah scrolls, or any of the Hebrew scrolls of *TaNaKh,* could easily discover that

14   Jos. Ant. 13.10.5-6.

15   Mintz., op. cit.

16   John 2:11,23; 3:2; 4:46-54; 5:36; :2,26; 7:31; 9:3,16; 10:25,38; 11:47; 12:37; 14:10-12; 15:24; 20:30-31; Matthew 4:23-24; 8:1-15; 9:18-30; 11:2,20-23; 13:54-58; 14:2; Mark 1:40-44; 6:2,14; 8:1-9,22-26; Luke 4:36; 5:12-14; 9:1; 10:13,19; 19:37; Acts 2:22,43; 4:30; 5:12; 6:8; 8:6,13; 10:38; 14:3; 15:12; 19:11-12; Romans 15:19; 1 Corinthians 12:10; 14:22; 2 Corinthians 12:12; Hebrews 2:4; 6:5.

name. Indeed, the Israelites did not always have a superstitious fear of pronouncing that name; they are told to "call upon the name of YHWH" (Joel 2:32) for deliverance/salvation. This Name was neither secret, nor would anyone easily forget the sequence of only four letters, two of which are the same. Some might say that it was the vowels which were secret, which would also be absent from the unpointed Hebrew Scrolls of *TaNaKh*, leaving the true pronunciation of the Name a secret. But the Toldoth speaks of the letters of the Name being secret. So it seems to denote instead the 72-letter secret Name of God, otherwise called the *Shemhamphorasch*. In the Toldoth, Jeschu is said to have discovered the Shem in the Holy of Holies in the Temple, and wrote down the Shem on parchment, secretly placed it inside his hip, and thereafter performed miracles by means of the Shem. The same secret name was also the source of Juda Ischariota's marvellous power to fly in the air. And, although it is not explicitly stated in the Toldoth, presumably this was also the secret source of magical[17] power used by Elijahu, whom Christians call Paul.[18] Presumably the Jerusalem temple was where Jeschu allegedly learned the letters of the *Shemhamphorasch*, since the *Toldoth* speaks of a great foundation-stone in that temple, which is notably present as the famed *Shettiya* underneath the Dome of the Rock in Jerusalem.[19] This *Shettiya* lies underneath the Dome of the Rock, which is located on the famous Temple Mount, a place greatly disputed by Jews and Muslims; the spot is known as the Noble Sanctuary to Muslims, being a very sacred site in Islam, where the Prophet Mohammed began his legendary Night Journey.[20] Jews also claim the site as a sacred spot in Judaism, since it is the place where Solomon had built the legendary first temple.[21]

---

17   Magical or miraculous; as far as I am concerned, the terms are functionally synonymous; the mere difference being the attribution to either divine or diabolical agency, according to one's religious prejudices. Magical or miraculous in this sense denoting the presence of the supernatural or paranormal.

18   Romans 15:19; 2 Corinthians 12:12 cf Toldoth Jeschu 10.

19   See Hancock, Graham., *THE SIGN AND THE SEAL.* (©1992 by Graham Hancock) (New York: Crown Publishers; TOUCHSTONE; Simon & Schuster: 201 East 50th Street, New York, NY).

20   The same site also contains the famed Mosque of Omar.

21   However archaeological evidence is not congenial to the historicity of any such temple, or even of Solomon or David. Critical scholars are now advocating a radical revision of the early history of Israel, based upon archaeological evidence.

The postexilic Jews rebuilt the temple on the same site, which was later embellished by Herod.[22] Today most Jews and also millions of Zionist Christians sincerely believe that the Wailing Wall is the remnant of that same temple. However this is almost certainly not the case. There are two things that strongly militate against this common and fond misconception. First is the express declaration by none other than Jesus himself that "not one stone shall be left upon a stone"[23] among all those illustrious buildings, in what is sometimes fondly referred to as "the Little Apocalypse". Christians typically point to the destruction of the Jerusalem temple as an instance of fulfilled prophecy, whereas by contrast critical scholars postulate a post-70 A.D. date for the composition of the Synoptic Gospels, to account for the phenomenon. But if the Wailing Wall is indeed a remnant of that Herodian temple, then where is the fulfillment of prophecy? It would still be pending. In fact, if the Wailing Wall truly is a remnant of the Jewish temple, then this would actually point to a pre-70 A.D. point of origin for at least one of the Synoptic Gospels,[24] if not for all three. Because otherwise we would not expect a post-diction containing such a precise and spectacular detail of non-fulfillment. The relevant evidence suggests instead that, most likely, all three Synoptic Gospels post-date the destruction of the temple in 70 A.D., and everyone knew that literally not one stone had been left upon another by the Romans. It is only in comparatively recent times that the belief that the Wailing Wall is a remnant of the Herodian temple has taken root among some Christians and Jews. The Chief Sephardi Rabbi has expressed doubts that the Wailing Wall is truly a remnant of Herod's temple.[25] And we can be reasonably certain that it definitely is not, based not only upon Christ's clear declaration that "not one stone shall be left upon a stone" of that temple-complex, but also because the Romans not only completely demolished Jerusalem, but they also built a temple to Jupiter there. In 131 A.D., the emperor Hadrian rebuilt Jerusalem, giving it the name of Aelia Capitolina, and placed it under the jurisdiction of Caesarea. He also erected a temple to Jupiter, and even

22   John 2:20.
23   Mt 24:2; Mk 13:2; Lk 21:6, according to the original Greek.
24   From which presumably the other two Gospels would have copied the Little Apocalypse.
25   Hancock., op. cit., pg. 388.

placed his own image in it, and commanded it to be worshipped.[26] In fact this is exactly the event that sparked the abortive Bar Kochbah uprising. After that rebellion was brutally crushed by the merciless Romans, all Jews were expelled from Jerusalem on pain of death. Even if the original Herodian temple had not already been destroyed completely in 70 A.D., it surely would have been by 135 A.D., or the year following. But in fact even before this, the temple to Jupiter had been built upon the very spot where the previous temple had stood. This was no doubt a great affront to the Jews, and even the Jewish Christian followers of the messianic movement may have interpreted this sacrilege as the very "abomination of desolation" spoken of by Daniel and Jesus.[27] Of course the only thing that doesn't fit is the timing of this event; in Daniel's prophecy, this was to take place within the time of the seventy weeks, or at the culmination of that period whereas this would be an anachronism, unless a person were using a different system of computation, such as those Jews who embraced Bar Kochbah as the Messiah. Once again we can see in this the rationale for the falsification of chronology vis-à-vis the prophecy of the seventy weeks, spoken of earlier, by the forged documents known as Ezra and Nehemiah. Hopefully the complete picture is now beginning to come into clearer focus. By substituting Artaxerxes for Xerxes in those texts, certain Jews could thereby justify latter-day messianic pretenders, up until the very time of Bar Kochbah. Without specifying which Artaxerxes, it became possible to make a false pretence that it was the later king, namely Artaxerxes Mnemon, who was the one spoken of therein, thereby justifying an even later *terminus ad quem* for Daniel's prophecy of the seventy weeks. By the very same token, the prophecy could thus be interpreted as being fulfilled in those very days, by the blasphemous and idolatrous Roman Emperor, who pompously had his own image placed in the temple to be worshipped. Interestingly however, this also evokes images from the Apocalypse, such as the great wild beast

---

26   Del Mar, Alexander., *THE WORSHIP OF AUGUSTUS CAESAR.*, (New York: 1900); reprinted by Kessinger Publishers. Available @ www.kessinger.net.; pg. 191 cf Dudley, Dean., *HISTORY OF THE FIRST COUNCIL OF NICE.* (A&B Publishers Group: Brooklyn, New York [NY] 11238; ISBN: 1-881316-03-3); pg. 89.

27   Daniel 9:27; Matthew 24:15; Mark 13:14.

and his image, which came to life.[28] Caligula also had a desire to have his image placed in the Jerusalem temple to be worshipped, but this travesty was averted.[29] The purport of all the above is that, most likely, the Wailing Wall, at which so many devout Orthodox Jews pray to God daily, is the remains, not of the Jewish temple, but of the Roman temple to Jupiter.

---

28 Revelation 13.
29 Jos. Ant. 18.8.1-9; War 2.10.1-5.

Talmud

Now we must proceed to consider the chronological evidence from the Talmud in favour of an earlier date for Jesus. But first we should learn a little bit about the Talmud. The Talmud is much more copious than TaNaKh; it is very voluminous, and could easily require years and even decades of study, to become fully acquainted with it. Just as the Torah is the foundation of TaNaKh, so the Mishnah is the foundation of the Talmud. The Mishnah, as an oral tradition, was in formation probably even from soon after the return of the Jews from Babylon to their native land. The final, written codification of the Mishnah did not occur until approximately the dawn of the third century C.E., under Rabbi Judah the Prince. He was the last of the great *Tannaim*, the compilers of the Mishnah. Rabbi Adin Steinsaltz has the following to say of the relationship between the Mishnah and the Talmud:

"The Mishnah is the foundation of the Talmud, and the Talmud is first of all an explanation and expansion of the Mishnah. It is organized around the Mishnah, interpreting and analyzing it. But the Mishnah's relationship to the Talmud is not merely organizational. The Mishnah is not just the text of which the Talmud is the commentary. The Mishnah provides the Talmud with both its conceptual and its factual foundation. All the provisions and laws in the Talmud are laid down in accordance with the Mishnah. Every Halakha has a source- and this source is generally the Mishnah. In every discussion or argument, there are factors that determine its correctness- and these, too, are found in the Mishnah."[1]

We can thus see from this how greatly and fundamentally important the Mishnah is in relation to the entire Talmud. We can also see somewhat of a distinction between the Mishnah and the Talmud; I had always thought that the Mishnah and Gemara were simply different parts of the Talmud. In a general sense this is true, but there is also a distinction. Rabbi Steinsaltz continues:

"The Talmud accepts the contents of the Mishnah as incontrovertible facts. The Talmud can find interrelationships and connections among the subjects, it can draw attention to problems, it can reconcile apparent contradictions- but it cannot disagree with the Mishnah. The Talmud looks to the Mishnah as the source for the certainty of its findings. The Mishnah serves as the ultimate arbiter of every problem and provides final proof for every assertion or theory. This special authority is not accorded solely to the Mishnah, but also to the other collections of the statements of the Tannaim- the Tosefta, Baraitot, Sifra, Sifrei, and other Halakhic Midrashim. All these provide the Talmud with primary source material to be scrutinized carefully and applied to the search for the solution of problems."[2]

So we can see from these passages that there is a distinction between the Mishnah and the Talmud. Rabbi Steinsaltz had earlier made such a distinction, when he wrote the following:

"The Mishnah (the scholars of which are called Tannaim) is written in a precise and very terse Hebrew style, presenting complex subject matter in concise form. Although the text of the Mishnah is itself usually clear, it does not cover every possible case, and many problems and questions arise whose solution cannot be found in the wording of the Mishnah alone. For three centuries (c. 200 C.E.-500 C.E.) after the

1   Steinsaltz, Adin {Rabbi}., *THE TALMUD. (THE STEINSALTZ EDI-TION)*; Rabbi Israel V. Berman, translator and editor. (1989; The Israel Institute for Talmudic Publications and Milta Books) (New York: Random House), pg. 3.
2   Ibid., pgs. 3-4.

compilation and editing of the Mishnah, the Rabbis (called Amoraim) and their students discussed and analyzed the Mishnah. Their questions, discussions, and solutions make up the Talmud."[3]

Although Steinsaltz does not draw attention to the fact, it should not be overlooked that Karaite Jews reject the Mishnah, the Tosephta, the Baraitoth, the Siphra, the Siphrei, and all the Halakhic Midrashim, as well as the Talmud; they hold only to the TaNaKh as sacred. This fact is potentially significant in reference to the fact that Mead alluded to "a distinctly Karaite Toldoth."[4] Unfortunately, without being able to examine an English translation of the text alluded to, I cannot be certain just exactly what Mead had meant by this. But if in this matter I can trust his scholarly judgment,[5] then it implies that the Toldoth Jeschu, or some essential form of it,[6] predates the Talmud, and possibly even the Mishnah. But if it is true indeed that Karaite Jews also shared a basic form of the Toldoth in common with Orthodox Jews, then this would point to a pre-Talmudic, if not a pre-Mishnaic, text or tradition.

A *midrash* (plural: *midrashim*) is an embellishment and expansion upon an earlier story; often with the intent to justify some new doctrine. A *halakha* (plural: *halakhoth*; also *halacha* and *halachoth*) is a practical law, as distinguished from *aggadah* or *haggadah*, which is an allegory. For example, in Galatians 4:21-31, "Paul" uses *haggadah* to justify his argument against circumcision; whereas the statement attributed to Jesus in Mark 7:15 is used as a *halakha* to justify the abrogation of a *kosher* diet. Of course such arguments would be rejected by the Mishnah and the Talmud; but these are illustrations of the principles. It is arguable that the account of Christ's temptation in the wilderness, as recorded in Matthew and Luke, are *midrashim* upon Mark's more concise record of that tradition in his Gospel.

But the Orthodox Rabbis consider the study of the Talmud to be the study of the Torah in the greater, more encompassing, sense. To them,

---

3 Ibid., pg. 2.
4 Mead., op. cit., pg. 316.
5 However, see chapter below on Mead's errors. This places his judgment on such matters in grave doubt.
6 Including possibly an oral tradition.

the Talmud clarifies the Torah. The voluminous quantity and intricate complexity of such Talmudic studies could easily justify decades of study, just to even "scratch the surface", as it were. The Talmud is essential to Rabbinical Judaism. It could be said that the Talmud makes explicit that which is implicit within the Torah. And, despite the fact that both the Mishnah and the Talmud developed for the most part after the destruction of the Jerusalem Temple by the Romans, when blood sacrifices could no longer be offered as a cleansing for sin, the Talmud is definitely aligned with the priestly tradition.[7]

According to Adin Steinsaltz, there are sixty tractates in the Mishnah, according to tradition. These tractates are grouped into six major sections, called orders.[8] He qualifies this by saying "However, the accepted division comprises sixty-three tractates. Three of them, *Bava Kamma, Bava Metzia,* and *Bava Batra* ("The First Gate," "The Middle Gate," and "The Last Gate"), are really the three parts of a large tractate called *Nezekin* ("Damages"), and the tractate *Makkot [Makkoth]* ("Lashes"), seems to have been a continuation of tractate *Sanhedrin*."[9] However, even counting the three tractates mentioned as parts of *Nezekin* as only one tractate, and counting *Makkoth* and *Sanhedrin* as only one tractate, I still counted sixty-five tractates, excluding the so-called "Minor Tractates", of which there are fifteen.[10] Interestingly, the tractate *Nezekin* is mentioned in the version of the Toldoth Jeschu found in Mead's book.[11] The Toldoth Jeschu presented above is essentially a reproduction of what is found in Mead's book; however all of the notes and the commentary are mine alone.[12]

There is a Jerusalem Talmud, and a Babylonian Talmud. The latter is more popular and more commonly used by Orthodox Jews. Rabbi Steinsaltz has this to say of the two Talmuds: "Both the Babylonian Talmud and the Jerusalem Talmud contain Gemara text on many, but

---

7   As opposed to the prophetic, or Ebionite, tradition, which was in opposition to all such blood sacrifices.

8   Steinsaltz., op. cit., pg. 37.

9   Ibid.

10   Ibid., pgs. 38-47.

11   Mead., op. cit., pg. 260.

12   I have also made a few emendations to the text, where warranted.

by no means all, of the tractates of the Mishnah. Some tractates appear with Gemara in both compilations of the Talmud, others appear with Gemara in one but not the other, and some have no Gemara in either."[13] He also writes: "In general, within an order, the tractate with the most chapters is placed first and the tractate with the fewest chapters comes last."[14] In other words, all other things being equal, the longest tractate within a given order is placed first, and the shortest being placed last. Interestingly, within the New Testament codex, the Pauline epistles are placed in the very same system of order. The same is also true of the Suras of the Koran. A study of the Koran reveals an overwhelmingly strong Talmudic influence.

Later on, Steinsaltz makes this admission in respect to the Talmud: "The Talmud was also subjected to government and church censorship, and most present-day editions still contain a considerable number of changes and omissions introduced by censorship. Indeed, almost every passage dealing with non-Jews must be suspected of having undergone some change."[15] It will be important to keep this in mind later, as we discuss some controversial traditions of the Jews. Steinsaltz also admits that there are manuscript variants of the Talmud: "It should also be noted that there are important variant manuscripts of the Talmud (among the most famous being the Munich manuscript [1334] of the entire Talmud), in which one occasionally finds illuminating variant readings."[16]

This brief introduction to the Talmud was necessary, since it impinges upon our subject-matter in some important ways, as we will see hereafter. So we will be discussing the Talmud in relation to the Toldoth Jeschu. But for now perhaps the most important point relevant to our central thesis concerns the fact that Simeon ben Shetach, who is mentioned as a contemporary of both Miriam and Jeschu (Mary and Jesus), was, according to Rabbinic tradition, also a contemporary of Alexander Jannaeus, otherwise also known as Alexander Jannai or Alexander

---

13   Steinsaltz., op. cit., pg. 37.
14   Ibid.
15   Ibid., pg. 50.
16   Ibid.

Yannai.[17] G.R.S. Mead also brings forward arguments in favor of the 100 B.C. date in the Toldoth, although his points are often obscure and complex.[18]

Jesus is often called "Ben Pandera" or "Jeschu Ben Pandera" in Jewish tradition. The appellation occurs frequently in the Talmud. And in the Toldoth Jeschu, it is Joseph Ben Pandera who is the real, biological father of Jeschu. It is curious that three of the four New Testament Gospels preserve the name Joseph as the father of Jesus, at least in the legal and nominal sense (Mark does not mention Joseph). As mentioned above, the Jews have a tradition of two Messiahs, one of whom is called the Son of Joseph.[19]

Jesus is of course most highly esteemed, beloved, and exalted among Christians; to them he is the very Son of God, the Lamb of God, the Word of God, the Wisdom of God, and the Image of the invisible God. In normative Christianity Jesus is regarded as God the Son, equal to God the Father. But in Judaic tradition Jesus is regarded as a notorious false prophet, an evil sorcerer, a deceiver, and an arch-villain. Only in Mandaean tradition is Jesus vilified in a similar manner. Most other traditions, if they speak of Jesus at all, at least esteem him as a holy prophet, a healer of the sick, or a wise philosopher. Unfortunately, even in our so-called "enlightened" society, most people have instinctively placed Jesus upon a pedestal of untouchable sacro-sanctity, and this makes it very difficult to proceed with any genuine historical inquiry into the true nature, character, teachings, or circumstances of the original, historical Jesus, without fear of some degree of societal censure or reactionary backlash from fundamentalists or the gatekeepers of cultural conservatism. Nevertheless we bravely pursue our inquiry unimpeded by the protests of *ignoramus neanderthalensis*. Some of the material we have yet to cover, and which we have already covered in our study of the Toldoth Jeschu, may appear somewhat prejudicial to the vested interests

---

17   Ibid., pg. 31.

18   Mead., op. cit., pgs. 135-151; 302-323.

19   Eisenmenger., op. cit., pg. 701. The term most likely refers to descent from the tribe of Joseph.

of certain ethnic or religious groups,[20] yet we nevertheless bravely proceed with our inquiry in the face of implicit censorship by those misguided by pseudo-political correctness. But if we are to proceed thus unimpeded in our inquiry, we must at least acknowledge that certain sensibilities may be offended by some of the material to be presented.[21] But unless plain language can be used herein, we would be so constrained that we would be hidebound by a constant recourse to widely circuitous circumlocutions of expression that would burden this work with a bulk and awkwardness of diction that ought to be obsolete in the postmodern era. Therefore we shall proceed without further ado.

Jews sometimes refer to Christians, and especially Roman Catholics, as Edomites. This is definitely not a compliment. The Edomites are cursed in TaNaKh as enemies of God and his people.[22] Edom is the same as Esau; Esau the brother of Jacob acquired the name of Edom (which means red in Hebrew) because he sold his birthright to Jacob for some red soup.[23] One reason why the Jews call Christians, and particularly Roman Catholics, Edomites, is because red is such a prominent color in Roman Catholicism. Cardinals of the Catholic Church traditionally wear red robes. Red was also a prominent color in the Roman Empire, and since the Roman Catholic Church became the official religion of that Empire, and also ruthlessly persecuted Jews, the Jews have always ever since thought of the Roman Catholic Church as a continuation of the Roman Empire. The Holy Roman Empire was certainly under Papal dominion. And even some Protestant authors have pointed out the paganization of Christianity within Roman Catholicism as "Mystery Babylon."[24] But there is also a deeper reason why the Jews call Christians Edomites. It is found in the traditions of the Talmud.

---

20   I.e., Jews.

21   And by what has already been presented in the Toldoth Jeschu, namely that Jesus was a bastard and a son of a whore, etc.

22   Ezekiel 25:14; Joel 3:19; Amos 1:11; Obadiah; Malachi 1:4; Psalm 137:7-9; Lamentations 4:21-22.

23   Genesis 25:29-34.

24   Woodrow, Ralph., *BABYLON MYSTERY RELIGION.* (1966; Ralph Woodrow Evangelistic Association, Inc.) 1992. ISBN: 0-916938-00-X (Ralph Woodrow, P.O. Box 124, Riverside, CALIFORNIA 92502). See also: *THE TWO BABYLONS.*, by Alexander Hislop. (1853; 1859) (New York: Loizeaux

"Why the Christians, in the Writings of the *Jews,* are denominated from *Edom* or *Esau,* may be seen in the Talmudic Lexicon, and the Dissertation of *Abarbenel.* We shall only say thus much of it here, that in the private Books of the *Jews,* which fall not easily into the Hands of Christians, it is said that the Soul of *Esau* pas'd into *Christ;* and that *Christ* was therefore as bad as *Esau;* and that we, who believe in him, and whom they therefore call *Esau* and *Edomites,* are no better."[25]

This quotation, taken from the *Traditions of the Jews,* by Johann Andreas Eisenmenger, reveals quite a lot about the attitude traditionally held by Jews of both Christ and Christians. And it should be carefully noted that Eisenmenger had access to an edition of the Talmud older than that used by Rabbi Adin Steinsaltz. And it would also be wise to recall Rabbi Steinsaltz' concessions respecting those passages of the Talmud that speak of non-Jews being subject to revision and alteration, for various reasons. Interestingly also is the fact that the Jews held a belief in some form of reincarnation, as the passage above proves. Indeed, there is a rather lengthy section devoted to the subject of transmigration in the same book.[26] This doctrine of transmigration or reincarnation is known as *Gilgul,* or *Gilgulim,* meaning "rolling" or "rollings", in the sense of revolutions of the soul. When I was a college student some of the Jewish students had confided to me that they believed in reincarnation, but at that time I did not suspect that it was any part of traditional Jewish beliefs. But we can also find the concept of reincarnation in Josephus' works.[27] According to Josephus, it was the Pharisees who believed in reincarnation. So from this evidence we can discern that at least some Jews held a belief in some form of transmigration or reincarnation as far back as the first century. And it was apparently sometime after the abortive Bar Kochbah uprising that the Rabbis incorporated transmigration into

Brothers. (or A&B publishers).; *ROMANISM AND THE GOSPEL.,* by C. Anderson Scott. (Philadelphia: Westminster: 1946).; *THE WINE OF ROMAN BABYLON.,* by Mary E. Walsh. (Nashville: Southern Publishing Association, 1945).; *FIFTY YEARS IN THE CHURCH OF ROME.,* by Charles Chiniquy. (New York: Christ's Mission; 1885; 1953).; *BABYLON THE GREAT HAS FALLEN.,* Watchtower Bible and Tract Society. (New York: 1963).

25   Eisenmenger., op. cit., pg. 755.
26   Ibid., pgs. 441-503.
27   Jos. War. 2.8.14.

calculations respecting when the Messiah was to come. This only makes sense in view of the fact that after that time, Daniel's prophecy of the seventy weeks was no longer of any use to them, since the time indicated by the prophecy would already have long passed, even with the notorious chronological juggling afforded by such forged documents as Ezra and Nehemiah. Therefore the demotion of Daniel from a place in *Nehevim* to one in *Kethuvim* thereafter became inevitable.[28]

It is debatable just when, where and how the Jews acquired a belief in transmigration. It may have been due to Greek influence, although most Greeks did not believe in reincarnation, but rather a handful of Greek philosophers, who apparently acquired the belief from Indian sources. But it is also at least possible that the belief may have come from Buddhist missionaries, who lived in various Middle eastern cities even for several centuries before the Common era. In this connection it should also be noted that some have speculated that the Essenes also believed in reincarnation, and that some of their beliefs were very similar to those of the Druids, who reportedly also held a belief in reincarnation. Alexandria was a very cosmopolitan city, swarming with a variety of cults and mystery schools. So there can be no doubt that there was a vigorous cross-fertilization of ideas all through that era and area.

There can be no doubt that the Jews have called Jesus a "bastard" and a "son of a whore"; this arose as a response to claims of his having been miraculously conceived in the womb of a virgin, and thus born of a virgin. In Zoroastrianism there are said to be a series of virgin-born saviors; and there is no doubt that Zoroastrianism has had a strong influence upon both Christianity and pre-Christian Judaism. Indeed, one suspects that the hints of Zoroastrianism to be found in the New Testament may be due more to traditions arising from pre-Christian Judaism. Rabbi Steinsaltz tries to downplay the influence of Persian religion upon Judaism:

"With regard to the Persians and their religion, we find that in general the Rabbis avoided debates with them, and only rarely is it possible to

---

28   Although I personally believe that this took place in the early third century, or later.

find references, sometimes critical, to the dualistic religion of the Persians and other related matters. From time to time the Persian priestly sect did indeed interfere with the lives of the Jews. But apart from periods of religious persecution, even this contact was limited and unimportant. The Jewish scholars possessed superficial knowledge of Babylonian and Persian customs, and of the customs and beliefs of those Arabian tribes which reached certain regions of Babylonia- but in no area can their influence be detected in any substantial way."[29]

Despite what Rabbi Steinsaltz has written here, a very strong Persian influence is discernible in portions of TaNaKh, most notably in the books of Daniel and Ezekiel. In all fairness, however, most likely Steinsaltz is referring to a period long after there had already been a strong impact upon Judaism from both Persian and Greek sources. The damage had already been done long before the codification of the Mishnah, to say nothing of the Gemara and latter portions of the Talmud.

But the accusation of illegitimacy in respect to Christ's paternity most likely arose as a reaction against claims of his being the Son of God in the most literal sense possible. We cannot be sure just when such claims were first made for him, but it most likely was long after his own lifetime. Even the New Testament preserves a faint memory of what may be called a pre-virgin birth tradition, for want of a better term. In other words, the virgin birth was not an original part of the Gospel message, but was rather the penultimate conclusion in a chain of logic reaching back to the original messianic claims. One can discern a sequence of exaltation of the presumed ontological status of Jeschu/Jesus in the minds of his disciples: first, he was the Messiah, the Son of man; therefore he was also the Son of God. But being the Son of God could be interpreted variously, from mere adoptionism, to a more exalted, pre-existent status as a celestial, arch-angelic or aeonian being; on up to being the Son of God in the literal sense of having been born of a virgin; but the ultimate apotheosis of Jeschu/Jesus was him being enthroned as God the Son, upon full equality with God. Of course this was not officially sanctioned until the Council of Nicaea in 325 C.E., and even after that there were still some dissenting voices in Christendom: but it had, for all intents

29   Steinsaltz., op. cit., pg. 16.

and purposes, become a *fait accompli*. However if we assume that the thesis herein is correct, with the corresponding corollary that the New Testament Gospels were probably not written until either very late in the first century, or more likely, early in the second century, then this certainly allows for a great length of time for legends and traditions to spring up around the beloved Messiah, until he virtually became an Archetype. Thus the legend of Jesus became larger than life. And if latter-day devotees of Sabbatai Zevi could lavish so much unabashed praise upon him, even within the cultural context of such a vehemently monotheistic form of Judaism, then it is even more understandable that those who had embraced the Messianic claims of Jesus, either in his own generation, or in subsequent generations, would thereby exalt him to such a superhuman status as to almost rival the Godhead.[30]

Considering the dark veil of obscurity surrounding Jesus, particularly if we assume that our primary thesis is correct, and that he lived a full century earlier than the time alleged according to canonical Christianity, it is difficult to discern exactly where and when and how such progressive stages in his deification took place historically. But it is more believable, at least in a general sense, that a man could thus be deified, if we grant a century longer to the process. It is also debatable just how much of this deification may have been due to Greco-Roman cultural influence, or whether the seeds of such were latent within Judaism itself.

But returning to the question of allegations of illegitimacy of Jesus, made by the Jews, there can be no doubt at all that such accusations were made; and we can be reasonably certain as well that those accusations were made in response to claims of the virgin birth of Jeschu/Jesus, with all that that implied: possibly even that he was a rival to the Godhead. This would have been heresy, apostasy, and blasphemy to most of the Jews. It would have been a violation of their most sacred commandment against giving an equal to God.[31] And even in the New Testament we can see

---

30   We ought to keep in mind the various heretical forms of Judaism rampant during that time, as well as the influence of mystery religions and Greek philosophy upon the movement.

31   Deuteronomy 6:4-5 cf Exodus 20:2-5; Deuteronomy 5:6-10.

that the Jews so understood the claims of Christians respecting Jesus.[32] And this despite clarifications to the contrary placed in the very lips of Jesus himself.[33] And as we will soon see, even by the latter half of the second century (when the New Testament texts were written according to my interpretation) there was already a raging dispute between Jews and Christians respecting Christ's paternity. Mead has this to say of the matter:

"For instance, the Christ (said the mystics) was born of a "virgin"; the unwitting believer in Jesus as *the* historical Messiah in the exclusive Jewish sense, and in his being *the* Son of God, nay God himself, in course of time asserted that Mary was that virgin; whereupon Rabbinical logic, which in this case was simple and common logic, met this extravagance by the natural retort that, seeing that his paternity was unacknowledged, Jesus was therefore illegitimate, a bastard (*mamzer*). Round this point there naturally raged the fiercest controversy, or rather it was met with the most contemptuous retorts, which must have broken out the instant the virginity of Mary as a physical fact was publicly mooted by the simple believers of the general Christian body. This particular dogma, however, must have been a comparatively late development in the evolution of popular Christianity, for the "common document" knows nothing of it, the writers of the second and fourth Gospels tacitly reject it, while some of the earliest readings of our Gospels distinctly assert that Joseph was the natural father of Jesus. For the *mamzer* element in the Talmud stories, therefore, we have, in my opinion, no need to go back further than the first quarter of the second century or so as the earliest *terminus a quo.*"[34]

Although Mead does seem to make a reasonably valid point here, I have a few reservations respecting exactly what he said here. First of all, I am not necessarily in agreement that it was as late as the first quarter of the second century when there were accusations of illegitimacy in respect to Christ's birth, particularly if we are to view Jesus as having been born about a century before the commonly-accepted time. Mead may

---

32   John 5:18; 10:30-33.
33   John 5:19; 10:34-36.
34   Mead., op. cit., pgs. 120-121.

be correct in surmising that such accusations were merely a response to the claims of a virgin birth, but here once again, Mead's scholarship is highly questionable, since he seems blithely oblivious to the prophecy that the Messiah would be born to a virgin.[35] The Greek translation of Isaiah was no doubt extant in the days of Queen Alexandra, and therefore a man claiming to be the Messiah of biblical prophecy could have been well understood as also implicitly claiming birth from a virgin. And in this connection, it is worth noting that, if Jesus, his family, and his earliest disciples were Greek-speaking Egyptian Jews, then they no doubt would have used the Greek texts of Isaiah, Daniel, and the other prophets. Secondly, Mead here protests too much. He claims that the second and fourth Gospels "tacitly reject" any such claim to virgin birth[36] but this is very far from proven; Mark omits any mention of a virgin birth, and so does John; but John's declaration that "the Word became flesh"[37] seems to implicitly endorse the virgin birth of Christ. It is true that some early readings found in Luke are more in accord with a strictly human paternity for Jesus, but these same readings are scornfully rejected as corruptions of the text by fundamentalists.[38] Mead also speaks here of a "common document" which today is more commonly called "Q"; formerly such hypothetical texts as the *Logia Kyriou* and the *Testimonia* were spoken of by Bible scholars. But once again, it is far from proven that any such texts ever existed; in fact, it seems much more likely that oral traditions were the basis for the Gospel texts. Not even the smallest fragment of any such hypothetical document has ever been discovered. I suppose that the closest thing so far found along these lines is a small fragment of a text found among the Dead Sea Scrolls,[39] which speaks of one who "will be called the Son of God, *and* they will call

---

35   Isaiah 7:14 (LXX).

36   And therefore divine paternity.

37   John 1:14.

38   Luke 2:33 reads in some copies "his father and mother" rather than the more common "Joseph and his mother"; some early copies of Luke also insert the words from Psalm 2, "This day have I begotten thee" in Luke 3:22, implying a merely "adoptionist" Sonship. But it remains to be seen whether or not these are the genuine original readings of these texts. We must be wary of merely adopting readings that are favourable to our own opinions.

39   4Q246.

him the Son of the Most High" etc., etc. When news of this fragment first leaked out, it stirred rumours of a possible link with the Gospels, especially the Gospel of Luke; but now[40] Scroll scholars interpret the text as most likely speaking of Antiochus Epiphanes, or his son, also called Antiochus; therefore it is now construed as an "antichrist" type of reading.[41] But this opens up another Pandora's Box, inasmuch as it touches upon what appears to be a relatively taboo topic; namely, that we can find, right within the very pages of TaNaKh, a clear teaching that the Messiah was to be born of a virgin, and the Son of God. And here once again we can see Mead's inadequacy to assess the issues with which he sought to deal. He was both naïve and also insufficiently acquainted with the Jewish Scriptures to see that in fact there are references to the Messiah as the Son of God therein. So his "mystical" interpretation of the virgin birth seems to be more the product of his own imagination, rather than of any real evidence. His theosophical prejudices dictated certain fallacious assumptions vis-à-vis Jesus and the alleged virgin birth, which led him down several false paths. But rather than get bogged down in Mead's numerous errors, absurdities, and insipid inanities, I would rather proceed to prove my point.

It has certainly become fashionable to claim that any idea of a virgin birth was necessarily a pagan idea, and had nothing to do with Judaism. But Judaism itself was not entirely untouched by foreign influences. There was a very strong Persian influence upon postexilic Judaism, and later a Greek and even a Roman influence. One can also discern Egyptian, Assyrian, Babylonian, and Canaanite influences. To pretend that Judaism was ever pure and unalloyed with any such foreign influences is to embrace Jewish fundamentalism. Indeed, one can find at least some prophetic basis for such a claim from within TaNaKh:

17 Therefore the Lord himself shall give you a sign: Behold, a maiden shall conceive, and bear a son, and shall call his name *Immanuel.*

(Isaiah 7:14 cp Matthew 1:23 cf Toldoth Jeschu 4)

40   After the entire surviving fragment has been published.
41   Wise, Abegg & Cook., op. cit., pgs. 268-270. Cf Shanks, Hershel., op. cit., pgs. 203-204. It could also refer to Julius Caesar, or his son, Augustus, who were worshipped as Gods by the Romans.

Immanuel in Hebrew means "God is with us".[42] There has long been debate raging between Jews and Christians over whether the Hebrew word *almah*, which I have here simply translated as "maiden" denotes a virgin in the proper sense of *virgo intacta*. Of course Christians claim that it means exactly that, while Jews say that the word does not necessarily denote a virgin woman or girl, but only a young woman or damsel. Therefore I have used the ambiguous word "maiden" which could mean either a virgin or simply a young woman. Possibly the sense was meant to imply rather that the Messiah was to be a firstborn manchild; the importance of the firstborn son was important in Judaism from the very beginning.[43] I realise that in the original context of the verse, the prophecy did not apply to the Messiah as such; but it became a standard practice of *haggadah* to apply two or more levels or layers of interpretation to biblical texts, particularly in respect to the Messiah. But in the Greek Septuagint translation of the verse, the Hebrew word is rendered *parthenos*, the Greek word for virgin.[44] Against this some Jews may argue that the Greek translation is incorrect, having been influenced by pagan Greek ideas; and/or that the text of the Septuagint has been corrupted by Christian scribes, who placed their own favoured reading into the text. Christians might well counter such charges by saying that not only is the Greek text correct, but that the Hebrew Massoretic text has been corrupted by Jewish scribes, who altered the reading from a more precise Hebrew word denoting a virgin, such as *bethulah*, to the more ambiguous *almah*. It is certainly true that the Hebrew Massoretic text has been altered in at least a few places; most notably, Isaiah 19:18 and Zechariah 12:10.[45] So it is not inconceivable that the Jews may have altered the text of Isaiah in this controversial verse, in order to defy the

---

42   Cf Isaiah 8:8,10.

43   Exodus 4:22-23; 13:2.

44   SEPTUAGINTA., op. cit., pg. 575. (vol 2; Duo volumina in uno).

45   The latter of which one can find the original reading of in John 19:37 and also partially in Revelation 1:7. The fact that the New Testament preserves the true original reading of Zechariah 12:10 is proven by the fact that, as the text stands in the Massoretic text of Zechariah, there is an abrupt and unaccountable change from the third to the first person right in the midst of the verse, which makes the reading incoherent and absurd; whereas the genuine reading is in the third person throughout.

Christians. Indeed, it could be argued that the very fact that we find *parthenos* in the Greek text of Isaiah 7:14 proves that the original Hebrew must have been *bethulah*, rather than *almah*.

Furthermore, the Hebrew Scriptures had already been translated into Greek, beginning in the third century B.C. Not only that, but the original time of the prophecy had already long expired,[46] thereby making any further *exegesis* upon it unmistakably *Messianic*. Therefore the prophecy had by now taken on truly *messianic* connotations; therefore the Hebrew translators may very well have deliberately used the Greek word *parthenos* to denote the belief then current that the Messiah was to be born of a virgin. Jews today can deny it and rant and rave against it all they want, but they prove nothing; they certainly prove nothing respecting people who lived so many centuries before their time, who had much different beliefs, customs, and expectations. It may even be argued that *parthenos* or *virgin* is the true meaning of *almah*, according to the very same Greek Septuagint translation. The belief in a virgin-born Messiah may have been due to Persian Zoroastrian influence. The story of the *magi* found in Matthew's Gospel may be an implicit acknowledgment of this influence, although there is also an implicit triumphalism and a shameless attempt to co-opt that tradition in Matthew. The idea of the virgin birth of the Messiah also seems implicit within Genesis 3:15; the fact that the promised Savior is to be the "Seed of the woman" seems to imply an expectation of a virgin birth for that messianic Savior. This very same theme is taken up later in the book of Enoch, which says: "And trouble shall seize them, when they shall behold this <u>Son of woman</u> sitting upon the throne of his glory."[47] This verse is rendered as merely "<u>Son of man</u>" by R.H. Charles, in his translation.[48] Despite the discrepancy

---

46   I.e., within 65 years of the time it was first uttered by Isaiah. Cf Isaiah 7:8,16.

47   Laurence, Richard., (translator)., *THE BOOK OF ENOCH THE PROPHET*. (Also otherwise known as I Enoch or the Ethiopic book of Enoch; translated by Richard Laurence in 1883; available from Adventures Unlimited Press; 2000; LXI:9); pg. 74.

48   Charles, R.H., *THE BOOK OF ENOCH*. (London: 1917; available from The Book Tree, Escondido, CALIFORNIA; 1999; LXX:5 [Charles' edition uses a different numbering system for chapters and verses than what is found in Laurence's edition; this latter numbering system may now be more standard in

of readings, and the unquestionable scholarship of R.H. Charles, I am more inclined to agree with Laurence's rendering of the verse. However, if the thesis herein is correct, and Jesus lived back in Hasmonean times, then he himself would not have known the book of Enoch, since it was not written until the reign of Herod I, as was also the book of Jubilees. Nevertheless there can be no question but that a later generation of followers of Jesus were influenced by these works; witness the quotation from Enoch found in the epistle of Judas.[49]

In any case there can be no real doubt that at least some Jews were expecting a virgin-born Messiah, possibly even in the days of Jesus himself, or even before that time. If so, then any claim to being the Messiah by Jesus would have at least implicitly included a claim to having been born of a virgin. And in the Bible, the idea of the virgin birth seems to be inextricably intertwined with the concept of divine paternity:

6 For unto us a child is born, unto us a son is given: and the government shall be upon his shoulder: and his name shall be called Wonderful Counselor, the Mighty God, Everlasting Father, Prince of Peace;

7 of the increase of his government and peace *there shall be* no end, upon the throne of David, and upon his kingdom, to order it, and to establish it with judgment and with justice from henceforth and forever. The zeal of the GOD of hosts shall accomplish this. (Isaiah 9:6-7)

While it is true that Jewish translations of *TaNaKh* will translate that passage differently, the meaning found above is consistent with what is found in the ancient Greek Septuagint translation.[50] The Latin Vulgate also accords with the Greek reading.[51] This certainly seems to be an expectation of a divine Messiah, right within TaNaKh itself. Of course most Jews today, especially Rabbis, would deny that there was ever any such intended meaning to such a passage. It is fashionable in some circles, notably among Grail authors, to deny that the Jews were ever expecting any kind of divine or even semi-divine Messiah. But an examination

---

biblical scholarship]).; pg. 81.

49 Judas (Jude) 14-15.

50 SEPTUAGINTA., op. cit., pg. 578. (vol. 2; Duo volumina in uno).

51 BIBLIA SACRA VULGATA., op. cit., pg. 1105.

of texts from TaNaKh and from the Old Testament Pseudepigrapha, such as Isaiah and Enoch respectively, reveals that the Jews (or at least <u>some</u> pre-Christian Jews) definitely *were* expecting at least some superhuman messianic figure to emerge and establish the kingdom of God on earth. Of course it is easy to dismiss such passages as merely archaic Eastern exaggerations and extravagant, poetic enthusiasms of the ancient Jews. But if we take this attitude towards the books of TaNaKh simply because they do not accord with contemporary interpretations of Judaic orthodoxy, then we are not only guilty of acquiescence to a shameless and blatant Talmudic revisionism, but we also make of TaNaKh a meaningless, worthless dead letter. In some cases even the clearest evidence will be dismissed unabashedly, if it clashes with the prejudices of the Grail author. A Michael Baigent can go on national television and say with a smile on his face that the words "Son of God" found on a Dead Sea Scroll do not mean anything divine. But what gives him the right to so pontificate, as if he is uttering an infallible *ex cathedra* pronouncement of Papal proportions? He must be quite a wonderful person indeed, if he can by mere *fiat* declare that words do not mean what they say. And people believe him, almost as if he were God in the flesh, or at least an angel of God. But he has merely succumbed to Talmudic revisionism. I realise very well that some people may also accuse me of revisionism, inasmuch as my theory requires Jesus to have lived a full century earlier than the traditionally accepted time. But to this charge I would respond that this is not revisionism, but rather an attempt at a historical, chronological reconstruction of events, or probable events. I do not claim infallibility.

But the concept of a Son of God can clearly be found within the pages of TaNaKh:

4 Who hath ascended into heaven, or descended? Who hath gathered the wind in his fists? Who hath bound the waters in a garment? Who hath established all the ends of the earth? What is his name, and <u>what is his son's name</u>, if thou canst tell?

(Proverbs 30:4, KJV)

7 I will declare the decree: the LORD hath said unto me, <u>Thou *art* my Son</u>; this day have I begotten thee. (Psalm 2:7 cf Hebrews 1:5)

12 <u>Kiss the Son</u>, lest he be angry, and ye perish from the way, when his wrath is kindled but a little. Blessed are all they that put their trust in him. (Psalm 2:12 cf Luke 7:45)

14 <u>I will be his Father, and he will be my Son</u>. (II Samuel 7:14 cp Hebrews 1:5)

And this idea of the divine Sonship of the Messiah also seems to be linked with the divinity of the Son:

6 Thy throne, O God, is for ever and ever: the sceptre of thy kingdom is a right sceptre.

7 Thou lovest righteousness, and hatest wickedness: therefore God, *even* thy God, hath anointed thee with the oil of gladness above thy fellows.

(Psalm 45:6-7 cp Hebrews 1:8-9)

Once again we are confronted with a different translation of the above passage in official Jewish translations of TaNaKh; yet the Greek text of Hebrews 1:8-9, and also the Greek text of the Septuagint rendering of the passage are both in accord with the meaning found above.[52] I recall that when I was a college student, I had a private conversation with a Jewish girl on campus, who was a friend of mine, about this passage. Her aspiration was to become the very first female Rabbi. She said that the passage means that God, or part of God, is in the Messiah, but not that the Messiah is himself God. I suppose that is a reasonable interpretation. The passage does place the Messiah in a position of subordination to God.[53] And it is certainly questionable and highly doubtful if any pre-Christian Jews ever thought of the Messiah as being upon an equality with God. But such passages as those above at least imply that the seeds of such an apotheosis were latent within the very texts of TaNaKh themselves.

---

52   Nestle-Aland., op. cit., pgs. 563-564. SEPTUAGINTA., op. cit., pg. 47. (vol. 2; Duo volumina in uno). N.B. the numbering of the Psalms is different in the Septuagint.

53   Psalm 45:7.

Whether or not the original intent of those texts was to thus place the Messiah within the Godhead we may never know (at least while still alive in the flesh). But suffice to say that the very ambiguity of the Scriptures are such that they allow for differences of opinion ranging from those of the *Ebionim* at one end of the spectrum (to whom the Messiah was only a man) to that of the Athanasian Creed, with Arianism as a medium between the two extremes. Be that as it may, by the latter half of the second century the concept of the virgin birth of the Messiah was in full bloom, and was quickly becoming the normative position of those calling themselves Christians. Of course by then the movement had already had a fairly long history, and had no doubt undergone significant thematic developments. Indeed, those Greek scrolls[54] of the New Testament represented a radical revisionism in a number of respects, particularly if the theory advocated herein be true.

But Jesus was very commonly called Jeschu Ben Pandera in Talmudic traditions, and also in the Toldoth Jeschu. In some versions of these Talmud stories, Ben Pandera is a Roman soldier; but in others, he is not a Roman, but a Greek soldier; as we learn from the following:

"Finally, in these Talmud Mary-legends we come to the thrice-repeated Miriam daughter of Bilga story, which runs as follows:

"Bilga always received his part on the south side on account of Miriam, daughter of Bilga, who turned apostate and went to marry a soldier belonging to the government of Javan, [Greece] and went and beat upon the roof of the altar. She said to him: 'Wolf, wolf, thou hast destroyed the property of the Israelites and didst not help them in the hour of their distress!'"[55]

---

54   It seems highly likely to me that most, if not all, of the texts of the New Testament were first written on scrolls, rather than codices, despite what some Christian apologists might claim to the contrary. The Dead Sea texts were written on scrolls, and some scholars have argued rather persuasively that at least some of them may have been written in the first century A.D. One argument sometimes used by advocates of Christian codices is that scrolls were somehow associated with pagan religion; however, this is a hollow argument, since all of the Hebrew Scriptures had been first written on scrolls, and even the Greek translations of those texts must have originally been inscribed on scrolls.

55   Mead., op. cit., pg. 165.

The very fact that it is a Greek soldier in this account places Mary (and hence Jesus) in Maccabean-Hasmonean times, rather than Roman times. This is very powerful evidence indeed. Mead comments further on this:

"In this case, however, it does not seem to be the Talmud or the Jews themselves who connect this story with Miriam, mother of Jeschu, but Dalman, who leaves us to suppose that it is one of the censured passages of the Talmud. What ground, however, Dalman has for bringing this story into relation with the Mary-legends I cannot discover [sic]; he seems to depend on Laible, who refers to Origen quoting Celsus as making his Jew declare that "Mary gave birth to Jesus by a certain soldier, Panthera." If, because of this, we are to take the above as a Mary story, it should be noticed that the "soldier" is of the "house of Greece," and therefore the date of the incident must be placed prior to the first Roman occupation of Jerusalem by Pompey in 63 B.C.; so that in it, in any case, we find a confirmation of the Ben Perachiah date."[56]

Here Mead errs by an ill-advised over-cautiousness, but we can safely disregard it for the time being. Instead it would be more expedient to clarify what he means here by "the Ben Perachiah date", since it relates directly with our central theme. Mead is referring to a story found in two tractates of the Babylonian Gemara, namely *Sota*, 47a, and *Sanhedrin*, 107b. The story is as follows:

"The Rabbis have taught: The left should always be repelled, and the right, on the other hand, drawn nearer. But one should not do it *as Elisha who repelled Gehazi or as Jeremiah repelled Baruch, or* as R. Joshua ben Perachiah, who thrust forth Jeschu with both hands. What was the matter with regard to R. Joshua ben Perachiah? When King Jannai [Alexander Jannaeus; Yannai] directed the destruction of the Rabbis [Jos. Ant. 13.14.2], R. Joshua ben Perachiah and Jeschu went to Alexandria. When security [for the Pharisees, probably under Queen Alexandra] returned, Rabbi Simeon ben Shetach sent him a letter to this effect:

---

56   Ibid., pg. 166. Once again we note Mead's incompetence; the passage so obviously refers to Mary the mother of Christ that Mead is fatuous for doubting it.

'From me, Jerusalem the holy city, to thee, Alexandria in Egypt, my sister. My spouse tarries in thee, and I dwell desolate.' Thereupon Joshua arose and came *back to Jerusalem*; and [but] *stopped and rested and stayed at* a certain inn in the way, in which they treated him [R. Joshua] with great respect. Then spake Joshua: 'How fair is this inn (*akhsanga*)!' Jeschu saith to him: 'But Rabbi, she (*akhsanga* = a hostess) has little narrow eyes.' Joshua replied: 'Thou godless fellow, dost thou occupy thyself with such things?' *and he* directed that 400 horns should be brought, and put him under strict excommunication. Jeschu ofttimes came and said to him, 'Take me back.' Joshua did not trouble himself about him. One day, just as Joshua was reading the Shema, Jeschu came to him, hoping that he would take him back. Joshua made a sign to him with his hand. Then Jeschu thought that he had altogether repulsed him, and went away, and set up a brickbat [idol] and worshipped it. Joshua said to him: 'Be converted!' Jeschu saith: 'Thus have I been taught by thee: From him that sinneth and maketh the people to sin, is taken away the possibility of repentance.' And the Teacher [Rabbi Joshua ben Perachiah] [*i.e.*, he who is everywhere mentioned by this title in the Talmud] has said: 'Jeschu had practised sorcery and had corrupted and misled Israel.'"[57]

This passage is of course of enormous importance to the thesis herein. In fact, the value of this passage, which occurs in two different tractates of the Talmud, cannot be overstated. These two tractates, *Sota* and *Sanhedrin*, also occur in two different orders of the Talmud; *Sota* is of the third order; and *Sanhedrin* is of the fourth order.[58] And here we learn that Rabbi Joshua ben Perachiah, Rabbi Shimeon ben Shetach, King Jannai, and Jeschu ben Pandera (Jesus) were all contemporaries. And it is important to keep in mind that the Jews would have had no reason to deliberately dislocate Jeschu from the time in which he really lived, placing him a full century earlier than the traditional Christian date. However, the Talmud does not blame the Christians for placing Jesus/Jeschu at a time later than he really lived, but instead seems blithely oblivious to such questions altogether, and has recourse to other objections against the alleged messianic status of Jesus. The very casual and unsolicited way

---

57   Ibid., pgs. 137-138.
58   Steinsaltz., op. cit., pgs. 42-43.

in which we find this evidence respecting Jeschu/Jesus in the Talmud argues in favor at least of its chronological setting, if not its polemics. Mead continues on from the same passage:

"This famous passage, if taken by itself, would of course fully confirm the hypothesis of the 100 years B.C. date of Jesus. The arguments for and against the authenticity of its statements embrace, therefore, practically the whole substance of our investigation. Let us first of all consider the face value of these statements. Jannai or Jannaeus (John), who also bore the Greek name Alexander, was one of the famous Maccabean line of kings, the son of John Hyrcanus I, and reigned over the Jews 104-78 B.C."[59]

According to Mead, Simeon ben Shetach and Alexander Jannaeus were not only contemporaries, but Simeon ben Shetach was the brother of Jannai's wife Salome.[60] Therefore apparently Alexandra-Salome was the same woman who was the widow of both Aristobulus and Alexander Jannaeus, and who reigned as queen for nine years, according to Josephus.[61] Presumably, according to the chronological scheme advocated herein, the final, seventieth week of Daniel's prophecy occurred some time during the nine-year reign of Queen Salome, otherwise also known as Alexandra; or at least that, according to the chronology commonly used by the Jews at that time, it was thus believed that the time of fulfillment had come. At least this is the rationale for the basis that Jesus made a claim to being the Messiah the Prince of the prophecy; and, even taking a critical view of the Toldoth, this is the implicit chronological setting of those events, or alleged events. We should also note that a chronology thus placing the *terminus ad quem* of Daniel's prophecy of the seventy weeks in Alexandra's reign is not quite as far from the accepted, standard chronology vis-à-vis the reigns of Persian kings than what is found in Josephus' earlier chronology,[62] to say nothing of his supposedly "corrected" chronology,[63]

---

59   Mead., op. cit., pg. 138. We must remember that here Mead is using the standard chronology, rather than the chronology of Josephus.
60   Ibid., pg. 139.
61   Jos. War. 1.5.1-4; Ant. 13.16.1-6.
62   Found in his *War of the Jews*.
63   Found in his *Antiquities of the Jews*.

which is even ten years further from the standard chronology, resulting in a chronology that is approximately forty-five years deviant from the standard chronology.[64]

It is notable as well that this passage, found in two different tractates of the Talmud, also places Jeschu in Egypt, specifically Alexandria. And the temple in Leontopolis, of which we spoke earlier, was located in the nome of Heliopolis, which was not really that far from Alexandria. Note also that the letter from Rabbi Simeon ben Shetach speaks favourably of Alexandria, calling it the "sister" of Jerusalem; this is in stark contrast to the image of extreme xenophobia and cultural isolationism portrayed by the likes of Robert Eisenman in his works. The passage also presents a timetable of sorts. If Jeschu and Joshua fled Jerusalem during the brutal persecution of the Pharisees by Alexander Jannaeus, but that "when security returned" Simeon ben Shetach wrote his letter, sending for Rabbi Joshua, and Jeschu accompanied him on his trip back to Jerusalem, then, if we can accept the passage as having any historicity whatever, Jeschu was still alive after the death of Alexander Jannaeus, in 78 B.C., according to Mead. Because security would not have returned to the Pharisees until after the death of Jannai (Jannaeus), and his widow

---

64   It should be clearly evident that my use of the term "standard chronology" in this context has nothing whatever to do with when Jesus supposedly lived, but rather the length of time that had elapsed from the decree of Cyrus to the days of Aristobulus the brother of Alexander Jannaeus. As noted above, Josephus in his *War* had said that Aristobulus began to reign 471 years and three months after the return from Babylon, which necessarily coincided with the decree of Cyrus; whereas, in his latter work, the *Antiquities*, Josephus adds ten years by saying that Aristobulus began to reign 481 years and three months after that time. By contrast, the standard chronology holds that the decree of Cyrus was issued in approximately 536 B.C., giving us a date of 54 B.C. for 482 years later, which is long after the actual time in which Aristobulus lived. The instance of the discrepancy in Josephus' earlier work can only be accounted for by the supposition that the Jews had been using a different system of chronology at an earlier time; from this it is not difficult to suppose that those living in the reign of Queen Alexandra-Salome may have used a still different chronology, and one which would have allowed for the *terminus ad quem* of Daniel's prophecy of the seventy weeks to be fulfilled in their time. The lengthening of the chronology in Josephus' latter work is most readily accounted for by supposing that he thereby sought to exalt Moses by ascribing to him a most venerable antiquity.

instituted a pro-Pharisee policy.[65] So if this passage from the Talmud is correct in terms of chronology, then Jeschu was still alive at that late date. The implication of this is that the events narrated in the Toldoth Jeschu must be supposed to have occurred during the reign of Alexandra, otherwise also known as Salome or Queen Helene (in the Toldoth); she having been twice widowed, by two brothers, Aristobulus and Alexander Jannaeus.

But it is worth noting that one of the Talmud tractates quoted from above, namely *Sota*, is primarily concerned with a woman accused of adultery.[66] So there is a strong presumption that the tractate spoke of Miriam the mother of Jeschu as an adulteress. The other tractate in which the same passage occurs, *Sanhedrin*, is primarily concerned with sins incurring the death penalty.[67] Adultery is, according to the Torah, a sin warranting the death penalty.[68] In a famous story found in the Gospel of John, the scribes and Pharisees bring a woman guilty of adultery to Jesus, saying that Moses had commanded that she should be stoned to death; they were testing Jesus, to see how much in accord with the Torah he was. Of course these men were outrageous hypocrites, since, in Leviticus, it says that both the man and the woman are to be put to death; but they only brought the woman. But Jesus made the famous reply "He that is without sin among you, let him cast the first stone at her."[69] It is certainly a beautiful story, whether or not it ever took place as a historical event. Christ's attitude at least was more compassionate and humane, more truly and fully human, than that of the Pharisees. This story occurs in John 8:2-11 in most Greek manuscripts of that Gospel; although there are some early texts of John that omit the story.[70] But the traditional placement of the story may have been purposeful, since later in the same chapter we can find a statement that seems to indicate controversies respecting the paternity of Jesus, with accusations of illegitimacy being implied in the subtext.

---

65   Jos. Ant. 13.16.1-6.; War. 1.5.1-4.
66   Steinsaltz., op. cit., pg. 42.
67   Ibid., pg. 43.
68   Leviticus 20:10.
69   John 8:7.
70   Nestle-Aland., op. cit., pgs. 273-274.

41 Ye do the deeds of your father. Then they said to him, We be not born of fornication; we have one Father, *namely* God. (John 8:41)

By the Jews answering Jesus by saying "We be not born of fornication", the implied subtext is that by contrast he is the product of fornication, in the minds of the Jews, to whom a few verses later Christ says "You are of your father the devil, and the lusts of your father you will do. He was a murderer from the beginning, and abode not in the truth, because there is no truth in him; when he speaketh a lie, he speaketh according to his own *nature*; for he is a liar, and the father of *lies*."[71] While it seems unlikely that there ever was such a conversation between Jesus and the Jews, nevertheless it represents the attitudes of mutual animosity that already existed by the second century A.D., the likely time of the composition of John's Gospel. The Evangelist thereby answers accusations of Christ's supposed illegitimacy with counter accusations of a diabolical, satanic spiritual paternity for the Jews, placed in the lips of none other than Jesus himself.

There is also another verse in the New Testament that seems to imply accusations of illegitimacy aimed at Jesus on the part of the Jews (or perhaps we should say those Jews who did not believe in his messianic status). This one is more buried under the surface, possibly due to constraints of propriety (or what is believed to be such) placed upon Bible translations. I realise that Christians may be upset by my reconstruction, but I am only seeking to establish truth. This other verse occurs in the Gospel of Luke.

14 But his citizens hated him, and sent a message after him, saying, We will not have this *bastard* to reign over us. (Luke 19:14)

In the King James, the italicized word is *man*, not *bastard*, as I have it. In the original Greek there is no corresponding word; some translations that seek a literal rendering have "this one" to translate the Greek word *touton*, which imports no more than that. But the fact is that typically, the Greek text is more descriptive; in idiomatic English, "this one" sounds suspiciously hollow, as if something is being left unsaid. Those who are

---

71   John 8:44.

more familiar with *Koine* Greek may assure me that the grammar is perfectly sound, which it probably is; nevertheless I still suspect that the original Greek text has been edited by Christian scribes here, since such scribes may well have been shocked to see *nothos,* the Greek word for bastard, being ascribed to Jesus Christ (although by the Jews in the parable), in this verse. Therefore their "pious" hands quickly erased the terribly blasphemous and unthinkable word from the text. I may be wrong, but to my mind, the word *bastard* seems more implied by the context, and really is no more speculative than the more conservative *man,* as found in the King James text. In both cases there is no corresponding, underlying Greek word to justify [fully justify] the presence of the word in the translation. But it is standard practice for Bible translators to insert what they believe are necessary or implied words, but usually these are denoted, as in the King James Bible, by being placed in italics. I feel that the word *bastard* is justified in this verse, provided that it is *italicized.* In any case I feel that this verse, together with John 8:41, proves that by the time that the Greek scrolls of the New Testament were written, the virgin birth idea was already dominant within the nascent Christian or proto-Christian community, together with the response that Jesus, so far from being of divine paternity, was a bastard. Naturally this charge only inflamed the zeal and fanaticism of the Christians, who in turn claimed that God had forsaken his beloved chosen people, and that now they (the messianic community) were the new chosen people. They were the remnant. Or so they claimed. In the Gospel of Nicodemus, the Rabbis explicitly accuse Jesus of illegitimacy:

6 But the elders of the Jews answered, and said to Jesus, What shall we look to?

7 In the first place, we know this concerning thee, that thou wast born through fornication; secondly, that upon the account of thy birth the infants were slain in Bethlehem; thirdly, that thy father and mother Mary fled into Egypt, because they could not trust their own people.

8 Some of the Jews who stood by spake more favourably, We cannot say that he was born through fornication; but we know that his mother Mary

was betrothed to Joseph, and so he was not born through fornication. (Nicodemus 2:6-8)

Although the Gospel of Nicodemus, otherwise also called the Acts of Pilate, was not written at least until the late third century, this passage at least clearly imputes an accusation of illegitimacy by the Jerusalem Rabbis, hurled against Jesus. The form of the accusation suggests influence from John 8:41, discussed above; the Gospel of Nicodemus clearly evinces literary influence from all four canonical Gospels. So Nicodemus makes explicit what is otherwise implicit within John and Luke.

But there can be no doubt that the Jews have accused Mary of adultery and fornication; even the Koran says that the Jews "uttered a grievous calumny against Marium".[72] G.R.S. Mead has the following to say on this topic:

"It is exceedingly difficult to classify these Mamzer legends or to treat them in any satisfactory chronological fashion, but it is remarkable that in them there seem to be two deposits of tradition characterised by different names for Jeschu- Ben Stada and Ben Pandera, names which have given rise to the wildest philological speculation, but of which the current meaning was evidently simply "son of the harlot," whatever may have been their line of descent. Ben Stada occurs exclusively in the Talmud, where it is the most frequent designation of Jeschu, though Ben Pandera is also found; Ben Pandera is found in the Toldoth Jeschu, and as we have seen in the Church Fathers, while Ben Stada is never met with in these sources."[73]

From this we can see that Ben Pandera is the more dominant, hence probably older, designation. But there can be no doubt that the Jews have accused Mary of fornication and adultery, and Jesus of being a bastard child. This is abundantly proven. Mead quotes from a passage in the Mishnah that proves this:

"Simeon ben Azzai has said: I found in Jerusalem a book of genealogies;

---

72   Koran Sura IV:156.
73   Mead., op. cit., pgs. 154-155.

therein was written: That so and so is a bastard son of a married woman."[74]

Lest this appear inconclusive, Mead continues:

"This Simeon ben Azzai flourished somewhat earlier than Akiba, and may therefore be placed at the end of the first and the beginning of the second century. He was one of the famous four who, according to Talmudic tradition, "entered Paradise"; that is to say, he was one of the most famous mystics of Israel. He was a Chassid, most probably an Essene, and remained a celibate and rigid ascetic till the day of his death. We might, therefore, expect him to be specially fitted to give us some information as to Jesus, and yet what he is recorded to have said is the very opposite of our expectations. Ben Azzai, we are to believe, declared that he had found a book of genealogies at Jerusalem- presumably then before the destruction of the city in 70 A.D. This book of genealogies can be taken to mean nothing else than an official record; nevertheless we are told that it contained the proof of Jeschu's bastardy, for "so and so" is one of the well-known substitutes for Jesus and Jesus alone in the Talmud, as has been proved and admitted on either side."[75]

To be sure, there are some wild anachronisms in the Talmud, and Christians and other critics may allege that the confusion in respect to chronology pertaining to Jesus is due simply to these anachronisms. But to merely remark upon anachronisms within Talmudic tradition is only an observation, not an explanation. It does not account for such anachronisms. And in fairness to the evidence it must be admitted that, in some instances, these anachronisms are leaning in the opposite direction; i.e., they place Jeschu at a time later than the commonly accepted time,

---

74   Ibid., pg. 153. It should be noted that Mead provides a note in his text that refers to *Jebamoth*, 49a as the Mishnaic source for this passage; Jebamoth is transliterated by Rabbi Steinsaltz as Yevamot in his guide to the Talmud (pg. 41). Yevamot is primarily concerned with sisters-in-law, levirate marriage, prohibited marriages, and forbidden sexual relationships.

75   Ibid., pgs. 153-154. Note that "so and so" as Mead expresses it, or "such a one" is a common expression in the Talmud for Jesus; this also evokes the verse in Luke, which says that "we will not have this one to reign over us", discussed above.

according to canonical Christian tradition. Mead himself admits this in his own book:

"The Ben Stada stories are mostly characterised by anachronisms which are as startling as those of the Ben Perachiah date, but which are its exact antipodes."[76]

However Mead accounts for this discrepancy in the following way:

"The Mishnah School at Led (Lydia) is said to have been founded by R. Eliezer ben Hyrcanus, the teacher of R. Akiba, and it was doubtless the great reputation of Akiba as the most implacable foe of Christianity which, in course of time, connected the name of Mary with stories of Akiba [Akiva] which originally were perfectly innocent of any reference to the mother of Jesus. Thus, in later times, we find tradition bringing Akiba and Miriam together in personal conversation, we find it still later giving her one of Akiba's contemporaries as a husband, and finally we meet with a curious legend in which Miriam is made the contemporary of a Rabbi of the fourth century!"[77]

Then shortly after this, Mead recounts a Talmudic story very similar in content to what is found in section 2 of the Toldoth Jeschu; in the Tolodth, it is Rabbi Simeon ben Shetach who inquires of Miriam, while in this other story, it is Rabbi Akiba:

"A shameless person is, according to R. Eliezer, a bastard; according to R. Joshua, a son of a woman in her separation; according to R. Akiba, a bastard *and* son of a woman in her separation. Once there sat elders at the gate when two boys passed by; one had his head covered, the other bare. Of him who had his head uncovered, R. Eliezer said, 'A bastard!' R. Joshua said, 'A son of a woman in her separation!' R. Akiba said, 'A bastard *and* a son of a woman in her separation!' They said to R. Akiba, 'How has thine heart impelled thee to the audacity of contradicting the words of thy colleagues?' He said to them, 'I am about to prove it.' Thereupon he went to the boy's mother, and found her sitting in the market and selling pulse. He said to her, 'My daughter, if thou tellest me

---

76   Ibid., pg. 155.
77   Ibid., pg. 156.

the thing which I ask thee, I will bring thee to eternal life.' She said to him, 'Swear it to me!' Thereupon R. Akiba took the oath with his lips, while he cancelled it in his heart. Then said he to her, 'Of what sort is this thy son?' She said to him, "When I betook myself to the bridal chamber I was in my separation, and my husband stayed away from me. But my paranymph [i.e., the bridegroom's best man] came to me, and by him I have this son." So the boy was discovered to be both a bastard *and* the son of a woman in her separation."[78]

By speaking of "a shameless person" it is evident to me that none other than Jesus was intended here. Despite this, Mead himself doubts that it was originally a Jesus story.[79] Mead believes that this is the probable source of that part of the Toldoth Jeschu.[80] This is certainly possible, but I feel that the Toldoth version is more ancient. Otherwise we would have to doubt Mead's assurances that there is indeed a "distinctly Karaite Toldoth"; the Karaites would never have accepted any Talmudic document as authoritative, or any document directly or indirectly derived from it. Therefore we are at a grave disadvantage by not being able to more directly examine Mead's sources. Mead also fails to note the anachronism evident in the passage above; i.e., that Akiba is made contemporary with Rabbi Joshua, who lived in the days of Simeon ben Shetach. This throws a serious monkey-wrench into Mead's argument and thesis.

Among the Rabbis of Orthodox Judaism, Jeschu (Jesus) was a terrible arch-deceiver, a sorcerer, a wicked idol-worshipper, who led many Jews astray, almost even a demon incarnate. They believe his crucifixion or hanging was a well-deserved punishment, and proved that he had been cursed by God.[81] They thus also believe that he is tormented and tortured in hell, in the midst of foul, boiling excrement.[82] The relevant portion of the story from the Talmud is as follows:

"Thereupon Onkelos went and conjured up the spirit of Jeschu. He asked

---

78   Ibid., pgs. 156-157. It should be noted that Mead has a footnote indicating that this is taken from Talmud tractate *Kallah*, 18b.

79   Ibid., pgs. 158-159.

80   Ibid., pg. 159.

81   Deuteronomy 21:22-23.

82   Mead., op. cit., pgs. 202-203.

him: Who is esteemed in that world? The spirit answered: The Israelites. Onkelos asked further: Ought one to join himself to them? The spirit said: Seek their good and not their ill. He who toucheth them, touches the apple of His eye. Onkelos asked: Wherewith art thou judged? The spirit said: With boiling filth."[83]

The Jews even have a tradition of Miriam (Mary) in hell.[84] So we can be reasonably certain that by the time these traditions arose, there had already been a division between two different groups of Jews that was so deep and bitter as to be beyond hope of any reconciliation. What had begun as two different interpretations within a single religion eventually resulted in the birth of two different religions entirely. We may also surmise that most likely, the bitterest elements of these traditions arose after the time when Christians began to persecute Jews. This would place such traditions, or the most scandalous and shocking of them, after the conversion of the Emperor Constantine in the early fourth century. On the other hand, one has but to read Josephus to see how deeply bitter were the struggles, contentions, and even armed conflicts that took place between mutually opposed groups of Jews, in what can only be described as civil wars, during the century of Hasmonean independence from Gentile dominion.

There is also apparently some evidence of a Jewish Christian movement before and during the time of Bar Kochbah. Mead writes the following: "For instance, in the recent revolt against the Romans led by Bar Kochbah (132-135 A.D.), Justin declares that this popular Messiah specially singled out the Christians for torture if they refused to deny that Jesus was the Messiah and utter blasphemies against him (c. xxxi.)."[85] This proves that there were Jewish Christians in Palestine in the early second century. Bar Kochbah acquired a very large following due to his endorsement as the Messiah by the Rabbi Akiba, who himself reportedly had 24,000 followers. Apparently Rabbi Akiba and Bar Kochbah were both crucified by the Romans, as were thousands upon thousands of other Jews. Many Jews were also sold into slavery. From that time forth

---

83   Ibid.
84   Ibid., pg. 163.
85   Ibid., pg. 123.

all Jews were forbidden to ever enter into the city of Jerusalem, upon pain of death. This was the beginning of the great Diaspora. The Greek word *diaspora* occurs in the epistle of James;[86] he addresses his letter to the "twelve tribes scattered in the *diaspora*". I am not hereby seeking to prove a second-century origin for that epistle, although I think it likely may originate from that time; however the term *diaspora* as used could have reference to the scattering in the aftermath of 70 A.D., or even to the general *diaspora* in the wake of the Babylonian Captivity. What I find interesting is, that a literal reading of the text implies that James' epistle was addressed explicitly to *Jewish* Christians, rather than to all Christians, unless one insists upon spiritualizing the meaning of what James wrote in the first verse of his letter.[87] But this fits in perfectly with the soteriological division within the New Testament noted above; James being classed with Matthew and Revelation as being in accord with a works-based salvation, in opposition to the Pauline-Johannine faction, who advocated a faith-based salvation. In fact, James insists upon both faith and works for salvation.[88] In fact, as noted above, this appears to be an attempt to reconcile the salvation through works apart from faith doctrine[89] with the opposing doctrine of salvation through faith apart from works.[90] So James was appealing to Jewish Christians, very specifically and explicitly. Interestingly, neither epistles of James or Jude make any reference whatever to the passion of Jesus, to say nothing of a substitutionary atonement. By contrast, the other epistles of the New Testament abound with this doctrine, as does also the book of Acts.[91]

---

86 Nestle-Aland., op. cit., pg. 588.

87 But of course fundamentalists will not do this, since it undercuts their system of exegesis; furthermore, if the first verse can thus be spiritualized, then this implicitly dilutes the pungency of the moral contents of that epistle.

88 James 2:14-26.

89 Matthew 25:31-46.

90 Ephesians 2:8-9.

91 Romans 5:1-11; 6:23; 1 Corinthians 1:17-18; 2:2; 10:16; 11:23-27; 2 Corinthians 5:19-21; Galatians 6:12-14; Ephesians 2:11-18; Philippians 3:18; Colossians 1:19-20; 2:13-14; Hebrews 9:24-28; 10:5-12; 12:24; 13:20; 1 John 1:5-10; 1 Peter 1:2,18-19; 2:21-24; 3:18; 2 Peter 2:1; Acts 2:38; 5:28-32; 8:32-35; 13:23-39; 16:30-31.

And of course we find the doctrine expressed, at least in a rudimentary form, in the Gospels.[92]

Jeschu (Jesus) is linked in the Talmud with every enemy of the Jews, such as Balaam, Ahitophel, Gehazi, Haman, and Titus. Jeschu ben Pandera, being the common appellation of Jesus Christ in the Talmudic literature, is a constant reminder of the accusation of illegitimacy of his conception and birth. The fact that such accusations arose long after the time of Jeschu, can also be proven from the very same circumstances which also prove, albeit obliquely, that claims to having been born of a virgin also probably long postdated his own time. There is a curious passage in the Torah[93] that there is apparently no Talmudic commentary upon, in relation to either Mary or Jesus. I can say this with full confidence, since, had there been any such relevant commentary, I have no doubt that Mead would have discussed it in his own work. And the passage is of such a nature that, since Mary was never openly accused of adultery or fornication, much less punished for it, she is thus vindicated of such charges altogether. Therefore it is inconceivable that Mary openly claimed to be a virgin mother in the days she was bearing Jesus, or even long after. In the Toldoth Jesus may claim descent from a virgin, but nowhere in the New Testament does he do so.

Before moving on it may be worthwhile to briefly take notice of what might be offered as an alternate theory respecting the origin of the accusations of illegitimacy respecting Jeschu/Jesus. Some may speculate or even postulate that Jeschu was charged with being a *mamzer* (bastard) because he could not prove that he was a lineal descendant of King David, as the Messiah was supposed to be. However we have presented information above that suggests that in fact Jeschu neither was nor ever claimed to be, a descendant of King David, since he was of Levitical descent. In fact there is a strong presumption that he was cognate to the Hasmonean dynasty, which was of priestly descent. So a variation of the same argument may be that Jeschu could not produce a genealogy proving his Levitical descent.[94] This brings to mind the Simeon ben

---

92   Mt 26:27-28; Mk 14:23-24; Lk 22:20 cf Jn 6:53-54.
93   Deuteronomy 22:13-21.
94   Ezra 2:61-63; Nehemiah 7:63-65 cf I Esdras 5:38-40.

Azzai passage, quoted from above, where "a book of genealogies" is mentioned, and somehow "proves" the illegitimacy of Jeschu. But it seems doubtful that any such scenario could have been the basis for the claims of illegitimacy hurled against Jeschu by the Rabbis. If it were a mere matter of lacking a Levitical genealogical pedigree, or proof thereof, it seems that the mere absence of any confirming genealogical text would have been duly noted without further ado. Jesus and his brother did not officiate at the Jerusalem temple, nor would they have desired to, as long as animal sacrifices were offered there. If we can credit the traditions respecting James the Just, then it is much more probable that he served as high priest in the temple in Leontopolis, Egypt, where no animal sacrifices were offered. The same is probably equally true of Jesus. So presumably they would have had no such need for a confirming Levitical genealogy, if they indeed lacked one. But if instead it were a question of Davidic descent, Jesus himself seems to have expressly disavowed such descent when teaching in the temple.[95] The very fact that this disavowal has survived the potential censorship of generations of Christian scribes only makes it that much more evidential.

I mentioned earlier that the Jews have a tradition of two Messiahs. Quite possibly some such tradition may have existed among them even as early as the first century B.C. This would have allowed for at least one of these Messiahs to not necessarily be a descendant of King David. The following passage is of some interest:

"And in the Treatise, *Mashiach uthechiath hammethim,* out of the Book *Tekkunim,* 'tis said, "Upon the Ox and the Ass, which are representatives of *Esau* and *Ishmael,* will come riding the two *Messias,* who will reign over them.""[96]

As noted earlier, one of the Messiahs is known as the Son of Joseph; the other is the more familiar Son of David.[97] While the Son of David is regarded as the "true" Messiah, this does not preclude another legendary messianic figure from attaining a stature within traditional Judaism

---

95   Mk 12:35-37 cp Mt 22:41-45 cf Lk 20:41-44.
96   Eisenmenger., op. cit., pg. 371.
97   Ibid., pg. 701.

that allows them to speak of "two Messiahs". As we have seen even in the Dead Sea Scrolls there is some mention of two distinct Messiahs. And while the Dead Sea Scrolls may shed some light upon our inquiry, albeit obliquely, yet it should be noted that those Scrolls for the most part seem to be normative with respect to the priestly tradition as such; in other words, we do not find an opposition to the very principle of blood sacrifices; instead, the opposition to the Jerusalem temple found in those texts is based upon the perceived corruption of the priesthood in Judaea. Yet even the Temple Scroll seems to envision a future time when blood sacrifices will be duly offered, but in a purified temple in a purified Jerusalem.

I wrote above that the idea of Jesus as a Levite dovetails rather nicely with some of the obscure facts brought forward in Mead's book. I will get to that presently. First we need to realise that Mattathias and all his sons, known collectively as the Maccabees, and their descendants, the Hasmoneans, were all Levites; for Mattathias was "a priest of the sons of Joarib" (I Maccabees 2:1); and only Levites could be priests according to the Torah. In fact, it is alleged by some that some of the political opposition to the Hasmonean rule in Judaea was due to the fact that these men were Levites, rather than descendants of the Davidic dynasty. But what Mead brings forward is relevant to this point respecting Jesus:

"But Ulla, a Palestinian Rabbi of the beginning of the fourth century, objects: Why all this precaution when Jeschu was plainly guilty of the charge? We have nothing to apologize for. On this the compiler of the Gemara remarks that Ulla is mistaken in taking this old tradition for an apology or a plea that every possible precaution was taken that Jeschu should have the fullest possible chance given him of proving his innocence. The real reason for all those precautions was that Jeschu was a person of great distinction and importance, and "near those in power" at the time, that is to say presumably, connected by blood with the Jewish rulers- a trait preserved in the Toldoth Jeschu, as we will see later on."[98]

Above I spoke of how the Rabbinical teaching of *Gilgulim* or transmigration became linked with messianic speculations after the time

98   Mead., op. cit., pg. 180.

of Bar Kochbah. There are a couple of relevant passages from the Talmud on this topic that are worth taking a look at. Here they are:

"And therefore it is, that our Rabbins, of Blessed Memory, have said, That the Son of David (*that is the* Messiah) cometh not, 'till all the Souls, which are in the Bodies, are at an End ('*till the Number of Souls, which are to be embodied, is completed;*) that is, 'till Souls cease to pass from one Body unto another. And by this we are plainly taught, that the Number of Souls is limited."[99]

"In the Treatise *Avodah hakkodesh* there is the following Passage. "Our Rabbins, of Blessed Memory, have revealed a great Mystery, touching the Delay of the Delivery (*or Restoration of the Jews*) and of the Coming of the *Messiah*. This they have done in the Sixth Chapter of the Talmud-Treatise *Jevamoth*, and in the First Chapter likewise of the Treatise *Avodah Sara*, where it is written, Rabbi *Asi* hath said, that the Son of *David*, that is, the *Messiah*, cometh not till all the Souls, which are to be embodied, have appear'd in the World: As it is said, *For the Spirit should fail before me, and the Souls which I have made.* And touching that Mystery, the Divines have taught from Tradition, that, before the Coming of the *Messiah*, every Soul shall be purified through the Mystery of the *Ibbur*."[100]

It is quite notable that the quotation immediately above speaks of a "delay" in the time of the "delivery", meaning the coming of the Messiah; it proves that the Jews knew that the real time when the Messiah was supposed to appear had already come and gone. As we have seen above, that was supposed to be 483 years from the time of the decree of Cyrus. Jesus is the only Messiah from the appropriate time period, according to the theory advocated herein, with the supporting evidence from hostile texts, such as the Talmud and the Toldoth Jeschu, proving the case. Could all this be merely coincidence? To say so strains all credulity, and the laws of probability. All the other would-be Messiahs failed miserably, and their followers dispersed. The last of the early Messiahs was Simeon Bar-Kochbah. But he also failed miserably, and no Jews

99   Eisenmenger., op. cit., pgs. 497-498.
100   Ibid., pg. 500.

today believe that he was or is the Messiah. Today he is more commonly called by Jews Simeon Bar-Kosiba. Although he led an uprising in the early second century, it would still have been possible, through some clever chronological juggling, to justify him as the Messiah spoken of by Daniel. But after his abortive uprising was crushed by the Romans, the Jews needed a new rationale to determine the coming of the Messiah. So it was only after this period that the messianic association with *Gilgulim* became part of Jewish tradition. And in fact this evidence is also in accordance with what Josephus wrote, since he identified the Pharisees as that sect of Judaism who embraced reincarnation.[101] And Orthodox Judaism is primarily derived from Pharisaic Judaism. Of course as to whether or not Jesus himself taught reincarnation, either openly or in secret, we can only speculate. But it is at least reasonably possible, if not probable, that transmigration may have been a dogma of the *Ebionim*, especially in view of their opposition to animal sacrifices. And there is at least a reasonable degree of probability that Jesus was one of the *Ebionim*.

Jewish Christians are sometimes called *Minim* in the Talmud. The Minim is a designation that Jews have used for heretics or apostates from Judaism. It is frequently, if not exclusively, used of Christians, particularly Jewish Christians. The Minim are cursed and hated by the Rabbinical Jews. G.R.S. Mead has this to say of the Minim:

"It is impossible to be certain whether all of the subsequent "Minim" Talmud passages refer expressly to Christians or not, for the word Min is in itself no certain guarantee, and it must ever depend on the context as to whether it can be taken in this precise sense or not. Since, however, Mr. Moses Levene, in his article on "Jesus and Christianity in the Talmud," quotes these passages as referring to the Christians, we cannot go altogether wrong in provisionally following his lead, for we may plead that according to common Jewish tradition they are taken in this sense, and this is all that concerns us at present."[102]

But here Mead is speaking of certain questionable Minim passages,

---

101   Jos. War. 2.8.14.
102   Mead., op. cit., pg. 210.

which may or may not refer to Christians. But there are definitely at least some Minim passages in the Talmud that undoubtedly speak of Christians. Mead continues:

"But besides these Minim passages there are others concerning which there can be no doubt as to against whom they are intended to be directed, and with these we will begin"[103]

Mead also quotes some passages from the Talmud that say that the books of the Minim should be destroyed:

"The books of the Minim are not to be kept from the fire on the Sabbath [sic], but must be consumed on the spot with the names of God contained therein. Rabbi Joses said: On a week day let the name of God be cut out and hidden away, and the remainder burnt. Rabbi Tarphon declared: May I be deprived of my children if I do not burn them with the names of God!"[104]

"Rabbi Ishmael said: If in order to make peace between husband and wife, the Law allows the name of God to be 'blotted out' [in the bitter waters; cf Numbers 5:11-31], how much more shall the books of these men [i.e., Minim] be destroyed who stir up enmity and angry feeling between Israel and their Father who is in heaven. To them the words of David may be applied: 'Do I not hate them, O Lord, that hate thee? Am I not grieved with those who rise up against thee? I hate them with perfect hatred, I reckon them my enemies. [Psalm 139:21-22]'"[105]

A little further on Mead quotes from another Talmud passage respecting the Minim:

"The post-Mishnaic Rabbis have taught: An animal, if slaughtered, even according to the Jewish rites, by a Min, is like an animal offered to idols. His (the Min's) bread is like the bread of a Cuthite (Samaritan) and his wine like that offered to idols. The books of the Law, the Prophets, and

---

103   Ibid.
104   Ibid., pg. 236. There is a footnote in Mead's work noting that this passage is taken from the Talmud tractate *Shabbath*, 116a.
105   Ibid., pg. 237. This is also from tractate *Shabbath*, 116a.

the Hagiographa which have been written by him, are like the books of magicians."[106]

And just a little further on we also read: "Rav Nachman said: We hold that a roll of the Law that has been written by a Min shall be committed to the flames"[107]

So the Minim were regarded as being impure and contaminated by false beliefs and practices, and that this spiritual corruption would render unclean whoever associated with them. Nevertheless the Minim had a reputation for curing diseases, as the following passage proves:

"A man must not carry or take from the Minim, he must not intermarry with them, and must not accept their cures for disease."[108]

There may be a hint that the *Minim* were suspected of altering passages within *TaNaKh*, which would render their versions unacceptable. Such versions were not regarded as trustworthy. Aside from this consideration, just having been in possession of the hated *Minim* would have rendered such texts impure, polluted, corrupted, ritually unclean, vile, evil, and undesirable. But the very fact that the *Minim* would have the very same books in common with the other Jews proves that they were themselves Jews, or at least that they held the sacred books of the Jews as sacred Scriptures. What other groups could this possibly apply to, other than both Karaites and Christians? Or to the Jewish antecedents of those two groups?

But the Karaites were distinct from the *Ebionim*, the *Notzrim*, and presumably, from the *Minim*. The Karaites did not have a reputation as healers, as did the Essenes and Therapeutae. But as we learn from the quotation from *Aboda Zara* above, the *Minim* did have a reputation for curing diseases, or at least offering such cures, or claiming such curative skills and powers. Therefore the description of the *Minim* seems to

---

106   Ibid., pg. 239. Mead has a footnote indicating that this passage is taken from the Talmud tractate *Chullin*, 13a.
107   Ibid., pg. 240. Mead has a footnote indicating that this is taken from the Talmud tractate *Gittin*, 45b.
108   Ibid., pg. 239. Mead has a footnote indicating that this passage is taken from the Talmud tractate *Aboda Zara*, 27b.

most closely correspond to what we would imagine the early disciples of Jesus to have been. Furthermore it was not the use of Greek rather than Hebrew that was at issue here; Greek-speaking Alexandrian Jews had used Greek translations of the Hebrew Scriptures for generations. And even Rabbi Adin Steinsaltz admits that "In the Mishnaic period there were scholars who permitted the use of Torah scrolls written in Greek."[109] In other words, it was the doctrine, rather than the language, culture or ethnicity of the Minim that was unacceptable to the Orthodox Rabbis.

Finally, we need to consider the evidence of the frequency of the anachronistic references to Jesus having lived in the days of Alexander Jannaeus in the Talmud. While it is true that there are a number of anachronisms in the Talmud, particularly in relation to Mary and Jesus, nevertheless what is interesting and in my view relevant, is that those anachronisms that place Jesus in Hasmonean times are much more common than contrary anachronisms, and thus appear to be statistically significant. Mead also noted this in his own way:

"If we are told that Jesus lived in the days of Nebuchadnezzar, we are not so astonished; for experience in contemporary apocalyptic and pseudepigraphic literature teaches us that Nebuchadnezzar is clearly a substitute for some other name. If even we are told that Akiba, one of the most famous of anti-Christian controversialists, at the beginning of the second century A.D. calls on Mary to witness to the illegitimacy of Jesus, we can understand that this is a pure device of haggadic polemical rhetoric, but when we are told that Jeschu was a disciple of Joshua ben Perachiah and lived in the days of Jannai, and find this date element cropping up again and again in many guises in Jewish tradition, we fail to find a satisfactory explanation in either of the above canons of exegesis."[110]

In other words, what Mead found significant, were not the anachronisms in and of themselves, but rather that this particular anachronism was statistically significant inasmuch as it would occur much more frequently

---

109   Steinsaltz., op. cit., pg. 16.
110   Mead., op. cit., pgs. 418-419.

throughout the Talmudic literature, thus indicating the possibility that it represented a genuine historical subtext. Together with the evidence from the Toldoth Jeschu, and all the other evidence presented herein, that possibility seems rather to become a probability.

What impresses me most about the evidence is the way that so many diverse elements, from diverse sources, converge in a quite unexpected and unsolicited way to confirm the thesis that Jesus lived a century before the commonly-accepted time. If all of the evidence originated from just one source then we would be justified in being greatly suspicious of it. But when we can see that in many cases otherwise innocuous details dovetail together so perfectly to confirm a postulate then we have grounds for saying that postulate is proven. An alternative yet coherent picture of Jesus emerges: Jesus, living in the days of Queen Alexandra, being himself a Levite, possibly even cognate to the ruling dynasty, claims to be the Messiah the Prince of Daniel's prophecy of the seventy weeks. He is an Ebionite, who, with his brother James, sometimes officiates as high priest at the Jewish temple in Leontopolis, Egypt. He manages to acquire a loyal following of disciples who remain faithful to him generation after generation, even though most of the Jews reject his messianic claims. However we must recognise that Jesus is significantly different from the other messianic pretenders of that era. None of them still have followers claiming that he was/is the promised Messiah. And while it is true that the latter-day Messiah Sabbatai Zevi still has some followers, they are not very numerous. Of course it can be argued that the influx of large numbers of Gentiles into the proto-Christian messianic movement and the subsequent events that led to the expansion of Christianity, such as the conversion of the Emperor Constantine to Christianity, were mere accidents of history; nevertheless the legacy of Jesus still lives on today, however corrupted or distorted.

THE LITTLE APOCALYPSE

In the Synoptic Gospels, we have what is sometimes fondly referred to as the "Little Apocalypse".[1] It is supposed to provide proof of the prophet-hood of Jesus, since therein he predicts, among other things, the complete destruction of the Jerusalem temple.[2] Having recently re-examined the respective passages, I am now convinced, in agreement with most critical scholars, that the Gospel of Mark contains the most archaic form of the little apocalypse. I was surprised by this, since what we find in Matthew is more complete, and for a long time I had thought it was probably the original. One *caveat* I do want to immediately express, however: I am also fully persuaded that the reference to "Daniel the prophet" in Mark 13:14 is definitely part of the original text, in contradistinction from the consensus of the Deutsche Bibelgesellschaft Stuttgart.[3] In fact, they do not even have a reference to Daniel in the apparatus. Nevertheless the reference to "Daniel the prophet" is intact therein in the corresponding verse in Matthew.[4] In any case the Majority text definitely does include the reference to Daniel in Mark 13:14.[5] In

1 Mt 24; Mk 13; Lk 21:5-36; cf 17:20-37.
2 Mt 24:2; Mk 13:2; Lk 21:6.
3 Nestle-Aland., op. cit., pg. 134.
4 Ibid., pg. 68.
5 Interlinear Greek-English New Testament (Third Edition); Jay P. Green, Sr. (editor & translator); Baker Books, a division of Baker Book House P.O. Box 6287, Grand Rapids, MICHIGAN 49516-6287. ISBN 0-8010-2138-3., pg.

fact, as we will soon see, the entire prophecy is ultimately based upon the very same prophecy of the seventy weeks we have been discussing throughout this text.

Matthew's version of the little apocalypse doubtless contains numerous expansions and embellishments, but in some cases at least it is quite possible that Matthew has recorded portions of a genuine oral tradition that Mark overlooked. For example, while Mark records Jesus as saying "and then they shall see the Son of man coming in the clouds with great power and glory", an obvious reference to Daniel 7:13-14, the corresponding passage in Matthew speaks of "the sign of the Son of man in heaven: and then shall all the tribes of the earth mourn, and they shall see the Son of man coming in the clouds of heaven with power and great glory", which seems to incorporate an expansion based upon Zechariah 12:10-14.[6] One could certainly argue that the author of Matthew simply had recourse to the earlier Jewish prophecies, and thereby supplied an appropriate *midrash* in the verse. But it is equally possible that he may have recalled portions of an oral tradition that had already incorporated such predictions. After all, Jesus himself must have been a student of biblical prophecy. Therefore he likely spoke at length of the prophecies of Zechariah, Daniel, Isaiah, Jeremiah, Ezekiel, Hosea, Joel, etc., etc. One item from Matthew in fact seems to point to the likelihood of an oral tradition as opposed to any written *Testimonia* or *Logia Kyriou* or hypothetical "Q" document as the source of the little apocalypse. I am referring to Matthew 24:28, where Jesus says "For wheresoever the carcass is, there will the eagles be gathered together." The perplexing thing about this verse is that, it bears absolutely no thematic relationship whatever to any verses immediately preceding or following it. In fact, nowhere in the entire discourse is this strange saying explained. However the very same saying occurs in Luke 17:37, where it is the conclusion of a discourse in which Jesus speaks of the return of the Son of man. In Luke, the verse makes sense; it implies that those who are taken away, are taken away to judgment.[7] But in Matthew, the saying exists

---

155.

6   Mt 24:30 cp Mk 13:26.

7   Rather than a hypothetical Rapture as is so popular today among funda-mentalists.

in complete isolation, with no explanation whatever: it is anomalous. This militates against the idea that Matthew was merely copying from some prior written text, since, if that were the case, the underlying text itself would also have anomalously included such a saying outside of any meaningful context; this seems far less likely, in my view, than Matthew remembering the saying as being part of an oral tradition which he was recording, but being unable to remember the entire context of that saying. He presumably only remembered the most dramatic saying from that portion of the little apocalypse tradition. And if it is argued that Matthew merely copied from Luke, then why would Matthew have omitted the context of the saying from his text? So that explanation does not make sense either.

In Luke's Gospel, the little apocalypse is broken up into two different sections; part of which occurs in chapter 17, with the remainder in chapter 21. Luke's version appears slightly heterodox compared with the much more standard form of it found in Mark and Matthew; in fact, in Luke, immediately before the first occurrence of any of the material, Jesus seems to replace the traditional apocalyptic expectations by a declaration that is fondly repeated by mystics: "The kingdom of God doth not come with observation; neither shall they say, Lo here *it is,* or lo, there *it is; rather,* behold, the kingdom of God is within you."[8] Some have translated the verse as "the kingdom of God is in the midst of you", meaning that the kingdom of God is present in the person of Jesus himself. Nevertheless the apocalypticism which is normative to the Synoptics is almost entirely absent from the Gospel of John. Despite this, we do find a form of apocalypticism in the Pauline corpus.[9]

Advocates of an early date of composition for the Gospels often do so with an implicit intent to thus "prove" the supposed predictive power of Christ, due to the seemingly dramatic fulfillment evident in the destruction of the temple in 70 A.D. However even if all three Synoptic Gospels predated the destruction of the temple, Christ's alleged predictive

---

8   Luke 17:20-21.
9   1 Thessalonians 4:13-18; 5:1-11; 2 Thessalonians 2:1-12; 1 Corinthians 15:51-54; Philippians 3:20-21; Romans 11:1-29; 1 Timothy 4:1-3; 2 Timothy 3:1-7.

power would be no more than that of Daniel.[10] In fact there can be no real doubt that the little apocalypse is primarily based upon the earlier prophecies of Daniel. Daniel, in the prophecy of the seventy weeks, spoke of the future destruction of the Jerusalem temple. For therein it is written "the people of the Prince that shall come shall destroy the city and the sanctuary"[11] I have translated the Hebrew word as "spoil" above, but the very same Hebrew word *shakhath* can also be translated as "destroy", and it is so translated in the King James Bible. But whatever view one takes of Daniel, this still makes Daniel a greater prophet than Jesus, since Jesus himself was only ultimately referring back to the prophecy of Daniel when he declared that "not one stone shall be left upon a stone, that shall not be thrown down."[12] He was merely reiterating what had already been written before his time. Therefore even a very early date of composition for the Synoptics is hardly evidential in the prophetic sense; much less so than is the case with Daniel, even attributing a very late date to that book. To a very large degree this takes the wind out of the sails of those who would thus seek to "prove" what a great prophet Jesus had been, by pointing to the clear fulfillment of a specific prophecy.[13] On the other hand, one suspects that perhaps critical scholars have insisted upon a post-70 A.D. date for the Synoptics, to preclude a supposed fulfillment of prophecy. But here there is a difficulty for them; because Daniel himself predicted the destruction of the temple.[14] And presumably this prophecy either occurred in the first year of Darius the Mede,[15] when the temple had already been destroyed by the armies of Nebuchadnezzar,[16] or in the days (or shortly after the days) of Antiochus Epiphanes. Even in the latter

---

10   And this would remain true regardless of whether Daniel originated from the sixth century B.C. or the second century B.C.; in either case, Daniel's prophecy of the ruin of the temple long preceded that of Jesus Christ.

11   Daniel 9:26.

12   Mt 24:2; Mk 13:2; Lk 21:6.

13   Assuming that one or more of the Synoptic Gospels (and hence the little apocalypse) predate 70 A.D.

14   And I know of no biblical scholars who will venture that Daniel post-dates 70 A.D.

15   Daniel 9:1. Not to be confused with Darius the Persian.

16   And thus most Jews were awaiting the rebuilding of the temple; even Daniel's prophecy spoke of the rebuilding of Jerusalem, including the street and the wall.

case, the writer of Daniel turned out to be genuinely prophetic, since he was able to predict the future destruction of the temple. Therefore critical scholars who cavil against an early date for the Gospels on this account are guilty of a major blunder and merely quibble about an altogether moot point. Indeed, from the Jews' perspective, Daniel successfully predicted the rise of the Roman empire as the fourth beast/fourth kingdom, thus sealing the Canonicity of that book within *TaNaKh*. The fall of the temple in 70 A.D. merely confirmed the prophetic character of the book in the eyes of the Jews, and presumably in the eyes of the Christians as well.

However there is another implicit reason why Christian apologists advocate an early date for the Gospels. The unstated but implicit assumption being that, if those texts were written at very early dates, then it increases the supposition that the events narrated therein, or some semblance of them, really occurred. And, all other things being equal, this is a valid assumption. However there is another perspective that belies any such confident assumption. First of all is the almost universal concession that those texts were first written in Greek.[17] This belies a Palestinian provenance for any of these texts, since Palestinian Jews did not commonly speak Greek.[18] If those texts were written and distributed at locations far removed from where the events were alleged to have taken place, this decreases their evidential value significantly. As far as the claims of miracles are concerned, to paraphrase an earlier writer, "It would have been a miracle if they had not believed in miracles." Greek originals of the Gospels suggests a point of origin somewhat far from Galilee, Judaea, Jerusalem, Samaria, or anywhere near Palestine. Not only that, but the theory advocated herein also sheds new light on the issue. If we assume, based upon the evidence presented above, that Jesus actually lived in the first century B.C., rather than the first century A.D., then it follows that even such an early date as 37 A.D. was long after the death of Jesus. Assuming that the above theory is generally correct, and

---

17   Against this the Syrian Orthodox Church insists that those texts were written in Syriac. There are also traditions of an original Hebrew of Matthew, and an original Coptic text of Mark. But the general consensus is that all these works were originally composed in Greek.

18   Cf Acts 21:37.

there was a messianic *kahal* of some sort, that decided at some point to "dislocate" Jesus from his true original time, and for the reasons stated above, then this would have largely been a sort of "political" decision; the true original date and time would have been known to the *kahal* and presumably also to all the followers of the movement, and the new time element would have been a novelty in their claims respecting Jesus. As such, it is not entirely inconceivable that a new date may have been claimed even shortly after the time in which the events supposedly took place; those texts likely being issued to those who were in no position to contradict their contents, due to differences of language and location, if not distance of time. Furthermore it is not altogether inconceivable that, since the dislocation was itself primarily a symbolic act, it may have openly been intended as such, initially.[19] Only over time did the new dates become commonly accepted, and the original date of Christ became all but lost, except in a few isolated Jewish traditions, as found in the Toldoth Jeschu, and portions of the Talmud.

I cannot claim without fear of contradiction that there were no earlier texts of the messianic movement; indeed the Gospel of the Ebionites seems like a potential candidate for such a text.[20] Possibly some future discovery, similar to that of the Dead Sea Scrolls or the Nag Hammadi Codices, will unveil an earlier messianic movement. Michael Wise has written a book about a Messiah before Jesus, entitled *THE FIRST MESSIAH*.[21] He calls this hypothetical Messiah Judah. But if Jesus really lived in the days of Alexander and Alexandra, then he would have been the first Messiah, of whom all the others were imitators.

---

19   Of course this explanation is offered in rebuttal to those who might, at some future time, point to incontrovertible evidence of very early Gospel texts. In the absence of this evidence, it is hardly necessary to predicate an early origin for the Gospels, and I would personally favour a late origin for them. But this explanation is offered for the sake of completeness. In fact, the utility of this explanation may be one more advantage to the thesis advocated herein. Furthermore those texts would still retain a valid historical subtext; it would merely be further removed from the explicit dates encountered therein.

20   But this is far from proven.

21   Wise, Michael., *THE FIRST MESSIAH*. (© 1999 by Michael O. Wise) (HarperCollins Publishers, 10 East 53rd Street, New York, NY 10022). http://www.harpercollins.com.

Finally, the many historical contradictions between the four Gospels can perhaps be best accounted for by the thesis postulated herein. After all, if Jesus really lived a century earlier than the time portrayed in those texts, then it is only natural, to some degree, that there would be conflicting accounts in respect to certain historic details of what supposedly happened. One final point might also be worth mentioning before moving on to the next chapter: the neutrality of the Koran in respect to the chronology of Jesus. There are many passages of the Koran that speak of Jesus, but none of them distinctly place him within Roman times. As far as the Koran is concerned, Jesus may have lived either in the Roman era of Judaean occupation, or in the Hasmonean era. In fact, according to Kamal Salibi, the Jesus[22] of the Koran was a prophet who lived five hundred years before the alleged time of Christ.[23] His book is actually quite fascinating, and I highly recommend it. However Mr. Salibi was apparently unaware of the *Toldoth Jeschu*, and he also accorded historicity to the apostle Paul. He does acknowledge a Jesus (Jeschu) living in the first century, but he ultimately depicts the Jesus of the New Testament as a composite figure. Nevertheless he challenges the geographical provenance of Jesus, as I have challenged the chronology.

---

22   Jesus is Issa in the Koran (Qur'an).

23   Salibi, Kamal S., *CONSPIRACY IN JERUSALEM: WHO WAS JESUS?* (© Kamal Salibi, 1998) (First published in 1988 in hardback as *Conspiracy in Jerusalem: The Hidden Origins of Jesus*) (Reprinted 2002 by I.B. Turis and Co. Ltd.) (2007 Tauris Parke Paperbacks, an imprint of I.B. Tauris & Co. Ltd. 6 Salem Road, London W2 4BU 175 Fifth Avenue, New York, NY 10010) (Distributed in the U.S.A. and Canada by Palgrave Macmillan, a division of St. Martin's Press) (Paperback edition first published in 1992). http://www.ibtauis.com.

Reappraisal

N ow that we have presented our case, we must review and reconsider the evidence, from a critical perspective. We have seen that from two Jewish sources, namely the Talmud and the Toldoth Jeschu, there is textual evidence that Jesus lived in the days of Alexander Jannaeus and his widow Alexandra, respectively. We have also seen that, according to Daniel's prophecy of the seventy weeks, the Messiah was to come 483 years after the decree of Cyrus, which gives a result of 53 B.C., which is clearly far too early for the Jesus of the New Testament. But when the 45-year discrepancy between the standard chronology and that of Josephus' *Antiquities* is taken into account, this gives a result of 98 B.C., which is even further removed from the purported time of Christ. The chronology of Josephus' *War* gives us a date ten years later, or 88 B.C., which of course is still far too early for Christ. But the differences in chronology prove that different systems of chronology were apparently used by the Jews at different periods of their history. Queen Alexandra, the widow of Alexander Jannaeus, reigned over the Jews from 76 B.C. to 67 B.C., according to the standard chronology. Considering the relative flexibility of the systems of chronology apparently used by the Jews in those times, it is reasonable to suppose that, if Jesus lived in the days of Queen Alexandra, and claimed messianic status in her reign, that this also may have coincided with calculations of the *terminus ad quem* of Daniel's prophecy of the seventy weeks employed by the Jews of that time. To this evidence is added the important evidence respecting the chronological falsification found in the Massoretic texts of Ezra and Nehemiah. Therefore a fairly strong circumstantial case is evident that Jesus lived in Hasmonean times, rather than in Roman times.

All of the above evidence is also further supplemented by evidence respecting the *Ebionism* of both James and Jesus, and the probability that they were Levites. This is further augmented by the probability that the Jewish temple at Leontopolis in Egypt was used by the *Ebionim* as a place to worship God in spirit and truth without any bloody animal sacrifices. This evidence is also further supplemented by a passage from the Talmud that speaks of Jesus as being "near those in power" which in turn implies consanguinity with the Hasmonean dynasty. Furthermore we ought to keep in mind that all this evidence is derived from multiple and diverse, independent, sources; this only increases the evidential value of such material. Therefore it is safe to say that a strong case exists that Jesus actually lived in the first century B.C., based upon very strong circumstantial evidence. Not only that, but we have also addressed possible reasons why disciples of Jesus would have chosen to depict him living in Roman times, instead of Hasmonean times. In fact, there would have been multiple motives to thus dislocate Jesus from his original timeframe: first and foremost, to claim that he had fulfilled messianic prophecy; secondly, to implicate the Romans and the Herods in the murder of Jesus; and thirdly, to associate Jesus with the legacy of John the Baptist. Therefore I feel that a reasonably strong case has been presented that Jesus lived in the first century B.C., based upon the circumstantial evidence. The question is: Is the evidence strong enough? In other words, is this evidence, as seemingly strong as it is, really strong enough to redate Jesus to the first century B.C.?

Ultimately each reader will have to render his or her own judgment respecting the relative strength of the evidence, and whether or not it is sufficient to redate Jesus back to the first century B.C. But one ought to consider how difficult it is to overcome the academic and cultural inertia that favours the commonly-accepted date for Christ. Aside from the blind faith of religious believers, even many of those who otherwise pride themselves upon their open-mindedness may be reluctant to redate Christ to the first century B.C., simply because it is too radical a change from their accustomed way of thinking. I certainly do not expect evangelicals and fundamentalists to be persuaded by my evidence, but even many of those who may cherish some alternate theory of Christ may find my evidence rather inconvenient, since it does not fit into a pattern already commonly accepted. This includes not only those fond of Grail theories, or those who may advocate a New Age interpretation of Christ, but also those who postulate any number of alternative academic theories, or subscribe to such. In some respects, to suggest that Jesus lived a century before the commonly-accepted time is one of the most radical revisions of Christ and Christianity yet proposed. As such, the idea may be unwelcome in many quarters. Nevertheless I felt that the evidence was sufficiently strong that it should be known. I have not claimed, nor do I claim, that the evidence is tantamount to absolute proof. In fact, it is possible that the theory may be disproved at some point. On the other hand, it is also possible that some future researcher may bring forward additional evidence in favour of the thesis advocated herein. I admit that much of the evidence above is obscure, oblique, occult, and recondite; nevertheless the very obscurity of the evidence is another consideration in its favour. When we can see so many different sources of evidence converge together to uphold a single theory, then the theory is strengthened by the heterogeneity of its sources, in evidential terms. But of course evidence is subject to interpretation.

I personally consider the evidence from Daniel's prophecy of the seventy weeks to be the single strongest strand of evidence; it is far stronger and more important, in my view, than both the Talmud and the Toldoth put together. This is precisely why I thought that it was worth representing the theory already otherwise advocated by G.R.S. Mead. A person can easily point out that, both the Talmud and the Toldoth are intrinsically hostile sources, and therefore are not exactly trustworthy in respect to the chronology of Christ. In other words, a charge of anachronism against such texts is not entirely unwarranted, either by way of carelessness or design. In fact, a person may notice, that in the Talmud passage from *Kallah*, quoted from above,[1] both Rabbi Akiba and Rabbi Joshua

---

1   Mead., op. cit., pgs. 156-157.

are contemporaries, even though historically they are separated by two centuries. Therefore this is a gross anachronism, and one may rightly charge inaccuracy to the Talmud on that account. Furthermore we are faced with a chronological uniformity in the case of the New Testament, which is a most formidable challenge to the revised chronology advocated herein. Of course this is taken account of by our suggestion that there had been a decision by a hypothetical messianic *kahal* to dislocate Jesus from his original timeframe, for various reasons, which have also been offered. Nevertheless such uniformity still seems like a strong barrier to overcome, especially in view of other contradictions evident between the four Gospel texts. In other words, the fact that, in so many instances, the Gospels often contradict one another, and yet, they all nevertheless agree on the time in which Jesus was crucified, and by whom, this seems to greatly strengthen the supposition that Jesus really lived in the days of Herod and Pilate.

Furthermore the evidence of the substitution of *Artaxerxes* for *Xerxes* in the forged Massoretic texts of Ezra and Nehemiah, although it lends itself to the theory advocated herein, does not necessarily require a re-dating of Christ; instead, a person could concede the chronological falsification,[2] and yet maintain that Christ was nevertheless born in the days of Herod; in that case, Christ would simply have been another latter day messianic pretender who happened to benefit circumstantially from a clever chronological falsification wrought by the Jews.[3] Furthermore we must remember the essentially reactive nature of such texts as the Toldoth Jeschu, and of those portions of the Talmud that speak of Mary and Jesus. Being essentially reactive in nature, they cannot in and of themselves supplant the proactive Gospel texts. What is lacking is any confirmation from any neutral historical source confirming Christ's historicity, either in the first century B.C., or the first century A.D. This is, admittedly, as much of a problem for a thesis advocating Christ in the first century B.C. as one advocating Christ in the first century A.D. Despite these realizations, the nagging suspicion that Jesus may

---

2   Which I definitely do regard as absolutely proven herein, in respect to those texts.

3   Either before, during, or after his own time. Ezra & Nehemiah were apparently written sometime between 46 B.C. and approximately 140 A.D.

have lived in the days of the Hasmoneans will not go away. While the evidence may not be quite as strong and clear-cut as we would wish, it is still nevertheless quite significant. The evidence dovetails together from so many different sources so well and fits together so well to present a harmonious portrait of Christ in Hasmonean times as to defy the "explanation" of it all being mere coincidence.

Christians will no doubt balk at what I have written respecting Paul. They will carp that I have not sufficiently proven my case against the historicity of Paul, and will probably use the excuse that Paul had some kind of eye disease, which was why he employed trusted disciples to act as his secretaries in the writing of many of his epistles. Yet there is a certain hollow irony in such a line of argument, since the very epistle which would no doubt be appealed to as the basis for such a claim[4] is one in which "Paul" makes a point of claiming explicit authorship.[5] For it is in Galatians in which we read "Where is the blessedness you spoke of? For I testify on your behalf, that, if possible, you would have plucked out your own eyes, and given them to me"; which is taken by some as referring to some strange and unidentified eye affliction that Paul was beset by. Yet towards the very end of the same epistle we read "You see how large a letter I have written unto you with mine own hand." Therefore the very epistle that would be appealed to as the basis for such an explanation is an exception to the rule. And, as noted above, the colophon, although it does not ascribe authorship to anyone else,[6] neither is Paul himself explicitly named as the author of the letter. It simply says "Written unto the Galatians from Rome". It is implied that Paul wrote the epistle, but not explicitly stated in the colophon. Christians might claim that before this time Paul had been afflicted by a strange eye disease, that was to humble him, on account of his many visions and revelations,[7] and that this may have been related to his three days of blindness from his vision

---

4   Galatians 4:15.
5   Galatians 6:11.
6   As most of the Pauline epistles are ascribed contrary authorship, discussed above. Galatians 6:11 pretty much ruled out ascription of authorship to anyone but Paul, however. Nevertheless Paul is not named as the author in the colophon.
7   2 Corinthians 12:7.

of Christ on the road to Damascus,[8] but that, after he arrived in Rome, he was healed. This is a convenient yet seemingly plausible explanation, yet the book of Acts itself does not give a hint of an ongoing eye affliction of any kind. We are told merely that Paul was three days and nights without sight.[9] Furthermore these Christians cannot come up with a credible explanation for why Paul, who was taught in Jerusalem by the prestigious Rabbi Gamaliel,[10] never saw or even so much as heard of the great wonder-worker from Galilee, in all his years, right in Jerusalem. It is interesting that the Toldoth attributes thirty years distance of time between Jeschu and Paul. This at least avoids the obvious problem just stated, which the New Testament account is burdened with. This is a fatal flaw in the scheme, which proves that Paul was a mere fiction. As far as I am concerned, I have superabundantly proven that Paul was a mere phantom. Of course this in and of itself does not prove that Jesus really lived in the days of Queen Salome-Alexandra, but it does eliminate one potentially huge obstacle. I also strongly suspect that the earliest form of the Toldoth omitted any mention of Paul. The form of the story suggests, on the contrary, that the climax of the story was the dragging of the corpse of Jeschu through the streets of Jerusalem. Of course everybody must know that this never happened; even the Jews who first told the story, wrote it down, and read it, had to have only relished the symbolic aspect of having victory over their ideological opponents. Because otherwise, if this had happened, then obviously no religion such as Christianity could ever have arisen. The followers of Sabbatai Zevi do not deny his "conversion" to Islam; they merely reinterpret it as an act of "occultation" in accord with their mystical beliefs. Likewise in the case of Jesus, there must have been a circumstance that at least allowed his disciples to claim, either in his own generation or in a later generation, that he ascended to heaven. Although this is generally depicted as a carnal bodily resurrection from the dead,[11] there is nevertheless a remnant of a tradition of a more spiritual interpretation within the texts of the New Testament itself.[12]

---

8   Acts 9:9; 22:11.

9   Acts 9:9.

10   Acts 22:3.

11   Mt 28:9; Lk 24:36-43; Jn 20:19-29; 21:7-14; Acts 1:3; Toldoth Jeschu 8.

12   Mt 22:30; Mt 12:25; Lk 20:34-38; 1 Corinthians 15:44-50; Hebrews 12:23; Revelation 20:4.

Therefore it is at least possible that the original claim was one of spiritual ascension to heaven, rather than of a bodily resurrection in strictly carnal terms. In fact, the Toldoth itself uses the term *ascension* rather than *resurrection*. And this despite the otherwise obviously carnal depiction narrated therein. Of course we can only speculate upon what may have really happened, and furthermore I have stated that I am not seeking to offer a complete explanation of the historical Jesus herein; I am merely offering evidence that Jesus may have lived in the first century B.C. But we may surmise that the circumstances were such that, at whatever point claims of a bodily resurrection were made on Christ's behalf, there was no possibility of a refutation. This may have been due to a number of different reasons, other than a claim of a miraculous resurrection.[13] Therefore the crude display of vengeful triumphalism in the Toldoth is juvenile, infantile, and absurd. It certainly undercuts the validity of the Toldoth as a serious historical text. Mead should have picked up on this, but he did not comment upon it. In fact, I strongly suspect that this was the very reason why the story was set in the days of Queen Salome-Alexandra.[14] The Romans themselves would hardly have been concerned if some upstart religious sect among the Jews claimed that their crucified Master had risen from the dead.[15] Furthermore in the days of the Roman occupation, the Jews no longer held the legal authority for a death sentence.[16] Therefore the rationale for the story dictated a setting in which a Jewish monarch was in a position of unchallengeable power. So the evidence from the Toldoth is not really all that strong, admittedly. I feel the same way about the passages from the Talmud, which abounds with so many blatant anachronisms. As stated above, if it were only for the Talmud and the Toldoth Jeschu, we could easily jettison the theory that Jesus lived 100 B.C.

But we also have Daniel's prophecy of the seventy weeks. This appears to

---

13   Which claim is rejected on holistic grounds.

14   Although technically, even this is not true; the Queen is merely named Helene therein, which places the story in an imaginal setting.

15   Unless this idea were associated with military opposition to Roman occupation. But against this we have the blatantly pacifist teachings of Christ: Mt 5:21-22,39-42; 26:52; Lk 6:27-36; cf Mt 22:15-21; Mk 12:13-17; Lk 20:19-26.

16   Jn 18:31.

give us some very strong circumstantial evidence in favour of an earlier date for Jesus. This is also particularly pungent when we consider the evidence from Josephus and from the Septuagint proving the lateness of Ezra and Nehemiah.[17] Once again this evidence does not prove that Jesus himself actually lived so much earlier than the commonly-accepted time, but such evidence is at least congenial to that theory. And we can be quite sure that Daniel's prophecy of the seventy weeks was very important to the earliest Christians. In fact, we can even find a couple of references to a prophetic period of seventy weeks in the Christian version[18] of the Testament of Levi. The relevant verses are as follows:

"And now I have learnt that for seventy weeks ye shall go astray, and profane the priesthood, and pollute the sacrifices."[19]

"And whereas ye have heard concerning the seventy weeks, hear also concerning the priesthood. For in each jubilee there shall be a priesthood."[20]

Although these are not explicit references to Daniel's prophecy of seventy weeks, nevertheless the literary parallel is obvious. And we can be quite sure that the *Testaments* are pseudepigraphal. The reference to "each jubilee" in the latter verse also betokens an implicit reference to the book of Jubilees, which was written in the Herodian era. And there can be no doubt about the anteriority of *Jubilees*, since in the Testament of Judah there is a reference to a battle between Jacob and his sons and Esau and his sons, which is narrated in *Jubilees*.[21] What is also interesting is that Levi is exalted above Judah in the *Testaments*. Not only that, but there appears to have been an attempt in *Levi* to reconcile the apparent discrepancy between the Levitical and Davidic descent of Jesus:

17   In fact that evidence strongly suggests that Ezra & Nehemiah were written after the works of Josephus. The same is also true of the New Testament texts.
18   It is generally admitted by critical biblical scholars that the *Testaments of the Twelve Patriarchs*, as they have come down to us, have been interpolated by Christians. They are based upon earlier Jewish texts. Fragments of some of these earlier texts have been found among the Dead Sea Scrolls.
19   Testament of Levi, 4:24.
20   Testament of Levi, 5:1.
21   Testament of Judah, 2:2-9; cf Jubilees 37 & 38. The account is excluded from Genesis.

"And by thee and Judah shall the Lord appear among men, saving every race of men."[22]

I suppose it is not surprising that the earlier, Aramaic version of the *Testament of Levi* excludes all these verses. Nevertheless there is enough of a literary parallel with the remainder of the surviving Greek texts to prove that the Greek texts were based upon earlier Aramaic texts.[23] The texts may have been originally composed in Hebrew.[24] However I would hasten to add that the introductions and notes to texts in the *Forgotten Books of Eden* collection are not very trustworthy.[25] Once again this material is admittedly obscure, but I felt it was at least worth mentioning.

Of course fundamentalist Christians, so far from being convinced, will no doubt rant and rave against what I have written, and no doubt also cite as "evidence" against it notable examples, such as a numerical parlour-

22   Testament of Levi, 1:14. These verses are taken from *The Forgotten Books of Eden.*

23   Wise, Abegg & Cook., op. cit., pgs. 250-260. The Words of Levi. (1Q21, Geniza Fragments, Mt. Athos Greek text, 4Q213-214, 4Q540-541).

24   Ibid.

25   The Forgotten Books of Eden. (© 1927 by Alpha House, Inc.) (Thomas Nelson). The very same observation also applies to the Lost Books of the Bible. (© 1926 by Alpha House, Inc.)(Thomas Nelson). Numerous examples could be given, but we will only cite the following: In the introduction to The Testaments of the Twelve Patriarchs, it is stated that the twelve books "are biographies written between 107 and 137 B.C. [sic]" But we are not told any reason for why these dates of composition are maintained; it is a mere pontification. Furthermore the views of the late Dr. R.H. Charles seem to have been misrepresented to some degree therein, since his name is invoked, but without reference to the fact that he elsewhere stated that in his opinion, the Testaments had been interpolated by Christian scribes, although based upon earlier Jewish texts. This view may be found in the more scholarly two-volume set of Old Testament Pseudepigrapha, edited by James H. Charlesworth, still available today. However even this latter, "more scholarly" treatment is of questionable value; for example, I noted that in the introduction to IV Maccabees therein, it was pointed out by the "brilliant" scholars that the Gospel of Mark had some literary affinity with IV Maccabees. Not only is this untrue, but the fact that the Gospel of Luke <u>does</u> have definite literary affinities to IV Maccabees was not mentioned. For so-called biblical "scholars" to commit such a blunder is equivalent to reading that automobiles run on kerosene (rather than gasoline) in an automechanics manual.

trick performed by Sir Robert Anderson "proving" that Jesus rode on a donkey into Jerusalem on the exact day predicted by Daniel centuries earlier.[26] Anderson, a dispensational premillennialist, is at pains to prove the authenticity of Daniel, and while he does admittedly offer some valid points, he still is notoriously guilty of misrepresenting the evidence, and even of an implicit Conspiracy of Silence respecting evidence contrary to his own cherished belief-system. Anderson postulates a hypothetical 360-day prophetic calendar, to bring Daniel's prophecy of the seventy weeks into perfect accord with the alleged time that Jesus rode into Jerusalem.[27] But Anderson completely disregards the 364-day calendar found in both *Enoch* and *Jubilees*. No doubt this was a function of his policy of silence respecting texts whose very existence demolished the version of Christianity advocated by him. Therefore in a *holistic* sense his evidence can be negated. It is also further negated by the rather obvious fact that the Jews knew that the year was 365 days long as far back as the eighth century B.C., if not for many centuries before that time.[28] But if anything, the evidence offered by Robert Anderson only serves to illustrate the point made above respecting the propriety of placing Jesus in the exact time in which the Gospels do. It is therefore even more

---

26   See his book *Daniel in the Critics Den*. However this can also be found online @http://www.newble.co.uk/anderson/daniel/dan1.html.

27   With the additional assumption that the *terminus a quo* of the prophecy was in the 20th year of Artaxerxes, as we read in Nehemiah 2ff. Therefore either Anderson was unaware of the evidence presented above respecting the chronological falsification of the Massoretic texts of Ezra & Nehemiah (which seems unlikely, since William Whiston, in his notes upon Josephus, stated his opinion that neither of those books appeared to have been extant earlier than the second century A.D., and Mr. Anderson was no doubt well acquainted with that edition of Josephus), in which case he was insufficiently diligent to adequately deal with his subject-matter intelligently; or he knew of the evidence, but remained suspiciously silent about it. He was also guilty of an implicit Conspiracy of Silence respecting the Book of Enoch, which demolishes his much vaunted Protestant Canon of Scripture.

28   Genesis 5:21-24. Critical scholars concede that Enoch was a solar cypher. The Ptolemaic Egyptians knew the true length of the year; they attributed to Hermes Trismegistus, (whom some also equate with the Hebrew Enoch,) 36,525 books. (See *The History of Freemasonry*, by Albert Mackey., pg. 51.) The exact correspondence of numbers to the true length of the solar year (365.25 days) is too much to be pure coincidence.

"perfect" than even the original *terminus ad quem* of Daniel's prophecy, based upon a natural, straightforward reading of the text. Therefore it suggests artificiality, rather than historic realism. This also undercuts the argument that Jesus probably lived during the commonly-accepted time, rather than in the Hasmonean era; at the very least, there seems to be an equal probability that Jesus could have lived at either time.

One other point is also worth noting. There are a few Talmud traditions of the stoning of Jesus.[29] What is curious about this is that, although there are no New Testament stories alluding to an actual stoning of Jesus, we are nevertheless told in the Gospel of John that the Jews took up stones to stone Jesus.[30] Not only that, but there is a story in which the apostle Paul is stoned, apparently to death.[31] Many Christians believe that Paul referred to this incident in 2 Corinthians 12:2-4, where he speaks of "a man in Christ caught up into paradise, who heard unspeakable words, which it is not lawful for a man to utter." My question is: Do we have here, a possible remnant of a tradition, that Jesus may have come to his demise in a manner somewhat different from what we are otherwise told? After all, crucifixion lends itself far more readily to a depiction of a fulfillment of such prophecies as Isaiah 53 and Psalm 22.[32] The agony of crucifixion lends itself far more readily to the poetic anguish expressed in such passages than being stoned with stones. And if Jesus were first stoned to death, and afterwards hanged on a tree, then this would be more in literal accord with what we find written in certain New Testament passages examined above.[33] I realise that this is a radical revision from what we have traditionally been taught to believe about the death of Jesus, but it is possible that it could be true.

Some may feel that I have dealt a death-blow to the historicity of Jesus.

---

29   Mead., op. cit., pgs. 176-178. These tractates are Palestinian *Sanhedrin*, 25c, and Babylonian *Sanhedrin*, 67a.

30   John 8:59; 10:31-39.

31   Acts 14:19-20.

32   It may be objected by some that Psalm 22 was not composed as a prophecy; while strictly speaking this may be true, nevertheless the Psalms were frequently interpreted as prophecies by many postexilic Jews. See the Dead Sea Scrolls.

33   Acts 5:30; 10:39; 13:29; Galatians 3:13; 1 Peter 2:24.

They may point to the silence of Josephus and Philo[34] as being fatal to any supposition that either Jesus or Paul ever lived as historic figures. And admittedly this is a major problem. However I would point out that if we redate Jesus to the Hasmonean era, the absence of historical records is not quite so glaring as if we suppose he lived in the Roman era of Judaean occupation. The reason is simple: the very presence of the Romans in Palestine would in and of itself double the likelihood of someone making a historical record of some kind respecting such a prominent messianic figure as Jesus Christ. In fact, the absence of any legitimate or credible Roman records of the trial and crucifixion[35] of Christ tends to circumstantially strengthen the thesis that Jesus lived in Hasmonean times. On the other hand, the absence of credible accounts of any provenance only serves to undermine the implicit assumption of Christ's historicity. In fact, some may speculate that both Jesus Christ and Christianity were invented as a Jewish response to the destruction of the Jerusalem temple in 70 A.D.[36] But the thesis presented herein has assumed the historicity of Jesus implicitly; this is another issue that is technically beyond the scope of our inquiry. Stated otherwise, if we proceed with the implicit assumption that there was indeed a historical Jesus, upon whom the Gospels and other texts of the New Testament were based, then we feel we have presented cogent evidence that Jesus lived back in Hasmonean times, rather than in the days of Herod and Pontius Pilate.

Admittedly, everything discussed above is a lot to take in. It is certainly challenging to reconsider so much that is otherwise usually taken for granted. Nevertheless I still feel that the evidence is sufficiently strong that it is worth some serious consideration by those who are genuinely seeking knowledge of the original, historical Jesus. The evidence is significant enough that it should be more widely known. Many may find

---

34   Neither of whom mentioned either Jesus or Paul. See discussion above on the *Testimony Flavium*.

35   Despite the efforts of Christian forgers as evinced in the New Testament Apocrypha and such disreputable works as the *Archko Volume*.

36   Christianity as a religion requires no animal sacrifices; therefore a temple as such is superfluous. This is based upon the one-time "perfect" and "final" sacrifice for sins by the Son of God-Messiah, etc., etc. *ad nauseum ad infinitum*.

the evidence sufficiently compelling to redate Jesus to the first century B.C. Gerald Massey, who wrote volumes about the Egyptian roots of civilization, and also wrote a book entitled *The Historical Jesus and the Mythical Christ*, in which he traced the New Testament depiction of Jesus back to ancient Egyptian roots, nevertheless conceded the historicity of the Jesus who lived 100 B.C. Even those who may find the evidence inadequate to thus redate Jesus must nevertheless admit that there is a significant amount of circumstantial evidence suggesting an earlier date for Jesus. I have tried to be fair to all the evidence. I rest my case. The verdict lies with the seeker of truth.

Mead's errors

Despite what may appear to be somewhat harsh criticisms of Mead's work on the subject treated above, both in the above text, and also to follow, I will state briefly that G.R.S. Mead paved the way for my own work; and without his earlier book mine would not exist. Therefore I owe an invaluable debt of gratitude to him for opening up this subject to non-specialists and bringing to light numerable obscure facts that shed light on the question of the chronology of Jesus Christ. Furthermore one would be well advised to consult his work to find the same subject treated from a much different perspective; the very fact that two different authors living a century apart could nevertheless both present significant evidence that Jesus may have lived a century before the commonly-accepted time only strengthens the evidential value of the theory thus advocated. Anyone who reads my text can clearly see how much I have relied upon Mead's earlier work, and it is fair to say that his book is essential reading on the subject. Mead's writing style and his perspective are greatly different from my own. And this is probably only partly due to the fact that he lived in a different time. I suppose there is a certain irony in the fact that two different authors, living a century apart from one another, have both written works discussing the possibility that Jesus Christ may have lived a century earlier than is commonly supposed. And while it is fair to say that without Mead's work mine would not exist,[1] I feel that I have

---

1 Or at least not in its current form.

brought forward significant evidence that was unknown or unnoticed before. In fact, I feel that Daniel's prophecy of the seventy weeks is the very heart of the evidence in favour of the thesis advocated herein. As such, I feel that I have greatly augmented the case that Jesus lived 100 B.C. And furthermore if it can be said that Mead's book is essential reading upon this subject, then I feel that mine is even more so.[2]

But in the service of truth I feel that it is necessary to point out some of Mead's more grievous errors, lest I be accused of implicitly endorsing what is otherwise insipid, inane, absurd, ridiculous, fatuous, obtuse, myopic, opaque, misguided, superficial, tedious, turgid, mischievous, and pseudo-scholarly. One has but to read the first few opening paragraphs of Mead's book to see how overlaid his perspective is with a syrupy sentimentalism that is guaranteed to lead him down a false path. He views the world through rosy Theosophical spectacles which color everything he sees with a hue that is unsuitable for historic realism. This I suspect is at the very root of the problem with Mr. Mead. It is ultimately his own form of religious blindness. Of course we cannot expect any writer to write outside of his own personal perspective; that would be quite impossible. And when we read a book with controversial subject-matter we at least expect a degree of excitement on the part of the author that we are not likely to find in the pages of an encyclopaedia entry. The book should at least be interesting, at least to those with some interest in the proposed subject-matter. It is the cardinal sin of any author to be boring. Anything but that can be forgiven. And although I have characterized certain aspects of Mead's book as "tedious" and "turgid" I nevertheless concede that his book is generally interesting to the first-time reader. After all the idea that Jesus may have lived 100 B.C. is pretty much a novel idea to most people, even today. Even if one has a view to "debunk" the theory, one first needs to be acquainted with the relevant evidence.

I have taken it upon myself to once again re-read Mead's book, to acquaint myself once more with his material, in order to write this chapter. I do not pretend that this review is in any way exhaustive, or even comprehensive; yet more along the lines of giving some of the most egregious examples

---

2   I hope the reader will forgive my apparent lack of humility, however justified.

of Mead's lack of genuine scholarship and objectivity. In the course of this reading I found it necessary to digress and write how irritating certain habits of his writing are. For example, Mead speaks over and over again of "tradition" as representing what today we would recognise as fundamentalism, or evangelical Christianity. Yet Mead appears blithely oblivious to the fact that most Protestants have been taught that "tradition" as such is something very strongly and emphatically condemned by Jesus Christ himself. In fact, anyone who even bothers to read the Bible can see passages in which Jesus absolutely condemns the Pharisees for rejecting the word of God and exalting the traditions of men.[3] Mead also briefly discusses the question of the historicity of Jesus, but without offering the slightest amount of real proof against the allegations of those who claimed that Jesus was merely a phantom. It seems to be a rather surprising oversight, since when he wrote and published his book the *ahistorical* model in respect to Jesus Christ was much more *en vogue* than it is today. Mead also has a distinct tendency to reject Christian sources outright and to favour Jewish sources as being more reliable. One also frequently gets the distinct impression that Mead is utterly out of his depth. But as we will see, Mead's occult beliefs cloud his judgment immeasurably. This is the real source of his confusion. And while Mead writes expansively on a new atmosphere of free inquiry[4] I personally have no doubt whatever that there were hardcore hellfire-and-brimstone preachers back then, just as there still are today. Mead seems to pause too long over mere trifles, and spends less time on real issues. His writing lacks precision. A person reading his book is likely to be even more confused after having read it. But of course these are just general criticisms; we will proceed with clear examples of Mead's many errors.

Speaking of the infamous *Testimonium Flavium*, Mead writes:

"For many years it has been abandoned by all schools of criticism, even the most conservative, and we have only to turn to any modern translation or text to find it definitely characterised as an interpolation or enclosed in brackets."[5]

---

3   Mt 15:1-11; Mk 7:1-13.

4   Which no doubt was true to some degree in 1903.

5   Mead., op. cit., pg. 60.

While what Mead wrote may have seemed true to him, nevertheless I thought it was worth pointing out that my edition of Josephus treats the passage as genuine. But what really proves Mead's pseudo-scholarship is what he has to say about the Protevangelion of James. Mead refers to a "recent brilliant study" by one Conrady on the "Book of James" otherwise known as the "Protevangelium" and Mead enthuses over the fact that this work "is already admitted by some to reach back as far as the middle of the second century"[6] and then proceeds to relate how Conrady has "demonstrated" that the Protevangelion is the original basis of the infancy narratives of Matthew and Luke.[7] Here Mead absolutely proves that he is out of his league and that he is merely a pseudo-scholar; he lacks even a sufficient familiarity with the documents in question to immediately recognise the sheer impossibility of what he is suggesting, or of Conrady's theories. First of all, it is quite impossible that this "book of James" could be in any way contemporary with any of the four Canonical Gospels, much less predate them; if it dates to the middle of the second century, then those texts must date to the middle of the first century, or not much later. But if, as Mead insists, the Canonical Gospels date to no earlier than some time in the second century, then this text must date to no earlier than the third century, if not later. In fact, not only does the character of the text clearly indicate that it must postdate the Canonical Gospels by a generation at least, if not by a century or more, but the very fact that Tatian's *Diatessaron* takes no notice of it also proves that it dates to a later time, or that it was regarded as spurious when Tatian composed his work. But anyone truly familiar with the New Testament will at once see the impossibility of supposing that such a document as the Protevanglion could be contemporary with any of the New Testament texts. For one thing, the Protevangelion shamelessly exalts Mary far above anything we read of in the New Testament. In fact, in the Gospel of Luke, when a woman declared "Blessed is the womb that bare thee, and the breasts that suckled thee" Jesus responds by saying "Yea, Rather, Blessed are they that hear the word of God, and keep it."[8] In other words, the very sentiment expressed is sharply rebuked by

---

6   Ibid., pgs. 63-64.

7   Ibid.

8   Luke 11:27-28.

Christ in the strongest possible terms. Such Mariolatry as is evinced in texts like the *Protevanglium* is completely foreign to the Canonical New Testament. But moving on from the milk, to the meat of the matter, the *Protevangelion* depicts Mary as a perpetual virgin. This at once instantly identifies it as a work contrary to, and of a completely different date from, the New Testament. And Mead, if he had been a genuine scholar, should have known this. There are a dozen passages in the New Testament that clearly negate the false dogma of the perpetual virginity of Mary.[9] In fact, it is quite obvious that the text of the Protevangelion made up the story that Joseph was an elderly widower, who already had children by his first wife, who married the very young virgin Mary, to account for the brothers and sisters of Jesus who are mentioned in the Gospels. Catholics today still believe the same ridiculous story, albeit the book it is found in is excluded from the Canon of Scripture. But neither Conrady nor Mead had a sufficient degree of scholarship to see the clear impossibility of the Protevangelion predating any of the Gospels. In fact, I have included in my note a reference to Matthew 2:13-21 precisely because none of these other children of Joseph are mentioned therein. In the colophon to the Protevangelium, James wrote that he fled and hid in the desert when Herod sought to slay the boys in Bethlehem. This implies that, according to that text, we are expected to believe that James was old enough to thus hide and provide for himself. This is obviously intended as an "explanation" for what is otherwise found in Matthew's Gospel, together with the other Gospels and New Testament documents that speak of brothers and sisters of Jesus. In fact, there is even more evidence that the Protevangelium postdates Matthew: the story of the martyrdom of Zechariah the father of John the Baptist, recounted in the sixteenth chapter, was obviously intended to explain Christ's declaration that the Pharisees would be guilty of the blood of all the righteous slain from the foundation of the world, from the blood of Abel to the blood of Zechariah the son of Berechiah, who was slain between the temple and the altar (Mt 23:35). The Protevangelion says that "Zechariah was murdered in the entrance of the temple and the altar, and about the partition" (Protevangelion 16:16). Clearly this

---

9   Mt 1:25; 2:13-21; 12:46-50; 13:54-57; Mk 3:31-35; 6:1-5; Lk 2:1-7; 8:19-21; Jn 7:3-5; Acts 1:14; I Corinthians 9:5; Galatians 1:19.

was intended to correspond to Christ's statement in Mathew, even though he was almost certainly referring to some now lost tradition of the martyrdom of Zechariah the son of Berechiah, who wrote the book of Zechariah. This is an instance that proves to me that Mead's scholarship is untrustworthy. This is an important point, because it calls into question many of his other statements, notably the point that there is an exemplar in Codex de Rossi 96 of a "distinctly Karaite Toldoth."[10] Since I cannot trust Mead's scholarly judgment I feel that it is highly questionable as to whether or not in fact there is any genuine exemplar of a Karaite Toldoth. The version of the Toldoth found in Mead's book is anything but Karaite. Perhaps Mead wanted to use a more complete version of the Toldoth. Once again, without being able to examine an English translation of the text in question, I have no way of determining whether Mead was correct about this or not.

But Mead further makes a gaudy display of his ineptitude by what he writes vis-à-vis the Gospel of Nicodemus, aka the Acts of Pilate.[11] Mead positively fawns over the suggestion by Rendel Harris that the Gospel of Nicodemus is a sort of "Homeric Gospel" in which Joseph of Arimathaea represents Priam, begging the body of Hector (Jesus) of Achilles (Pilate). Despite the fascinating novelty of such a suggestion, it is entirely unwarranted by the evidence. A mere two verses in the Gospel of Nicodemus are devoted to Joseph asking the body of Jesus from Pilate, and it simply follows the norm of the Gospel of John. Mead ought not to have had a fondness for such vanities; it only makes him lose credibility in the eyes of those more acquainted with the relevant subject-matter.

But the really gigantic error committed by Mead which really takes the cake is his completely insipid, inane, absurd, ridiculous, and idiotic suggestion that Jesus never claimed to be the Messiah. Lest this outrageous claim not be believed, I will quote Mead's own words on this:

"But in my opinion these Messianic disputations seem to be due to later developments, and to be part and parcel of doctrinal polemics between Jews and Judaeo-Christians; <u>for I have never been able to believe that</u>

---

10 Mead., op. cit., pg. 316.
11 Ibid., pgs. 65-66.

historically Jesus himself could have made any claim to be the Messiah. If the power of the great teacher, round whose transcendent person all these marvellous traditions and disputes have grown up, is rightly held to have been the power of a Master of Wisdom, not to speak of still more transcendent claims put forward on his behalf, then it can hardly be believed that he would have claimed to be what he could have foreseen would never be admitted by those to whom the Messianic tradition chiefly belonged. True, he may very well have taught a more universal view of Messianism, but that he should have claimed to have been the Messiah of prophecy, in any sense in which the Jews could have understood the idea, without that prophecy turning out to be a bitter mockery, can hardly be believed of a wise and merciful Teacher."[12]

Here we have a perfect example of everything that is wrong with Mead's entire approach and perspective. He is completely unsuited to any real historical inquiry; he has no sense of history. Mead has the unmitigated gall, not to say the arrant stupidity, to say that he cannot believe that Jesus ever claimed to be the Messiah, despite the united testimony of all Jewish and Christian sources, that, despite their otherwise vehement mutual opposition, at least agree on the point that Jesus did claim to be the Messiah in no uncertain terms. But here we arrive at the very heart of Mead's delusion, which robs his work of any real value. Mead cannot get past his own delusional belief in Jesus as a "Master of Wisdom" which leads him to such an unspeakably absurd conclusion. And not only that, but here Mead implicitly contradicts himself as well; for after all, if Jesus truly was so "transcendent" as Mead insists, then why, pray tell, would it have been so much of a "mockery" for him to lay claim to the title of Messiah? And here also we see that Mead's superficiality and lack of adequate research has led him down a dark, false path, and to an erroneous (not to say insane) conclusion. For if Mead had only known that Daniel's prophecy of the seventy weeks had very explicitly pointed to the very time when these other Jewish texts allege that Jeschu lived, he would have realised that it was precisely the Messianic claim that was at the very root of Christ's appeal to his followers. Mead here reveals his ineptitude in gaudy colours. He is bound by his own theological,

12   Ibid., pgs. 317-318.

theosophical shackles, which kept him from seeing what should otherwise have been quite obvious. And Jesus would not have been very much of a "Master of Wisdom" if he was not sufficiently clear about whether or not he laid claim to being the Messiah. Furthermore if he had not laid claim to such a title and office, he would not have come to such a tragic end, either at the hands of the Jews, or the Romans.[13] Every particle of history, everything that even has the slightest hint of historic legitimacy, militates against what Mead so freely froths at the mouth over here. It is really an insult to the intelligence to even read such trash. If this sounds like a harsh criticism, it is nevertheless fully warranted. The truth is I am really being too kind. Mead insists that Jesus, being a Master of Wisdom, would not have laid claim to being the Messiah.[14] But if Jesus really lived right at the very time when the Messiah was supposed to come, according to a key prophecy of the book of Daniel, then it would have behooved him to thus lay claim to messianic status, if he sought to impress himself upon the Jews in any real way. And if he really was such a transcendent Master of Wisdom as Mead alleges, then he could have done whatever was required to convince the Jews that he was indeed the Promised One. But Mead here wants to have his cake and eat it too. Either Jesus was a Master of Wisdom or he was not. If he was, then why would he not have claimed to be the Messiah? Benjamin Crème has thus laid claim for Lord Maitreya as being the Messiah for the Jews, the Christ for the Christians, the Imam Mahdi for the Muslims, the Kalki Avatar for the Hindus, and the Maitreya Buddha for the Buddhists. Is Lord Maitreya so much greater than Jesus? Of course the Theosophists sought to make similar claims generations ago for Krishnamurti.[15] I would also point out that Jesus nowhere claimed to be a "Master of Wisdom" as Mead would have it. His occult beliefs are a gloss, an overlay upon contrary beliefs, like a *palimpsest.* But the Messianic claims are the original, whereas claims of

---

13   I.e., assuming that the thesis herein is wrong and Jesus lived in the Roman era of Judaean occupation.

14   Even though according to Mead's own theory, together with abundant evidence presented herein, Jesus lived at the very time when, according to one of the Hebrew prophets, the Messiah was to come. If Jesus had not laid claim to being the Messiah during such a time, he would have been a Lord of folly, not a Master of Wisdom.

15   But I'm sure that now they would prefer to sweep this under the rug.

Jesus being a so-called "Master of Wisdom" are the overlay.[16] So here we can clearly see that Mead's occult religious beliefs cloud his judgment.

Mead also inadvertently insults Karaite Jews, by stating that the Talmud is the "chief means whereby the Jews have preserved themselves as a nation ever since the time of the final destruction of their Temple"[17] which implies that Karaite Jews are not worthy of any consideration at all. If anything, Karaite Judaism is far more justified than the Rabbinical superstructure of the Talmud, and the extravagant and absurd claims of the Rabbis that such a teaching was given to Moses on Mount Sinai. Mead also once again contradicts himself, by attributing a late date to Daniel on the one hand,[18] and then in the course of the very same discussion, on the very next page in his book, he claims that the Rabbis held that "there was no prophet after Malachi"[19] which, if admitted to be true, is an implicit argument against Mead's late date for Daniel. And would not those Rabbis who lived so many centuries ago be in a far better position to judge the authenticity or otherwise of Daniel? But Mead presumes to know better. Such insufferable arrogance is irksome, especially when it is united with such boundless ignorance.[20]

Mead's statement about James not really being Christ's brother has already been discussed above, albeit briefly. This is another major instance of Mead's ineptitude; and I dare say it seems to be directly related to his lack of perception in respect to the clear teaching of the New Testament that Christ had brothers and sisters. And this is one teaching that we can be absolutely certain is quite archaic, and most likely to be true historically. But it also appears to be Mead's crude and inadequate attempt to deal with those passages in the Pauline corpus that speak of the brothers of

---

16 Cf Mark 14:61-62.

17 Mead., op. cit., pg. 68.

18 I.e., 164 B.C.; Mead., ibid., pg. 74.

19 Ibid., pg. 75.

20 Although I have written above that judging the matter holistically, I am more inclined to view Daniel as a late pseudepigraphon, I am also perfectly content to be proven wrong, or thought to be wrong, and that the book of Daniel is completely genuine. The critics of Daniel have not adequately answered the arguments in favour of the book's authenticity. In either case Daniel foretold of the temple's destruction.

Christ as Paul's contemporaries, which, if allowed to be taken literally, would crush his theory.[21] Compared with these gigantic blunders, any other errors of Mead are merely comparative trifles. Therefore I will not bore the reader with the minutiae of Mead's idiosyncratic approach to this controversial subject-matter. Furthermore a dalliance over such errors will no doubt only make me appear to be mean-spirited and petty, especially when it is added to what may appear to be some exceptionally harsh criticisms. Nevertheless I feel that my criticisms, both of Mead and of others, are fully warranted by the circumstances. And since I have endeavoured to provide obscure evidence in favour of a controversial theory I do not exactly expect to be treated with "kid gloves" myself. I am fully welcome to legitimate criticisms of my thesis, and indeed I feel that I have even pointed out some of the chief weaknesses of the evidence myself. One is unlikely to find a similar degree of candor among authors who advocate a controversial theory. Typically such authors will omit any contrary evidence, or any discussion of any of the difficulties associated with their pet theory. Or if these things are addressed at all, it is usually only in a cursory and inadequate way. Furthermore I do not care to dance around chief points, but rather would get to the meat of the argument right away. Therefore my direct approach may be refreshing to some, but perhaps may seem unstylish to others. Nevertheless hopefully the reader feels more informed after having read my book than before.

---

21   I.e., assuming the historicity of Paul. But see discussion above.

Afterword

Hopefully I have made a contribution to the quest for the historical Jesus by what I have written above. I feel that I have unearthed some little-known (or previously unknown) information that is relevant to the question of precisely when Jesus lived. And despite my seemingly harsh criticisms of Mead above, I am nevertheless indebted to him for his research along these lines. The interpretation of evidence is often highly subjective, but I feel that I have offered the reader a reasonably strong case for Jesus having lived a century earlier than the commonly-accepted time, according to critical-historical canons of interpretation. As stated above, this inquiry was not intended to answer all of the key questions posed by the problem of the historical Jesus. Instead I have sought to limit myself, as much as possible, to a tightly-argued thesis that Jesus may have lived back in Hasmonean times, and to show how diverse, obscure elements of tradition relating to Jesus converge together in a very unexpected way to confirm that thesis. Nevertheless I would now like to tie up a few loose ends.

Above I spoke of an alleged contradiction between what "Paul" wrote in Galatians, and what is recorded in the book of Acts, which some have used to confirm the historicity of Paul. I gave a reference in the notes, but did not explain the discrepancy in detail. In Galatians, "Paul" claims that after his vision, he went to Arabia, and then returned to Damascus.[1] Then after three years he went to Jerusalem to see Peter, and stayed with him fifteen days.[2] He claims he saw no other apostles, except for James the brother of Christ.[3] "Paul" then protests that before God he does not lie.[4] This is suspicious in itself, since a man speaking the truth is unlikely to so protest, unless he expects that others will controvert his testimony. Then he says that he did not return to Jerusalem until fourteen years later, with Barnabas and Titus.[5] This account at least appears to be somewhat different from what is narrated in Acts, and so some have found fault with the book of Acts on that account.[6] In the book of Acts, we are led to believe that, immediately after being baptized by Ananias, Paul preached that Jesus was the Messiah, and went to Jerusalem soon after, but that all the disciples were suspicious of him, until Barnabas vouched for him. We get the impression that Paul became familiar with all the apostles, who were still in Jerusalem.[7] Admittedly the two accounts do seem to differ significantly, which in a strange way, seems to uphold the historicity of Paul.[8] Admittedly this kind of a discrepancy does seem to verify rather than nullify the alleged historicity of Paul.[9] I suppose I could be justly accused of special pleading if I were to argue that the discrepancy had been deliberately written into the text of Galatians in order to "solidify" the seeming

1 Galatians 1:17.
2 Galatians 1:18.
3 Galatians 1:19.
4 Galatians 1:20.
5 Galatians 2:1.
6 Most notably Kamil Salibi, who wrote *CONSPIRACY IN JERUSALEM: WHO WAS JESUS?* drew attention to this discrepancy, and from this argued that the account in the book of Acts was a falsification. But others have argued more convincingly that Paul was more likely the one who was lying. But after due consideration of all the evidence, I was finally led to the conclusion that Paul was merely a completely invented character.
7 Acts 8:1; 9:1-29.
8 Because if Paul were merely a completely invented character, we would expect his epistles to reflect the outline portrayed in the book of Acts, rather than contradict it.
9 Because in this instance the nature of the contradiction is historical, rather than doctrinal. The latter examples of contradictions rather militate against the assumed historicity of the individual in question.

historicity of Paul in just this way. But if Paul really was an invented figure, then it is possible that this was the case. Then again the very same thing could be said about the "fossil" passages that seem to confirm the historicity of Jesus. If Galatians was not written by Paul,[10] then why would the writer of that text write something contrary to the presumably earlier text of the book of Acts? Assuming the priority of Galatians is really no solution; the contradiction remains nevertheless. In that case we would have to ask why the writer of Acts wrote an account so much at odds with the earlier text of Galatians. This is definitely a problem for fundamentalists, however much they may ignore it. But it is also a problem if we deny historicity to Paul. Because the implicit assumption that follows from the postulate that Paul was merely an invented figure is that the book of Acts predates all of the Pauline literature. Conversely, the assumption that the Pauline corpus[11] predates the Book of Acts is more congenial and congruent to the contrary assumption that Paul was a historic figure. However the book of Acts does not give a precise timetable for all of the events that it narrates. It may be argued that it is very unlikely that Paul would only have met Peter and James, rather than any of the other apostles, but if there had been suspicion surrounding Paul, as the account in Acts states, then this is quite possible. In other words, the two accounts, although seemingly contradictory, are not necessarily as contradictory as some have supposed. In other words, the writer of Galatians, who is unidentified in the colophon,[12] who no doubt was a powerful figure within the Pauline faction, wrote freely what he chose. In other words, I do not consider this difficulty to be fatal to the supposition of the ahistoricity of Paul. But we can see that, according to the chronological correspondence, Paul's ministry really was closer to about thirty years later than the time of Christ, just as the Toldoth said. Of course in the New Testament the entire timeframe is approximately a century later than what is found in the Toldoth, but otherwise this thirty year lapse between Christ and Paul is common to both sources. But we are of course speaking of a time when Paul's ministry had been

---

10   I.e., assuming that the above theory is correct, and Paul was merely an invented figure.

11   Or portions thereof.

12   Although it is implicitly to be assumed that is was Paul; Galatians 6:11.

going on for years, possibly decades. So there still is a problem with why Paul never had seen or so much as even heard of Jesus all during his years in Jerusalem. Furthermore there are doctrinal contradictions within the Pauline corpus, that seem to indicate diversity of authorship, as claimed above. For example, as noted before, the Thessalonian epistles seem to depict a carnal concept of resurrection, whereas in 1 Corinthians, "Paul" says that Christ became a spirit.[13] We would do well to recall that the colophon to 1 Corinthians identifies the writers of that epistle as Stephanas, Fortunatus, Achaicus, and Timotheus (Timothy). But this spiritual concept of Christ's resurrection is further contradicted in Colossians, which says of the risen Christ that "in him dwelleth all the fullness of the Godhead bodily."[14] The colophon to Colossians identifies the writers of that epistle as Tychicus and Onesimus.[15] Romans, which was written by a woman,[16] does not have the misogynistic teachings found in some of the Pauline epistles.[17] These are a few clear examples that point to diversity of authorship of the Pauline corpus. And there is even a possible example of a passage that points to the prior existence of at least one of the Gospels therein. In the famous chapter on the resurrection found in 1 Corinthians, we read: "For I delivered unto you first of all that which I also received, how that Christ died for our sins according to the Scriptures; and that he was buried, and that he rose again the third day according to the Scriptures"[18] The problem is, although one can find some passages that at least seem to foretell Christ's passion in the Old Testament,[19] there is nothing therein that specifies a period of "three days" before the Messiah would rise from the dead. True there is a passage from Hosea that reads: "After two days will he revive

---

13   1 Corinthians 15:45.

14   Colossians 2:9.

15   And therefore of different authorship from 1 Corinthians. The Thessalonian epistles, just like Galatians, are implicitly attributed to Paul, who is nevertheless not named in the colophon as the writer.

16   Phoebe, a deaconess. See colophon.

17   I.e., 1 Corinthians 7:1; 11:3; 14:34-37; 1 Timothy 2:9-15; 5:9-15; 2 Timothy 3:6.

18   1 Corinthians 15:3-4.

19   Isaiah 53; Psalms 22, 69.

us: in the third day he will raise us up, and we shall live in his sight."[20] However the context of the passage in Hosea is completely contrary to an assumed messianic interpretation.[21] Therefore it is just barely possible that the four authors of first Corinthians were referring back to a written Gospel that was already extant and accepted as Scripture by the early believers; in fact, the plural "Scriptures" implies two or more such Gospels already written at the time when first Corinthians was composed. This indirectly argues in favour of the thesis that Paul was an invented figure, and those epistles attributed to him were written at a time later than we would otherwise have expected, had he existed and therefore wrote the epistles ascribed to him.

Aside from the question of Paul's alleged historicity, some people may feel unsatisfied by what I have written above because I have not attempted to present a more complete picture or answer some still lingering questions, such as: What does my theory say about the historicity of other New Testament characters, such as the twelve apostles, Mary Magdalene, Joseph of Arimathaea, etc.? But such questions must remain unanswered for now; I have not set out to pinpoint every possible detail of what Christ's life and ministry would have been like, had he lived a century earlier. I have merely sought to present the key evidence that this may have been the case.

Some may be disappointed that I did not write more about the sons of Jesus, and the implications of such "sons" mentioned in the Toldoth for the various Grail theories circulating around today. But quite frankly there was not much that could be written along these lines, especially in such a preliminary study; there are only the two brief passages in the Toldoth confirming that Jeschu had progeny. There is nothing whatever written about Jeschu's wife, or if he had any daughters. Neither are we told anything about his sons, other than that they accompanied him to Jerusalem for the Passover on his last sojourn there. Suffice to say that, the evidence accrued above allows for a Grail bloodline, but one originating approximately a century earlier than commonly supposed.

---

20   Hosea 6:2.
21   On the other hand, the controversial Jesselsohn Stone may vouch for a messianic interpretation of Hosea 6:2 in the days of Herod I.

Furthermore this bloodline was most likely of Levitical rather than Davidic descent.

Before closing, I want to briefly address an issue that may be raised by some persons: the silence of Josephus respecting Jesus. In other words, if we disregard the infamous *Testimonium Flavium* as a notorious forgery, as do most reputable historians, scholars, and literary critics, then not only is there an absence of any clearly identifiable passage respecting Christ in the writings of Josephus placing Christ in the first century, but neither is there any such passage we can readily identify as speaking of Christ in the first century B.C. But this is not necessarily as much of a problem as some may insist; Josephus is similarly silent respecting the decree of Claudius commanding all Jews to depart from Rome. And we have two independent sources confirming this decree; namely, the work of Suetonius, and the book of Acts. Therefore if Josephus could remain silent about a decree so materially affecting his people, then it is not quite so far-fetched that he would also remain silent about a messianic figure like Jesus.

Some may find some of my evidence stronger than other portions. I have sought to be as thorough as possible, without including anything superfluous or ridiculous. I have also sought to present my case with some degree of restraint, lest I weaken my case by overstating it. Various trails of evidence have been suggested for further research by others. I have recently discovered that there has been fairly recently (1999) been another book on the theme that the original, historical Jesus lived about a century earlier than the commonly-accepted time; the book is called *Jesus One Hundred Years Before Christ,* and the author is Alvar Ellegard. The book has received mixed reviews, and without having read it myself I cannot comment upon it, other than what I have read about it in such reviews. One critical review said that Ellegard argued that the references to Jesus in the New Testament were such that they seemed to portray a figure fairly far in the past, rather than someone who recently ascended to heaven. While in general this may be true, the problem of Galatians 1:19 and 1 Corinthians 9:5 remain, where the apostle Paul speaks of having met "James the brother of the Lord" in the first instance, and in the latter instance, referring to "brothers of the Lord" as persons contemporary with himself. Not having read the book I do not know precisely how Ellegard deals with this problem, or if he even addresses it. Other reviews have said that he traces Jesus back to the Teacher of Righteousness of the Dead Sea Scrolls, to the point of identity. But this in itself would appear problematical, since, according to the chronology of the Damascus Document, the Teacher of Righteousness appeared in approximately 176 B.C., or <u>two</u> centuries before Christ supposedly lived, according to canonical sources. Furthermore while Ellegard places the writing of the canonical Gospels in the second century (a position I tend to agree with), he places such documents as 1 Clement, Hermas, Barnabas, the Didache, the Apokalypse, and the Pauline corpus within the first century, and this relative chronology vis-à-vis textual origins appears to be seriously skewed. However his book may be worth reading.

But most importantly, I have read no notice that Mr. Ellegard has pointed out any of the distinctive evidence presented herein, respecting Daniel's prophecy of the seventy weeks, or the chronological falsification found in the canonical texts of Ezra and Nehemiah. Therefore I have made an original contribution to the subject herein. And here I will make an end.

Bibliography

ABINGDON'S STRONG'S EXHAUSTIVE CONCORDANCE OF THE BIBLE, TOGETHER WITH HEBREW, CHALDEE & GREEK DICTIONARIES., (1890, James Strong. Madison, N.J.) (James Strong,1822-1894) Key-word comparison © 1980 by Abingdon. Hebrew Dictionary, © 1890, James Strong. Abingdon. Nashville.

Apocrypha, King James Version.

Bible; Holy Bible; various translations, chiefly the King James; together with emendations based upon the original languages, according to the best available sources, including the following:

Nestle-Aland., NOVUM TESTAMENTUM GRAECE.
(© 1979 Deutsche Bibelgesellschaft Stuttgart)
(26th critical edition; Druck 1988).

BIBLIA HEBRAICA STUTTGARTENSIA.
(© 1983 Deutsche Bibelgesellschaft Stuttgart)
(EDITIO FUNDITAS RENOVATA)
Editio secunda emendata opera W. Rudolph et H.P. Ruger.

SEPTUAGINTA.
(© 1979 Deutsche Bibelgesellschaft Stuttgart)
Alfred Rahlfs, editor. (Duo volumina in uno).

BIBLIA SACRA VULGATA.
(© 1969 Deutsche Bibelgesellschaft Stuttgart)
(IUXTA VULGATAM VERSIONEM).

Interlinear Greek-English New Testament.
Third Edition (© 1996 by Jay P. Green, Sr.)
Published by Baker Books, a division of Baker Book House Company.
P.O. Box 6287 Grand Rapids, Michigan. 49516-6287.
ISBN 0-8010-2138-3.
(Greek text © 1976 by the Trinitarian Bible Society, London, England).

THE BOOK OF ENOCH THE PROPHET.
(Richard Laurence, translator; 1883)
Published by Adventures Unlimited Press
One Adventure Place
Kempton, Illinois 60946 http://www.adventuresunlimitedpress.com.

THE BOOK OF ENOCH.
(R.H. Charles, translator; 1917)
Published by The Book Tree 1999.
The Book Tree Escondido, California 92033. www.thebooktree.com.

THE BOOK OF JUBILEES.
(R.H. Charles, translator; 1917)
Published by The Book Tree 2003.
ISBN 1-58509-238-X.
The Book Tree
P.O. Box 16476
San Diego, California 92176. www.thebooktree.com.

THE LOST BOOKS OF THE BIBLE AND THE FORGOTTEN
BOOKS OF EDEN. (© 1926, © 1927 by Alpha House). Thomas
Nelson.
ISBN 0-529-03385-2.

Budge, E.A. Wallis., *BANDLET OF RIGHTEOUSNESS: AN ETHIOPIAN BOOK OF THE DEAD.* London: Luzac & Co. 46 Great Russell Street, W.C.
1929. Published by Kessinger Publishers. www.kessinger.net.

Del Mar, Alexander, *THE WORSHIP OF AUGUSTUS CAESAR.*
First published in 1900.
Published by Kessinger Publishers. www.kessinger.net.

Dudley, Dean., *HISTORY OF THE FIRST COUNCIL OF NICE.*
(A&B Publishers Group Brooklyn, New York 11238)
ISBN 1-881316-03-3.

Eisenmenger, Johann Andreas., *ENTEDECKTES JUDENTHUM. (THE TRADITIONS OF THE JEWS).*
Johann Andreas Eisenmenger, 1654-1704. In 1732-1734, John Peter Stehelin had selections from *Entedecktes Judenthum* translated into English and printed in two volumes as *Rabbinical Literature: or, Traditions of the Jews;* reprinted in 1742 and 1748.
Reproduction of the 1748 edition by Michael A. Hoffman II © 2006.
ISBN-13: 978-0-9703784-4-6. ISBN 10: 0-9703784-4-0.
Independent History and Research P.O. Box 849
Coeur d'Alene, Idaho 83816 www.RevisionistHistory.org.

JOSEPHUS: THE COMPLETE WORKS.
Josephus, c. 37 A.D. - 100 A.D. (translated by William Whiston; William Whiston, 1667-1752)
(© 1998 by Thomas Nelson Publishers)
ISBN 07852-5049-2.

Mead, G.R.S., *DID JESUS LIVE 100 B.C.?*
First published by University Books in 1903.
(© 2005 Cosimo, Inc. COSIMO CLASSICS)
Cosimo, P.O. Box 416 Old Chelsea Station
New York, NY 10113-0416. www.cosimobooks.com.
ISBN 1-59605-376-3.

Salibi, Kamal., *CONSPIRACY IN JERUSALEM: WHO WAS JESUS?*
First published in 1988 in hardback as *Conspiracy in Jerusalem: The Hidden Origins of Jesus.* Paperback edition first published in 1998.
(© 1998 by Kamal Salibi) Published in 2007 by Tauris Parke Paperbacks an imprint of I.B. Tauris and Co. Ltd. 6 Salem Road, London W2 4BU
175 Fifth Avenue, New York, NY 10010 www.ibtauris.com.
Distribute in the United Stated and Canada by Palgrave Macmillan, a division of St. Martin's Press 175 Fifth Avenue, New York, NY 10010.

Shanks, Hershel., *UNDERSTANDING THE DEAD SEA SCROLLS.*
(© 1992 by Biblical Archaeology Society) Edited by Hershel Shanks.
Random House, Inc., New York, NY.
ISBN 0-679-41448-7.

Suetonius, *THE LIVES OF THE TWELVE CAESARS.*
Suetonius, c. 69 A.D. - 130 A.D.
Penguin Classics Edition, translated by Robert Graves.

Steinsaltz, Adin {Rabbi}., *THE TALMUD. (THE STEINSALTZ EDITION);*
Rabbi Israel V. Berman, translator and editor. (1989; The Israel Institute for Talmudic Publications and Milta Books) (New York: Random House).

Wise, Michael, with Martin Abegg, Jr. & Edward Cook., *THE DEAD SEA SCROLLS: A NEW TRANSLATION.* (© 1996 by Michael Wise, Martin Abegg, Jr. and Edward Cook) (HarperCollins Publishers, 10 East 53rd Street, New York, NY 10022). http://www.harpercollins.com.

Wise, Michael., *THE FIRST MESSIAH.*
(© 1999 by Michael O. Wise) (HarperCollins Publishers, 10 East 53rd Street, New York, NY 10022). http://www.harpercollins.com.

About the Author

Michael Thomas was born in Salem, Massacusetts, in 1960. A key turning-point in his life was a born-again religious experience as a college freshman. This led to a series of misadventures and misfortunes that resulted in great emotional turmoil and financial loss. As he learned more about the Bible more and more questions arose, which could not be answered by anyone. Finally he rejected the biblical belief-system altogether in 1992. Since then he has explored many alternative paradigms and has embraced a more universal form of spirituality. He has an interest in many unconventional theories and human interest themes. He currently resides in Portland, Maine.